Fifty years of *Insight*

ATF THEOLOGY
Adelaide
2011

ACU Series

1. *Faith and Reason,* 2004 edited by Anthony Fisher OP and Hayden Ramsay.
2. *A Short Guide to Writing a Thesis: What to do and what not to do,* 2011 by Gerald O'Collins, SJ.

Fifty years of *Insight*

Bernard Lonergan's contribution to philosophy and theology

Edited by Neil Ormerod, Robin Koning

and David Braithwaite

National Library of Australia Cataloguing-in-Publication entry

Title: Fifty years of Insight / edited by Neil James Ormerod, Robin Konig, David Martin Braithwaite.

ISBN: 9781921817304 (pbk.)

Series: ACU series ; 2.

Notes: Includes index.

Subjects: Lonergan, Bernard J. F.--Criticism and interpretation.

Other Authors/Contributors:
Ormerod, Neil.
Konig, Robin.
Braithwaite, David Martin.

Dewey Number: 230.2092

Cover and layout design by Astrid Sengkey

An imprint of the ATF Ltd
PO Box 504
Hindmarsh, SA 5007
ABN 90 116 359 963
www.atfpress.com

Contents

Contributors

Mark D Morelli is Professor of Philosophy and the Director of the Graduate Program in Philosophy at Loyola Marymount University in Los Angeles. He is the founding editor of *Method: Journal of Lonergan Studies*, a co-editor of Lonergan's *Understanding and Being* and *The Lonergan Reader*, author of *Philosophy's Place in Culture: A Model* and *At the Threshold of the Halfway House: Bernard Lonergan's Encounter with John Alexander Stewart*, and Director of the Los Angeles Lonergan Center.

Elizabeth Murray is Professor and Chair of the Department of Philosophy at Loyola Marymount University, Los Angeles, California. She is author of *Anxiety: A Study of the Affectivity of Moral Consciousness* (1986); and co-editor of *The Lonergan Reader* (1997) and Lonergan's *Understanding and Being* (1980, re-edited 1990). She is the author of over twenty publications on Lonergan, and on other thinkers including Kierkegaard, Nietzsche, Freud, and Sartre. She is founder and current president of The Lonergan Philosophical Society. She also has a long-time interest in the role of philosophy in Jesuit higher education.

William Mathews, SJ has taught courses on philosophical anthropology and narrative selfhood for many years at the Milltown Institute, Dublin. In his *Lonergan's Quest* (University of Toronto Press, 2005) he explored the startlingly strange desire involved in the authoring of *Insight*. He is currently working on a book relating the dynamism of consciousness (Lonergan's transcendental notions) with Memoirs, Biographies, Journals and Spirituality. Longer term interests include an exploration of emergence and finality with references to cosmology, nature, culture and economics.

Robin Koning, SJ is a systematic theologian on the faculty of Jesuit Theological College, part of the United Faculty of Theology in the Melbourne College of Divinity. His doctoral research, examining the usefulness for theology of anthropologist Clifford Geertz's understanding of culture, draws significantly on Lonergan's account of culture.

Anthony (Tony) J Kelly, CSsR is a Redemptorist priest and a professorial fellow in the Faculty of Theology and Philosophy of Australian Catholic University, having been previously Head of the Sub-Faculty of Philosophy and Theology. His many books and articles show a strong Lonerganian influence, the latest being *The Resurrection Effect: Transforming Christian Life and Thought* (Orbis, 2008). Since 2004, he has been a member of the International Theological Commission. He is attached to the Canberra campus of the University.

Neil Ormerod is Professor of Theology at Australian Catholic University, based at the Strathfield campus. He is the author of a number of books, the latest including *Creation, Grace and Redemption* (Orbis, 2007) and, with Shane Clifton, *Globalization and the Mission of the Church* (T&T Clark, 2009). He has published articles in *Theological Studies, Irish Theology Quarterly* and *Pacifica*. His published work draws extensively from the thought of Bernard Lonergan and Lonergan scholar, Robert Doran.

Meredith Secomb is currently a doctoral student in theology at the Australian Catholic University (Melbourne), having completed Bachelor and Master degrees in Theology at Yarra Theological Union over the preceding years. For some time, she conducted a private practice as a clinical psychologist, working at the interface of psychology and spirituality. Meredith has published on the topics of Catherine of Siena, the contemplative foundation for social action, and a Lonergan-based approach to therapy. She has presented papers at Lonergan and psychological conferences both in Australia and overseas.

David Legg is currently Head of Faculty for Religious Studies at St Peter's College, Auckland, New Zealand. His study of Lonergan's work started in 1964 after reading *Insight*, while he was engaged in the study of Aristotle and Aquinas in Australia. His doctoral research was in the Logic of Questioning as developed by Lonergan in *Insight*. His present interest is in applying Lonergan's methodology to explicate philosophical problems, especially those found in modern and traditional cosmologies, including Indian and Islamic thought. As an educator he has developed programmes applying Lonergan's approach in teaching philosophy to secondary school students. He is presently involved with the New Zealand Ministry of Education in bringing the study of philosophy into the state secondary school curriculum.

Philip McShane is a Professor Emeritus of Mount St Vincent University, Halifax, Nova Scotia, and has been working in Lonergan studies since 1956, when he completed graduate work in mathematical physics. He is the author of more than a dozen books on Lonergan's contribution to culture, and the editor of two of the volumes of Lonergan's *Complete Works*: Volume 18, *Phenomenology and Logic*, and Volume 21, *For A New Political Economy.*

Sean McNelis is a part-time Research Fellow and a full-time doctoral student at Swinburne Institute for Social Research at Swinburne University of Technology in Melbourne, Australia. He has over 25 years experience in housing management, housing policy and housing research. His interests include: social housing policy, in particular housing finance, rental systems, housing for older persons and housing co-operatives; the foundations of housing research and housing policy; and, the economic and philosophic writings of Bernard Lonergan, in particular his groundbreaking insights into functional collaboration, emergent probability and macroeconomic dynamics.

Tom Halloran was introduced to Lonergan's *Insight* while a student in Rome in the years following Vatican II. He was fortunate in being able to follow up his interest in Lonergan's thought through the annual workshops and several years of classes at Boston College. Prior to coming to Australia in 1987, he taught a variety of theological and philosophical subjects in both University and Pastoral Ministry's settings. His longstanding interest in the methodology of Bernard Lonergan continues through the Australian Lonergan Workshop Committee, of which he is currently Secretary. Tom lives in Canberra with his family and is very involved with his local parish

Introduction

Bernard Lonergan is one of the greatest Catholic intellectuals of the twentieth century. His writings cover an enormous range of topics including philosophy, theology, science, history, art, education and economics. His collected works, currently being published by Toronto University Press, will number over twenty volumes. However, for most people he is best known for two works, *Insight: A Study of Human Understanding* and *Method in Theology*. If these were the only two works he ever wrote, his reputation would be undiminished, marking him as a unique mind capable of the most profound philosophical and theological analyses. Perhaps because of the profundity of his writings he nonetheless remains an intellectual *terra incognita* for many people. He has a well-deserved reputation for being difficult to read, particularly if one's starting point is *Insight*. It is not that his writing is particularly dense or obscure, but his appeal to mathematical and scientific examples often leave an unprepared mind floundering. His writing assumes a reader who is at the 'level of the times', abreast of the scientific and cultural achievements of the day. It is this, more than the complexity of the writing, that makes for the greatest difficulty for a novice reader.

These present essays represent contributions from leading international and Australian scholars in the area of Lonergan studies. They were brought together to mark the fiftieth anniversary of the publication of *Insight*. Though a little later than one might have liked, these essays reflect on the contribution of Lonergan's thought, principally *Insight*, but also his later work in *Method* have made to philosophy and theology. The essays contained in this work cover three general areas—philosophy, theology and what one might broadly call culture.

Mark Morelli takes up Lonergan's image of the 'half-way house', a half-way house between idealism and empiricism, and the different half-way house which locates idealism between empiricism and what Lonergan calls critical realism. In particular he is interested in identifying this latter half-way house with the absolute idealism of Hegel, rather than the critical idealism of Kant. His work presents a positive appreciation of the contribution of Hegel to Lonergan's understanding of critical realism.

Elizabeth Murray also explores Lonergan's metaphor of the half-way house to examine the nature of intellectual conversion and its place within Lonergan's thought. Along the way she engages with the thought of a number of major philosophers, including Kierkegaard, Kant, Husserl, Heidegger and Fichte. Her argument is that intellectual conversion involves a two-fold movement, the moment of withdrawal to immanence and the moment of transcendence to objectivity. Further, intellectual conversion is not a final achievement. The horizon of critical realism must be gained and regained through rationally self-conscious and free commitment.

William Mathews' contribution examines how Lonergan's argument in *Insight* overcomes the Kantian problematic which split phenomena and noumena and sought to rule out the possibility of metaphysics. This involves appropriating Lonergan's notion of objectivity, as he notes, 'Mastering the meaning of the principal notion of objectivity involved in my own experience a fairly major intellectual conversion with which I struggled for many years and continue to struggle'. Mathews illustrates his argument with extensive reference to scientific insights, particularly the work of Crick and Watson in discovering the structure of DNA. In seeking to replicate in oneself their journey of discovery one can uncover elements of one's own intentional operations which ground a solution to the Kantian problematic.

Robin Koning undertakes an examination of Lonergan's understanding of consciousness and compares and contrasts this with an understanding of consciousness found in the writings of Karol Wojtyla (later Pope John Paul II), particularly his work, *The Acting Person*. This is a significant issue because of the concerns raised by Pope John Paul II in his encyclical *Fides et ratio* on the modern 'turn to the subject'. While Wojtyla may not be as thematic as Lonergan in his examination of the topic of consciousness, Koning finds a number of similarities in their approaches, as well as differences. In particular he concludes that Wojtyla means by reflexive consciousness what Lonergan means by consciousness *tout court*, revealing some fundamental convergence in the views of Lonergan and Wojtyla on consciousness.

Anthony Kelly presents the first theological contribution to the collection, suggesting that the Christian phenomenon needs a more explicit place in Lonergan's *Method.* In this regard, von Balthasar's aesthetic phenomenonology of God's self-revelation appears to be the polar opposite to Lonergan's method based in the phenomenology of self-transcending consciousness. By referring to Jean-Luc Marion's recent phenomenology, particularly his notion of 'saturated phenomena', Kelly detects in all this a benign dialectic at work, even in the work of Lonergan himself, which can lead to a further enrichment of his theological inheritance.

Neil Ormerod takes up one of Lonergan's more philosophical contributions, that of contingent predication, concerning the relationship between creator and creature, to analyse the more theological issue of the relationship between the persons of the Triune God and creature. Such a stance has been developed in Lonergan's Latin writings recently made available in English translation in his collected works. Ormerod compares this approach to that adopted by Karl Rahner based on Rahner's account of 'quasi-formal causality'. He seeks to contribute to the debate between Lonergan scholars Robert Doran and Charles Hefling recently published in *Theological Studies.*

Following Kelly's suggestions in relation to the work of von Balthasar, Meredith Secomb deploys insights from both Lonergan and Hans Urs von Balthasar to examine the notion of a personal 'call' or vocation. Both these theologians embraced the Ignatian principle of serving God in a concrete way and both endorsed the Ignatian means for discerning God's call. However, they present quite different emphases in their recommendations for how people should attend to God's call. While Balthasar argued that people found fulfilment in discovering God's 'idea' or mission for their lives, Lonergan recommended that people be attentive to their consciousness in pursuing God's call. Secomb refers to the distinction between these emphases as, respectively, the 'call-writ-large' and the 'call-writ-small'.

David Legg explores the relationship between cosmology, theology and the universe, with a particular focus on the question: What is the universe? His initial interlocutors in this exploration are Emmanuel Kant and Ludwig Wittgenstein before turning to Lonergan's *Insight* for an understanding of the universe as a whole. He concludes that while Kant restricted our knowledge of the universe to his theory of 'perception', and Wittgenstein restricted what we could say about the world to the 'bubble' of language-games, Lonergan affirmed the reality of the universe of everything, as it really is, based on the unrestricted desire to know, expressed in our questioning.

Longstanding Lonergan scholar Philip McShane seeks to locate the larger cultural significance of Lonergan's work. Identifying the emergence of what Lonergan refers to as the 'second stage of meaning' with what Karl Jaspers refers to as an 'axial age', McShane asks what new axial age will characterise the emergence of a 'third stage of meaning' based on interiority as achieved in Lonergan's writings. As always McShane's essay is challenging, probing and wide-ranging over the full corpus of Lonergan's achievement. He asks us to consider not just the next fifty years but the next seven hundred years when a Lonergan-like lady in the Orient may find Lonergan as Lonergan found Aquinas. Typically the footnotes of this essay are an essay in themselves and worth pursuing.

We are particularly pleased to include the essay by Sean McNelis, the only contributor to explicitly consider Lonergan's contribution to economic thought. McNelis outlines the unique aspects of Lonergan's economics and its basis in his notion of a scheme of recurrence as developed in *Insight*. He argues that Lonergan's heuristic, the scheme of recurrence, poses a challenge for current social and economic research, particularly where it is dominated by common sense thinking. The essay illustrates some unique aspects of this heuristic: the ordered hierarchy of technology, economics and politics; the distinction between the patterns of an economy and the coincidental motivations of participants; the functional relations between series of groups of activities; the normativity immanent within the productive process; and the democratic focus of Lonergan's analysis. In particular McNelis seeks to apply these insights to the question of social housing.

In the final contribution, Tom Halloran contends that 'functional specialisation' is Lonergan's greatest contribution to philosophy and theology. Articulating his stand in a manner that recalls Lonergan's stand in 'Finality, Love, Marriage', Halloran writes, 'In the *recent fermentation* of *catholic praxis* on the *meaning and redemption of history*, the basic component of novelty would seem to be a *development in methodical collaboration*. Quite other factors, no doubt, account for the intense and widespread interest aroused in so-called Lonergan studies, but the ground of *the existential problem* must be placed, I think, in *one's judgement of value* with respect to functional specialisation.' As was the case in 1943, Halloran finds little evidence of the invited, relevant collaboration.

The editors would like to thank all the contributors for their contributions and patience in the publication of this volume. In particular Neil Ormerod would like to thank his fellow editors, David Braithwaite and Robin Koning for their careful reading and correction of the text, and for ensuring some sense of uniformity in the referencing used by our contributors.

Chapter 1

Lonergan's Debt to Hegel and the Appropriation of Critical Realism

Mark D Morelli

When I was my pursuing my graduate studies at the University of Toronto in the 1970s the Thomists there were highly suspicious of Lonergan. Despite his obvious dissatisfaction with Kant, Lonergan acknowledges more concretely and more thoroughly than Kant the methodological primacy of the synthetic unity of apperception.[1] As Lonergan puts it, in more familiar terms, if I weren't present to myself, nothing would be present to me.[2] Lonergan's affinity with Kant on this point is a violation of the Gilsonian proscription against getting involved in any significant way with Kant's Copernican Revolution.[3] But these Thomists were doubly

1. 'Kant deduced or postulated an original synthetic unity of apperception as the a priori condition of the 'I think' accompanying all cognitional acts' (Bernard Lonergan, *Collected Works of Bernard Lonergan*, volume 3, *Insight: A Study of Human Understanding*, edited by Frederick E Crowe and Robert M Doran (Toronto: University of Toronto Press, 1992), 365); (hereafter, *CWL* 3, *Insight*). 'Indeed, consciousness is much more obviously of this unity in diverse acts than of the diverse acts, for it is within the unity that the acts are found and distinguished, and it is to the unity that we appeal when we talk about a single field of consciousness and draw a distinction between conscious acts occurring within the field and unconscious acts occurring outside it' (*CWL* 3, *Insight*, 349).
2. 'Moreover, there is a third meaning of "presence": you could not be present to me unless I were somehow present to myself' (Bernard Lonergan, *Collected Works of Bernard Lonergan*, volume 5, *Understanding and Being*, edited by Elizabeth A Morelli and Mark D Morelli; revised and augmented by FE Crowe with the collaboration of Elizabeth A Morelli, Mark D Morelli, Robert M Doran, and Thomas V Daly (Toronto: University of Toronto Press, 1990), 15); (hereafter *CWL* 5, *Understanding and Being*).
3. Reporting Gilson's position, Gerald McCool writes: 'For the Kantian who makes consciousness the starting point of his philosophy can never be led out into the extra-mental world by the force of logical argument . . . No method that begins in consciousness, even precisely as Maréchal . . . can ever legitimately emerge from

troubled by Lonergan. Lonergan seemed to them to be not only post-Kantian—that was bad enough—but also post-Hegelian, and that was just too much. Lonergan's post-Kantianism made them suspicious, but in his post-Hegelianism they found the sufficient reason for dismissing him.

If the Toronto Thomists were wrong to dismiss Lonergan, they were right about his kinship with Hegel. Lonergan is, indeed, not merely post-Kantian but also post-Hegelian. Obviously, this has not meant to Lonergan scholars what it meant to those Toronto Thomists, for Lonergan's post-Hegelian philosophy has not scared us off. Still, our sticking with Lonergan despite his Hegelianism cannot be attributed to our having grasped fully the significance of his Hegelianism since little work has been done on Lonergan's relationship to Hegel.[4] So, if we are unfazed by Lonergan's Hegelianism, that is probably for other reasons. My own suspicion is that we are untroubled because we trust that Lonergan's philosophical position, however post-Hegelian it may be, is nevertheless still fundamentally Thomistic. The Toronto Thomists were scared off by Lonergan's Hegelianism, because it seemed to them too far removed from their Thomism and incompatible with it, whereas we stick with Lonergan, not because of the Hegelian elements in his thought but rather in spite of them, because we regard him as still authentically Thomistic.

There is some irony here, and it invites further interesting questions: How does the Aquinas of the Toronto Thomists differ from Lonergan's Aquinas? Why was the Aquinas of the Toronto Thomists so radically incompatible with Hegel? In what way is Lonergan's Aquinas compatible with Hegelian idealism? Does Lonergan's kinship with both Aquinas and Hegel have any implications for the appropriation of Lonergan's Critical Realism? It is impossible to address all of these issues adequately in a brief essay. Instead of attempting the impossible, I propose to focus here on

consciousness. Direct and immediate realism is the only valid starting point for a realistic Thomistic metaphysics' (Gerald A McCool, SJ, *From Unity to Pluralism: The Internal Evolution of Thomism* (New York: Fordham University Press, 1992), 162).

4. The single lengthy study of Lonergan's relationship to Hegel is Jon Michael Nilson's *Hegel's* Phenomenology *and Lonergan's* Insight*: A Comparison of Two Ways to Christianity*, a doctoral dissertation written under the direction of John S Dunne at the University of Notre Dame in 1975. Nilson has a good number of insights into the relationship, in particular, of Hegel's *Phenomenology of Spirit* to Lonergan's *Insight*, but he tends to conceive both philosophies as 'systems'—which, I would argue, is true of neither in the ordinary meaning of 'system', and his comparisons and contrasts remain for the most part descriptive and so underestimate the import of both the similarities and the differences between the two thinkers.

Lonergan's relation to Hegel and on the bearing of his debt to Hegel upon the appropriation of his Critical Realism.

First, I shall offer just one especially compelling bit of evidence of Lonergan's debt to Hegel. That debt is, as the Toronto Thomists rightly discerned, a large one. Secondly, I shall consider the implications of Lonergan's debt to Hegel for our understanding of Lonergan's well-known claim that idealism is the halfway house between materialism and his own Critical Realism. This claim is easily misinterpreted, and I shall summarise here an argument I have made elsewhere that the idealism of the halfway house through which we must pass on the way to Critical Realism is not a version of subjective idealism but is, in fact, Hegelian Absolute or Objective Idealism. If I am correct, Lonergan's debt to Hegel has important implications for our appropriation of his Critical Realism. Thirdly, then, I shall turn from Lonergan's relation to Hegel to our relation to this relation, and shall discuss briefly the fear of idealism associated with the discovery of the role of insight in human knowing. I shall distinguish an unreasonable fear of subjective idealism, on the one hand, that vanishes as inertial confrontationalist presuppositions are abandoned; and, on the other hand, a reasonable fear of Absolute Idealism that takes hold only once the inertial confrontationalist presuppositions are overcome.

Lonergan's debt to Hegel: a bit of evidence

First, then, let us consider a bit of evidence of Lonergan's large debt to Hegel. It is easy enough to show that the Toronto Thomists' suspicions were well-founded, even if their subsequent dismissal of Lonergan was not. A single citation from *Insight* will suffice to show this. In the footnote on the last page of Chapter 12 on 'The Notion of Being', Lonergan declares that 'characteristic features in the very movement of [Hegel's] thought have their parallels' in *Insight*, and that the 'whole argument' of *Insight* 'proceeds from *an sich*, through *für sich*, to *an und für sich*', in the manner of Hegel's *Phenomenology of Spirit* and *System of Logic*.[5]

We must leave for another occasion the exploration of the dynamic structural similarities between the argument of *Insight* and the very movement of Hegel's thought in his two greatest works, for the issue is made complicated by divergent ideals and different terminologies. But we need only notice how deeply into Lonergan's argument in *Insight* Hegel penetrates to realise that Lonergan's debt to Hegel must have important

5. *CWL* 3, *Insight*, 398.

implications for the appropriation of his Critical Realism. In order to bring those implications into focus, let us turn to Lonergan's claim in the Introduction to *Insight* that his standpoint of Critical Realism is reached by entering into and then going beyond the halfway house of idealism.[6]

Absolute idealism as the halfway house

There is more than one type of idealism, and Lonergan did not specify the type that characterises the halfway house.[7] It is very tempting to assume that the idealism in question is the Critical Philosophy of Kant which Lonergan evidently seeks to counter in *Insight*.[8] But, as I have argued elsewhere and at length, the idealism through which we must pass on our way to Critical Realism cannot be Kant's Critical Philosophy but must be the Absolute Idealism of Hegel to whom Lonergan owes the dynamic structure of the argument which he undertakes to refute Kant.[9] I shall

6. *CWL* 3, *Insight*, 22.
7. It should be noted that Lonergan typically speaks of 'idealism' without qualification, and one must determine from the context which idealism—Critical Idealism or Absolute Idealism—he is criticising. Moreover, Lonergan commonly emphasises the implicit anticipations of the position in Kant, rather than the counterpositional commitments. This emphasis tends to blur the fundamental difference between Critical Idealism and Absolute Idealism by emphasising their shared oversight of the role of judgment. A similar ambiguity afflicts his reference to 'idealism', without qualification, as the halfway house in the quotation from the Introduction to *Insight*. However, in *De Intellectu et Methodo*, the unpublished lecture notes from the course at Gregorian University, Rome, (first draft, 1959), Lonergan does actually distinguish between 'Kantian criticism' and 'idealism'; see *Understanding and Method*, translated by MG Shields (Lonergan Research Institute, 1990, unpublished), 109. Both fail to appropriate judgment, but only in 'idealism' is truth decisive.
8. Lonergan borrows the image of idealism as the halfway house between Critical Realism and materialism directly from Maréchal. See *CWL* 5, *Understanding and Being*, 277. However, as I shall attempt to show in what follows, we should not jump to the conclusion that, since Maréchal in his *Cahiers* was crafting a Thomist response to Kant, it is Kant's Critical Idealism that has the design and the furnishings required for an idealism that is to serve as the halfway house. The image also occurs in Leo W Keeler's *The Problem of Error from Plato to Kant: A Historical and Critical Study* (Rome: Pontifical Gregorian University, 1934), 6, which Lonergan reviewed in the 1935 volume of *Gregorianum*. However, the image is not Keeler's but occurs in a quotation from AE Taylor's *Plato* and is used with reference to the Eleatic doctrine.
9. See my article, 'Going Beyond Idealism: Lonergan's Relation to Hegel', in *Lonergan Workshop*, 20, *The 'Not Numerous Center': For* Insight*'s 50th Anniversary and* Method in Theology*'s 35th Anniversary*, edited by Fred Lawrence (Boston: Boston College, 2008), 305–36.

provide just the skeleton of my argument here and invite you to consult the longer article where it is fleshed out.

The idealism that serves as the halfway house between materialism and Critical Realism cannot be rooted in the basic counterposition.[10] If it is so rooted, it cannot be considered fundamentally superior to, or a significant advance beyond, incoherent realism. If it is to be properly speaking a halfway house, it has to lie beyond immediate, confrontational realism, whether of the naïve sort or of the more sophisticated Scholastic sort. But Kant's Critical Philosophy remains rooted firmly in the basic counterposition, and so it does not differ fundamentally from confrontational realism.[11] Despite his 'Copernican shift,' Kant retains the ideal of knowing as immediate confrontation with an 'already-out-there-now-real', for it is Kant's discovery of the impossibility of realising this ideal that leads him to restrict the human mind to knowledge of phenomena and drives him into the *cul-de-sac* that is the antinomies of pure reason. As Lonergan put it in *Insight*, Kant's Copernican Revolution was a half-hearted affair.[12] In Kant there is a residual empiricism; for him, immediate confrontation at the level of experience, or intuition, remains decisive, at least ideally.[13]

Hegel's Absolute Idealism, in contrast, is not rooted in the basic counterposition.[14] Hegel rejects the ideal of knowledge as immediate confrontation and pursues an ideal of knowledge as comprehensive and coherent understanding.[15] He rejects intuitionism and affirms the

10. See *CWL* 3, *Insight,* 413 on the elements of the basic counterposition.
11. 'Kant's philosophy is not built in a way that is compatible with the fact that the decisive element is truth. Because, for possible knowledge, the criterion in Kant always is the possibility of connecting it with an intuition. And that is why you get into these logical difficulties in Kant. But they are only symptomatic' (*CWL* 5, *Understanding and Being,* 278).
12. *CWL* 3, *Insight*, 438.
13. *CWL* 5, *Understanding and Being*, 277–78.
14. *CWL* 3, *Insight*, 372.
15. The ideal of comprehensive coherence in Hegel corresponds to the ideal that is the good or end of the second level of cognitional operation in Lonergan: 'Intelligence as such seeks a complete explanation of all phenomena: it aims at understanding everything. Hence it is constantly making distinctions in order to comprehend all these distinct realities in all their aspects. The end of intelligence is the whole complex of intelligible relations such that the universe may be understood in its unity.' This good is the end of 'systematic intelligence' which invites comparison with Hegel's notion of system: 'In saying "systematic" we do not mean to suggest some abstract system consisting of propositions from which everything can be deduced. 'Systematic' as we are using it is intended to connote an understanding of the whole concrete universe

discursive, mediating, constructive nature of intellect as intelligence.[16] Hegel's *Phenomenology of Spirit* is, on one interpretation at least, an account of Spirit's transcendence of confrontationism's presupposition of a primordial subject/object dichotomy.[17]

Still, if Hegel has abandoned knowing as immediate encounter, appropriated the pure and unrestricted desire to know, and rejected objectivity as extroversion, he has nevertheless failed to appropriate, as Lonergan notes repeatedly, the grasp of the virtually unconditioned and judgment of fact. Hegel's notion of being may be comprehensive in connotation, but it is restricted in denotation.[18] Accordingly, on its ascent beyond incoherent realism Absolute Idealism stalls, so to speak, on the level of understanding, and it may be described as quasi-positional or transitional.

Hegel's Absolute Idealism, then, is not counterpositional; it is basically positional but nevertheless incomplete. The sign of its incompleteness, it should be noted, is not to be found in its abstractness, because for Hegel, as for Lonergan, abstraction is not impoverishing but enriching. It is not the bloodlessness of Hegel's intellectual ballet that is the indicator of its incompleteness; rather, it is the superhuman poise required of the dancers. The quasi-positionality and transitional character of Hegel's Absolute Idealism is reflected in its notorious instability; it is a philosophy whose distinguishing feature is a too-precarious balance that manifests itself most vividly in Hegel's so-called 'speculative propositions'. In Hegel's pursuit of an ideal of the union of union and non-union, of the identity of identity and difference, we witness a heroic but ultimately unsuccessful struggle to work out the epistemological and metaphysical implications of the discovery that intellect is intelligence.

Of course, Hegel didn't regard his philosophy as transitional and only quasi-positional as Lonergan did. Despite its instability Hegel regarded his

---

distinguished according to all its many aspects and the intelligible relations of each of its parts, hence an understanding of the entire universe as something that is one' (Lonergan, *Understanding and Method*, 93–94).

16. 'Pure thinking knows that it alone, and not feeling or representation, is capable of grasping the truth of things, and that the assertion of Epicurus that the true is what is sensed, must be pronounced a complete perversion of the nature of mind' (Georg Wilhelm Friedrich Hegel, *Hegel's Philosophy of Mind*, translated by AV Miller (Oxford: Clarendon Press, 1971), 224).

17. Of course, Lonergan objects to Hegel's 'necessitarian' depiction of this process of superseding the subject/object dichotomy.

18. *CWL* 3, *Insight*, 398.

philosophy as absolute. What I have described as the residual instability of a transitional philosophy Hegel took to be the intrinsic dialectical tension of the Absolute itself which has reached its fully self-conscious, explanatory self-expression in Absolute Idealism. For Hegel, this tension is ontological. But the plethora of highly precarious conceptions or mixed conceptual results that characterise Hegel's system has generated perduring controversies in Hegel scholarship.[19] That the 'speculative proposition' in its various formulations generates these controversies, even among committed Hegelians, suggests that it does not in fact satisfy the immanent criterion of truth that is Hegel's own intelligent *Geist*.[20] This perduring spiritual discomfort has evoked valiant efforts to articulate a 'Hegelian Middle' that remains nevertheless elusive; and it has led even the most astute readers of Hegel to tip the balance to the right, like Kierkegaard, or to the left, like Marx and, more recently, Alexandre Kojève.[21] From Lonergan's

19. In Hegel's logic-in-motion, for example, Lonergan discerns such a mixed result: 'True, the same concept is always conceived in the same way, and there is no movement in concepts considered logically. Nevertheless, if they are considered in a concrete way as they exist in the human mind, they undergo continual modification because concepts do not exist independently of the intending and the understanding of a concrete human being . . . Hence, with a greater or lesser advance in understanding, concepts undergo greater or lesser development and change. To recognize this fact is to recognize the fundamental point in the solution of the problem of historicity' (*Understanding and Method*, 54). Again, Hegel's logic in its entirety, in virtue of the identity of thought and being, is a transitional *metaphysics* which, Lonergan claims, is *connotatively comprehensive* but *denotatively restricted*. The intending of the *Logic* is a hybrid of transcendental notion and determinate category. Lonergan writes in *Method in Theology* that 'the most fundamental difference in modes of intending lies between the categorial and the transcendental. Categories are determinations. They have a limited denotation. They vary with cultural variations . . . In contrast, the transcendentals are comprehensive in connotation, unrestricted in denotation, invariant over cultural change . . . They are comprehensive because they intend the unknown whole or totality of which our answers reveal only part' (*Method in Theology* (New York: Herder and Herder, 1972), 11). In Lonergan's terms, then, Hegel's intending is transcendental inasmuch as it is comprehensive in connotation, inasmuch as Hegel finds the whole, the totality, in every part; but it is categorical inasmuch as there is only the single virtually unconditioned which is the Absolute.
20. Thus, for example, Hegel's philosophy provides evidence for both the 'epochal' and the 'absolutist' interpretations of his eschatology. Is Hegel's philosophy *its* time comprehended in thought, or is it *time* comprehended in thought? See Daniel Berthold-Bond, *Hegel's Grand Synthesis: A Study of Being, Thought, and History* (Albany: SUNY Press, 1989), especially Chapter 7.
21. See Emil Fackenheim, *The Religious Dimension in Hegel's Thought* (Boston: Beacon Press, 1967), 76: 'From the outset and throughout, the Hegelian system seems faced with the choice between saving the claims of an absolute and therefore all-

standpoint, these controversies are intractable within the closed circle of the Hegelian System and so provide fodder for unending commentary. Their resolutions require transcendence of the residual dialectical tension that perpetually threatens the integrity of the 'speculative proposition' and whose opposing poles are the Hegelian System itself, on the one hand, which is a seamless fabric of internal relations, and discrete matters of fact, on the other. In short, their resolutions require a different ontology.

This is a serious limitation. But it is not attributable to the counterpositionality of Hegel's idealism. It is, rather, a consequence of its incompleteness. Hegel's Absolute Idealism shares with Lonergan's Critical Realism at least five noteworthy differences from Kant's counterpositional Critical Philosophy. First, while both credit Kant with the discovery of the primacy of the unity of apperception, both criticise him for failing to exploit fully the implications of this discovery.[22] Accordingly, in the second place, following JG Fichte, both reject Kant's postulation of the *Ding an sich* behind phenomena and his residual empiricism, and both affirm the enriching role of intellectual mediation. Thirdly, then, following Aristotle in the *De Anima*, both affirm the original unity of subject and object and the doctrine of knowing by identity.[23] In the fourth place, both affirm an immanent criterion of objectivity; the criterion of objectivity lies not outside human consciousness but within it.[24] Finally, both understand

---

comprehensive philosophic thought, but at the price of loss of any actual world besides it, and saving the contingent world of human experience at the price of reducing philosophic thought itself to finiteness.' See Chapter 4 on 'The Hegelian Middle' and right- and left-wing interpretations.

22. See *CWL 5 Understanding and Being*, 15 where Lonergan writes: 'you could not be present to me unless I were somehow present to myself.' On Kant, see *CWL 3 Insight*, 365. See 362–66 for Lonergan's contrast of his position with Kant's.
23. See *Hegel's Philosophy of Mind*, 180–81: 'However, the Knowing of truth does not itself, to begin with, have the form of truth; for at the stage of development now reached, it is still *abstract*, the formal identity of subjectivity and objectivity. Only when this identity has developed into an actual difference and has made itself into the identity of itself and its difference, therefore, only when mind or spirit steps forth as an immanently developed totality, not till then has that certainty *established* itself as truth.'
24. In the Introduction to his *Phenomenology of Spirit*, Hegel writes: 'But the essential point to bear in mind throughout the whole investigation is that these two moments, 'Notion' and 'object', 'being-for-another' and being-in-itself', both fall *within* that knowledge which we are investigating. Consequently, we do not need to import criteria, or to make use of our own bright ideas and thoughts during the course of the inquiry; it is precisely when we leave these aside that we succeed in contemplating the matter in hand as it is *in and for itself*. But not only is a contribution by us superfluous, since Notion and object, the criterion and what is to be tested, are present in consciousness

Kant's critique of pure reason to be, not the critique of the human mind it purports to be, but a critique of a long dominant historical conception of the human mind and ideal of knowledge.[25]

Kant's Critical Philosophy is properly-speaking counterpositional and, from Lonergan's standpoint, in this regard it is fundamentally wrong. Kant didn't know about insight; because he didn't know about insight, he remained a confrontationist.[26] In addition to being deficient in this fundamental way, Kant's philosophy is incomplete in other ways, the most notable being the absence from it of a doctrine of rational judgment. But it

---

itself, but we are also spared the trouble of comparing the two and really *testing* them, so that, since what consciousness examines is its own self, all that is left for us to do is simply to look on. For consciousness is, on the one hand, consciousness of the object, and on the other, consciousness of itself; consciousness of what for it is the True, and consciousness of its knowledge of the truth. Since both are *for* the same consciousness, this consciousness is itself their comparison; it is for the same consciousness to know whether its knowledge of the object corresponds to the object or not. The object, it is true, seems only to be for consciousness in the way that consciousness knows it; it seems that consciousness cannot, as it were, get behind the object as it exists for consciousness so as to examine what the object is in itself, and hence, too, cannot test its own knowledge by that standard. But the distinction between the in-itself and knowledge is already present in the very fact that consciousness knows an object at all. Something is *for it* the *in-itself*; and knowledge, or the being of the object for consciousness, is, *for it*, another moment. Upon this distinction, which is present as a fact, the examination rests' (*Hegel's Phenomenology of Spirit*, translated by AV Miller (Oxford: Oxford University Press, 1979), 53–54). See *CWL* 3 *Insight*, 659–62 on the immanent source of transcendence.

25. *CWL* 5 *Understanding and Being*, 20. Lonergan remarks that Kant's critique (the KRV) 'was not of the pure reason but of the human mind as conceived by Scotus . . .' See *Collected Works of Bernard Lonergan*, volume 2: *Verbum: Word and Idea in Aquinas*, edited by Frederick E Crowe and Robert M Doran (Toronto: University of Toronto Press, 1997), 38–39. Philosophers after Kant may be sorted into two groups: those who believe Kant to have critiqued the human mind, and those who believe Kant to have critiqued an *historical conception* of the human mind or *a particular ideal of knowledge*. Hegel and Lonergan may be counted among those in the latter group. Hegel locates Kant at the limit of the standpoint of Understanding in his *Phenomenology of Spirit*.
26. While Lonergan says that 'Kant, Aristotle, and St Thomas all knew about insight', he also immediately identifies a difference 'between Kant, on the one hand, and Aristotle and Thomas, on the other': 'Kant's a priori is . . . absolutely independent of experience . . . In Aristotle and St Thomas, on the other hand, the insight and the concept are distinguished, and the phantasm, the image, causes the insight. In Kant there is no talk of the insight, but only of the concept, the image, and the concept governing the image. Kant's synthetic a priori presupposes that the insight already exists and that the concepts are already formed. Given those presuppositions, one controls one's images, but the images do not cause the insight' (*CWL* 5 *Understanding and Being*, 31). In short, Kant knew about the consequences of insight, but not about the event.

is not the missing doctrine of judgment in Kant's Critical Philosophy that precludes its serving as the halfway house on the way to Critical Realism; it is its counterpositionality.

Hegel's Absolute Idealism, on the other hand, is quasi-positional, and so it is a transitional position. It is not properly-speaking counterpositional, and in this fundamental respect it is not deficient, although it, too, remains incomplete. Hegel, to an extent sufficient to push him beyond Kant's Critical Philosophy into Absolute Idealism, knew about insight, in the same unthematised way that Aristotle, as Lonergan asserted, knew about insight, even though neither Hegel nor Aristotle seems to have known about the grasp of the virtually unconditioned and judgment.[27]

It is Absolute Idealism, then, that is to serve as the halfway house between the 'two quite different realisms' distinguished by Lonergan. There is an incoherent realism that is half-animal and half-human, for which immediate intuitions, either sensitive or intellectual, are decisive; on the other hand, there is a coherent, fully human realism, for which rational judgment is decisive. Whereas incoherent realism is merely the static midpoint between materialism and idealism, Absolute Idealism is the halfway house, the transitional position, between materialism and the coherent Critical Realism beyond idealism. To reach Lonergan's Critical Realism, then, we must enter into and go beyond Hegel's Absolute Idealism. But the entry into and movement beyond Absolute Idealism is both a daunting intellectual challenge and a fearsome personal one.

Insight into insight and the fear of idealism

Recently, Richard Liddy published an account of his own gradual entry into the standpoint of Critical Realism.[28] It is the story of his personal struggle to appropriate Lonergan's position. For the title of his book Liddy borrowed the phrase 'Startling Strangeness' that occurs in the very paragraph in the Introduction to *Insight* where Lonergan speaks of two quite different realisms and identifies idealism as the halfway house on the way to Critical Realism. In his autobiographical account, Liddy describes a fear of idealism that arose in him subsequent to his discovery of insight and of the mediative and constructive functions of conscious and intentional operations. In light of the requirement that we enter into and

27. *CWL* 5 *Understanding and Being*, 18.

28. Richard M Liddy, *Startling Strangeness: Reading Lonergan's* Insight (Lanham: University Press of America, 2007).

go beyond Absolute Idealism in order to reach the standpoint of Critical Realism, this fear of idealism and its relationship to the appropriation of Critical Realism warrant closer scrutiny.

It may seem odd or inappropriate to shift the focus from the idealism of the halfway house, its philosophical superiority to Kant's Critical Philosophy, and its residual incompleteness, to the experience of fear associated with the break with confrontationism. Surely, of primary importance are the distinction between the two realisms and its philosophical implications; whether or not a fear is associated with this discovery may seem to be a minor issue. But we should recall that the Critical Realism that Lonergan promotes is not to be regarded as a system of mere concepts, nor even as a theory in the strong sense. The movement from incoherent to Critical Realism is not merely a change of mind or the adoption of a different *Begrifflichkeit* effected by the exercise of an isolated cognitive faculty; it is a personal transformation, a conversion of the concrete, existing subject.

While it may be premature to declare that the Age of Theory has ended—for even so-called 'postmodernism', far from being a positive alternative to classicism, is still in reaction against its failures—it is clear enough that the Age of Theory is on its last legs. Indeed, one might argue that the instability of Hegel's System is itself a consequence of his own futile attempt to find room in the static systems of conceptualism for the dynamic flow of interior intellectual life. Hegel insisted that his Absolute Idealism is not to be regarded as another in the series of Philosophies of the Understanding, as he called them, but as an objectification of a self-developing dynamism, albeit of a dynamic *Begriff*. Similarly, Lonergan insisted that his Critical Realism not be viewed as yet another conceptual product of the Age of Theory, but as an objectification of the normative unfolding of concept-generating conscious intentionality. If Hegel nudged Wolffian static, conceptual system, which found its ultimate criterion in the principle of non-contradiction, toward greater concreteness by insisting upon the dynamic flexibility of Kant's Categories of the Understanding and by regarding Kant's antinomies not as dead-ends but as signs of the need for a new beginning, Lonergan has pushed Hegel's peculiar logic-in-motion toward greater concreteness by nudging us beyond the flexible Categories to their preconceptual generative principles. The Critical Realism Lonergan offers is not a self-conscious, self-mediating, dynamic system of interrelated concepts but the dynamic standpoint of a deliberate and methodical existential subject. When we treat the concrete fear of idealism that is said to accompany insight into insight as a marginal concern, we operate within a structure of relevance characteristic of the Age of Theory, with its faculty psychology, but no longer appropriate in the Age of Interiority, with its qualitatively differentiated conscious continuum that is the concrete unity of consciousness.

The fear of idealism arises as a function of the combination of insight into insight with horizonal preconditions. As it happens, many students of Lonergan seem to have arrived at their breakthroughs with three prior horizonal commitments, each of which, when combined with insight into insight, may generate fear of idealism. The first is the prior commitment to confrontationism, often in a putatively Thomist guise, without which there would be no need for a breakthrough. The second is a prior commitment to Christian theism, usually in its specifically Catholic form. The third is a prior, inescapable respect for concrete fact. In combination with pre-existing confrontationism, insight into insight evokes one sort of fear of idealism that dissipates fairly quickly. In combination with either or both of the other two commitments, insight into insight evokes another sort of fear of idealism, one that initiates and qualifies a prolonged personal and intellectual struggle.

The first sort of fear is expressed as a fear of being trapped in one's own subjectivity. The roots of this fear do not lie in insight into insight, pure and simple, but in the combination of insight into insight with inertial confrontationist presuppositions. For insight into insight, by itself, entails the realisation that knowing is not immediate confrontation, that objectivity is not extroversion, and that being is not a subdivision of the 'already out there now'. The fear of being trapped in one's own subjectivity, however, presupposes a *Gegenstand* or object standing over against or in opposition to the subject, an object of the type postulated by Kant, and it entails an epistemological 'problem of the bridge'. This first sort of fear of idealism is the one Liddy identifies as emerging with his discovery of insight, and he reports that it was dissolved when he realised that the idealism he was fearing, in his words, 'still holds on to the idea of reality as "out there". . . '[29] Because he understood that the idealism he feared was just as counterpositional as the incoherent realism he was leaving behind, his fear dissipated.

This first sort of fear, then, is, in its most vulgar form, an unreasonable fear of solipsism and, at its most sophisticated, it is an unreasonable fear

29. Liddy, *Startling Strangeness*, 206.

of Kantian Critical Idealism. The realisation of its unreasonableness and its dissipation, then, do not signal either an entry into or a passage beyond the halfway house on the way to Critical Realism. The dissipation of this unreasonable fear of counterpositional idealism merely clears the way, I would say, for the emergence of a second sort of fear of a different sort of idealism, a fear of the quasi-positional, transitional, Hegelian Absolute Idealism of the halfway house. That is to say, insight into insight does not propel one through and beyond the halfway house of Absolute Idealism; on the contrary, it merely situates one at its threshold.

This second fear is a reasonable one and, as such, is not so easily alleviated. Now, either the pre-existing commitment to theism joins with insight into insight to evoke the fear that a real distinction cannot be drawn between divine and human subjectivity, or the pre-existing respect for fact combines with insight into insight to elicit the fear that being is just a tissue of internal relations, or both join with insight into insight to elicit a fear of the implications of Absolute Idealism. One now confronts the precarious balance, the instability, and the mixed results of the transitional position, and the residual dialectical tension between the ideal of comprehensive coherence and concrete and discrete matters of fact. The pseudo-problem of gaining access to being from without is replaced by the real problem of dividing being from within. That is to say, a pseudo-problem of objectivity, previously framed imaginatively in terms of 'inside' and 'outside', is replaced by a genuine problem of objectivity framed now in terms of unimaginable immanence and transcendence. The unreasonable fear of counterpositional idealism is gone, but a reasonable fear of quasi-positional idealism remains, and it should remain. It is this fear that initiates and qualifies the prolonged personal and intellectual struggle to go beyond idealism.

As Lonergan observed in 1958, in his first set of lectures on *Insight*, 'if you frankly acknowledge that intellect is intelligence, you discover that you have terrific problems in epistemology'.[30] These terrific problems arise as a consequence of insight into insight. That is to say, insight into insight evokes them; insight into insight does not solve them. Moreover, these terrific epistemological problems are not safely quarantined within an isolated cognitive faculty. They infect the concrete, existing subject. So it is that, when Lonergan discovered insight in the summer of 1930 while reading Stewart's *Plato's Doctrine of Ideas*,[31] he did not immediately

30. *CWL* 5 *Understanding and Being*, 19.

31. Lonergan reported his discovery by way of Stewart in the question session that

declare himself a Critical Realist, but found himself at the threshold of the halfway house of Absolute Idealism, and he feared he was becoming an idealist. Again, Lonergan reports that he sought assurance that he wasn't an idealist when he 'got hold of the idea that knowledge is discursive',[32] and the fear that he might be an idealist was still present, by his own admission, years after his discovery of the act of understanding, when he was arriving at the conclusions he set forth in *Insight*.[33] In the Preface to *Insight* Lonergan alludes to his twenty-eight-year search, from the beginning of his philosophical studies in 1926 until the completion of *Insight* in 1953. I think it is fair to say that the last twenty-three-and-one-half years of that twenty-eight-year search—from his discovery of insight in the summer of 1930 while reading Stewart until the completion of *Insight* in 1953—were spent in the halfway house of idealism, engaged in the terrific epistemological struggle required to move beyond it.[34] As Lonergan remarked in the Halifax Lectures, 'The intrusion of epistemological problems in a real, significant way is a disturbing event'.[35]

So it is that, despite the essential role of insight into insight in the appropriation of his Critical Realism, Lonergan regarded his doctrine of judgment as his greatest contribution to philosophy. Insight into insight

---

took place on June 19, 1979, at Boston College. 'Aristotle and Thomas held that you abstracted from phantasm the *eidos*, the *species*, the idea. And my first clue into the idea was when I was reading a book by an Oxford don by the name of J. A. Stewart who in 1905 had written on Plato's myths and in 1909 on Plato's doctrine of ideas. And he explained the doctrine of ideas by contending that for Plato an idea was something like the Cartesian formula for a circle . . . and that exemplified an act of understanding to me, and the idea was getting what's in behind the formula for the circle. So you have something in between the concept and the datum or phantasm. And that is the sort of thing that you can't hold and be a naïve realist . . .' The transcription of the tape-recording of the question session is held by the Lonergan Research Institute in Toronto and was done by Nicholas Graham.

32. Bernard Lonergan, *Caring About Meaning: Patterns in the Life of Bernard Lonergan*, edited by Pierrot Lambert, Charlotte Tansey and Cathleen Going (Montreal: Thomas More Institute Papers, 1982), 110. Also in *Caring About Meaning*, 108, Lonergan remarks that, while Husserl's 'account of knowledge was never purely constructive', his is. 'It is all construction. Saying it is all construction enlarges the notion that human knowledge is discourse. When I say "critical realism is not a half-way house between materialism and idealism but idealism is the half-way house between materialism and critical realism", it is the same thing again.'
33. Lonergan, *Caring About Meaning*, 110–11.
34. On Lonergan's reading of Stewart's book on Plato's doctrine of ideas, see my book *At the Threshold of the Halfway House: Bernard Lonergan's Encounter with John Alexander Stewart* (Boston: The Lonergan Institute, 2008).
35. *CWL* 5 *Understanding and Being*, 351.

may dispel the myth of confrontationism and dissipate the fear of counterpositional idealism. But with the elimination of that myth and the abating of that unreasonable fear there come to light terrific epistemological problems, and there emerges another, reasonable fear. The epistemological problems are finally resolved, and this reasonable fear is finally alleviated, only with the discovery of the virtually unconditioned and judgment of fact. As one's entry into the halfway house of idealism is occasioned by insight into insight, as one's dwelling in the halfway house is characterised by a struggle with a genuine problem of objectivity, so one's passage beyond the halfway house of idealism is accomplished only with the discovery of the grasp of the virtually unconditioned and judgment.

By way of conclusion, let us return briefly to the irony with which I began and the questions it evoked. Why is the Aquinas of the Toronto Thomists so radically incompatible with Hegel? I would say it is because Hegel breaks with confrontationism, and they, like Kant, do not.[36] Their Aquinas is, therefore, radically incompatible with Hegel who breaks completely with confrontationism. In what ways is Lonergan's Aquinas compatible with Hegelian idealism? Lonergan's Aquinas, like Hegel, breaks with confrontationism, and both, following Aristotle, affirm the doctrine of knowledge by identity.[37] Does Lonergan's kinship with both Aquinas and Hegel have consequences for our appropriation of Lonergan's Critical Realism? I think it has important and far-reaching consequences. It requires that we distinguish an unreasonable fear of idealism that is to be dismissed from a reasonable fear of idealism that is to be appropriated. That reasonable fear of idealism initiates and qualifies our pursuit of solutions to the terrific epistemological problems that follow upon the discovery that intellect is intelligence. It ushers us into

36. See *Collected Works of Bernard Lonergan*, volume 4, *Collection*, edited by Frederick E Crowe and Robert M Doran (Toronto: University of Toronto Press, 1988), 192–203, for Lonergan's discussion of Kant and Gilsonian Thomism.

37. *CWL* 3 *Insight*, 372, for Lonergan's acknowledgement of Hegel's rejection of confrontationism. Hegel evidently derives his understanding of knowing by identity from Aristotle's *De Anima*. See, in this connection, Alfredo Ferrarin, *Hegel and Aristotle* (Cambridge: Cambridge University Press, 2001). In his *History of Philosophy* Hegel gives no attention whatsoever to the positions of Aquinas. See his extensive treatment of Aristotle in his *Lectures on the History of Philosophy*, volume 2: *Plato and the Platonists*, translated by ES Haldane and Frances H Simson (Lincoln: University of Nebraska Press, 1999), 117ff. Compare his one-paragraph treatment of Aquinas in his *Lectures on the History of Philosophy*, volume 3: *Medieval and Modern Philosophy*, edited by Robert F Brown, translated by RF Brown and JM Stewart, with the assistance of HS Harris (Berkeley: University of California Press, 1990), 58.

and beyond the halfway house of Hegel's Absolute Idealism. It abates only with the completing achievement of a doctrine of the grasp of the virtually unconditioned and judgment that is the final moment of the ascent to the rationally self-conscious standpoint 'above the clouds' that is Lonergan's Critical Realism.

Chapter 2

Rational Self-Consciousness: A Peak Above the Cloud

Elizabeth A Murray[1]

In honour of the fiftieth anniversary of the publication of Lonergan's *Insight*, it would be salutary to consider his original intention in writing that work. The aim of his book is stated clearly in both its preface and introduction. It is a complex aim, which Lonergan states succinctly in the preface: 'the aim of the work is to convey an insight into insight',[2] and which he articulates over twenty-one pages in the introduction. He modestly describes his work as 'essay in aid of self-appropriation'.[3] He identifies self-appropriation as one's own rational self-consciousness taking possession of itself as rational self-consciousness. In the original preface to *Insight*, which appeared in print in the first issue of the journal *Method* in 1985, Lonergan identifies rational self-consciousness as 'a peak above the clouds'.[4] He develops this imagery further when he adds: 'Yet if man can scale the summit of his inner being, also he can fail to advert to the possibility of the ascent or, again, he can begin the climb only to lose his way'.[5] The reader of *Insight* then is invited to commence or, as the case may be, to advance on a trek to scale the summit of one's own rational self-consciousness and to take possession of that summit.

1. A revised version of this paper titled 'The Second Moment of Intellectual Conversion' appeared in *Lonergan Workshop (2008)*, 21 (2009): 277–94.
2. *Collected Works of Bernard Lonergan*, volume 3, *Insight: A Study of Human Understanding*, edited by Frederick E Crowe and Robert M Doran (Toronto: University of Toronto Press, 1992), 4 (hereafter *CWL* 3 *Insight*).
3. *CWL* 3 *Insight*, 16.
4. Bernard Lonergan, 'The Original Preface of *Insight*', in *Method: Journal of Lonergan Studies*, 3 (1985): 3.
5. Lonergan, 'The Original Preface of *Insight*', 3.

Lonergan's preliminary characterisation of this trek to the peak, however, presents a difficulty. The climb is described in two ways which may or may not conflict—as a momentous event in one's intellectual life and as a gradual process of development. On the one hand, we appear to be invited to perform a single decisive act:

> The crucial issue is an experimental issue, and the experiment will be performed not publicly but privately. It will consist in one's own rational self-consciousness clearly and distinctly taking possession of itself as rational self-consciousness. Up to that decisive achievement all leads . . . But though the act is private, both its antecedents and its consequents have their public manifestation . . . more than all else the aim of the book is to issue an invitation to a personal, decisive act.[6]

In considering the first possibility that self-appropriation may hinge on the performance of an act, a second question emerges: what is the nature of that act? In the above quotation the phrase 'clearly and distinctly' echoes Lonergan's point in the preface that insight is the source of what Descartes called 'clear and distinct ideas'.[7] Is this decisive act an act of insight? His fuller statement of the nature of self-appropriation later in the introduction supports this interpretation, for he talks of the *discovery* of two distinct realisms.[8] He refers also to St Augustine's *discovery* that the real is not any kind of body.[9] Or, is the key act of self-appropriation an act of decision, of deliberately orienting oneself? Lonergan's talk of rational self-consciousness taking possession of itself as rational self-consciousness strongly suggests so.

On the other hand, the trek to the summit is described as a gradual ascent. Lonergan insists: 'The labor of self-appropriation cannot occur at a single leap. Essentially, it is a development of the subject and in the subject, and like all development it can be solid and fruitful only by being painstaking and slow.'[10] Further, he characterises *Insight*, his 'essay in aid of self-appropriation',[11] as a 'book designed to aid a development'.[12] So the

6. *CWL* 3 *Insight*, 13.
7. *CWL* 3 *Insight*, 4.
8. *CWL* 3 *Insight*, 22.
9. *CWL* 3 *Insight*, 15.
10. *CWL* 3 *Insight*, 17.
11. *CWL* 3 *Insight*, 16.
12. *CWL* 3 *Insight*, 18.

self-appropriation of one's own rational self-consciousness is a gradual development, not a single leap.

Lonergan's preliminary remarks on his aim in *Insight* present us with the question of the nature of self-appropriation. Are we to understand self-appropriation to be a matter of the performance of a memorable act, a key insight or a decision, or is it a matter of one's personal development? Is self-appropriation a gradual process that involves a series of pivotal insights and decisions? In terms developed later in *Insight* and in *Method in Theology*, is self-appropriation of rational self-consciousness primarily a genetic or a dialectical self-transformation?

Lonergan wrote *Insight* from a moving viewpoint. The appearance of inconsistency in his initial account of self-appropriation is a function of his pedagogical approach. *Insight* is not a closed conceptual system. As he explains, a single book 'may be written from a moving viewpoint, and then it will contain, not a single set of coherent statements, but a sequence of related sets of coherent statements.'[13] In the spirit of Gödel, Lonergan operates from a moving viewpoint 'that successively sets up contexts only to go beyond them.'[14] He would have his interpreters qualify his earlier statements in light of his later statements. It would be facile to quibble about apparent inconsistencies in his introductory remarks. I bring out this seeming difficulty in the text in order to tease out an underlying and remaining question. Is self-appropriation primarily a matter of gradual intellectual development or is it primarily a dialectical process of radical transformations?

In Lonergan's account of the appropriation of truth, he describes a three-part process that involves both gradual intellectual development and existential commitment. 'To appropriate a truth is to make it one's own.'[15] The process of appropriation involves *learning*, the gradual accumulation of habitual insights; *identification*, the performance enabled by making the insights one's own; and *orientation*, the decision to adhere to what has been rationally affirmed as true. This last essential element of appropriation is not put in terms of conversion in *Insight*, but we can identify in it the deliberate choice of a radically different horizon. Without this personal commitment the achievement made possible through the painstaking accumulation of insights may slip away. Lonergan writes:

13. *CWL* 3 *Insight*, 18.
14. *CWL* 3 *Insight*, 18.
15. *CWL* 3 *Insight*, 581.

> But once we have reached the truth, we are prone to find it unreal, to shift from the realm of the intelligible and the unconditioned back into the realm of sense, to turn away from truth and being and settle down like good animals in our palpable environment.[16]

Self-appropriation of rational self-consciousness is a process of intellectual development that requires personal transformation and deliberate existential commitment. In his 'Lectures on Existentialism' Lonergan describes at some length how philosophic development involves conversion, a transformation of one's entire mode of life.[17]

Scaling the summit of one's inner being, then, involves a long climb that includes leaps. Certain necessary leaps are occasions of severe exposure in which one leaves safe ground only to confront the challenge of regaining balance on an opposite pinnacle. The leaps are necessary not in the sense that anyone making the ascent will automatically make them, but rather that if one is to reach the summit one must make them. The required leaps are dialectical moves in the process of the self-appropriation of rational self-consciousness. And if one is to stay at the summit a reorientation of oneself to the new-found truth must be made and remade.

The crucial discoveries one makes in the process of self-appropriation are specific to each of us. Each is a function of one's intellectual development and context, the philosophies one has been schooled in, the conflicts of one's time, and the ideal of knowledge under which one labours. For Augustine it was the discovery that he had been trying to imagine God, and that God could not be any kind of body, not even the minimal body of an unlimited white light. While the pivotal insights in one's intellectual development may be materially unique, there are certain intellectual transitions indispensable to the appropriation of rational self-consciousness. Let us turn to another image Lonergan employs in his introduction to *Insight*, the image of the halfway house.

An overview of the ascent to be made and its way stations is provided in the following account of self-appropriation:

16. *CWL* 3 *Insight*, 582.
17. *Collected Works of Bernard Lonergan*, volume 18, *Phenomenology and Logic: The Boston College Lectures on Mathematical Logic and Existentialism*, edited by Philip J Mc Shane (Toronto: University of Toronto Press, 2001), 289–91 (hereafter *CWL* 18 *Phenomenology and Logic*).

> For the appropriation of one's own rational self-consciousness . . . is not an end in itself but rather a beginning. It is a necessary beginning, for unless one breaks the duality in one's knowing, one doubts that understanding correctly is knowing. Under the pressure of that doubt, either one will sink into the bog of a knowing that is without understanding, or else one will cling to understanding but sacrifice knowing on the altar of an immanentism, an idealism, a relativism. From the horns of that dilemma one escapes only through the discovery—one has not made it yet if one has no clear memory of its startling strangeness—that there are two quite different realisms, that there is an incoherent realism, half animal and half human, that poses as a halfway house between materialism and idealism, and on the other hand that there is an intelligent and reasonable realism between which and materialism the halfway house is idealism.[18]

The peak Lonergan would have us reach is the worldview of critical realism. In order to reach that summit one must pass through other positions. He identifies two halfway houses, that of naïve realism and that of idealism. Let us consider both in a preliminary fashion.

The first halfway house is naïve realism which is an advance over materialism, but nevertheless as a philosophic position, remains incoherent. Both materialism and naïve realism are forms of empiricism. The latter is an advance over the former, because while both view knowing as a matter of perceiving the real, the latter allows a role for human intelligence. Materialism, which has a history dating back to the Presocratic atomists, is generally a reductionism that issues in varieties of perspectivism, relativism, or scepticism. Typically materialism does not recognise any role for understanding in knowing. So-called 'mental acts' are simply neurological events. The only legitimate science of the mind is the study of the brain.

Lonergan credits naïve realism with being half-human, that is, with recognising some role for understanding in knowing. A prominent representative of such a position is Gilson whose Scholastic realism is unabashedly dogmatic. Knowing the real involves a role for intellect as that which abstracts concepts from sense perception. Gilson assumes the overriding principle, *Nihil in intellectu nisi prius fuerit in sensu* (nothing is

18. *CWL* 3 *Insight*, 22.

in intellect unless it is first in the senses). Abstract concepts are abstracted from sense and the mind contains these mere shadows of the real. We bridge the gap between the abstract concepts in the mind and the concretely real through the addition of an intellectual vision. For Gilson we reach the concrete because the 'concept of being is "seen" in the data of sense'.[19] His wholesale rejection of the Kantian critique of such intellectual *Anschauung* is based on the self-evident fact of our perception of the real. To argue otherwise is to arbitrarily adopt an idealist starting point.[20]

While Lonergan distinguishes materialism and naïve realism in the introduction, in later works he tends to conflate the two and refer simply to empiricism or to naïve realism. Varieties of empiricism, such as materialism, dogmatic realism, physicalism, phenomenalism, and pragmatism, share certain fundamental tenets. To move from one empiricist position to another may involve an advance in philosophic argumentation and the insights required for such developments, but the fundamental horizon is not thereby gainsaid. The fundamental assumption is that in sense-experience we directly perceive reality, which seems to be the natural view of people everywhere. As Lonergan remarks, 'some form of naïve realism seems to appear utterly unquestionable to very many'.[21] Yet, this view is the result of a failure to distinguish between what is natural in our knowing as extroverted animals surviving in our habitats, and what is natural in our knowing as intelligent and rational human beings. But this brings us to the limit of the empiricist horizon. In order to continue the ascent, to advance to the next halfway house, a dramatic, dialectical move is required.

Let us return at this point to the quote featured from the introduction. Lonergan names a second halfway house: 'there is an intelligent and reasonable realism between which and materialism the halfway house is idealism'.[22] Note that he does not situate this second halfway house as midway between naïve realism and critical realism, but as midway between materialism and critical realism. The significance of this detail is twofold. First, he views materialism, which thrives in post-modern continental

19. Bernard Lonergan, 'Metaphysics as Horizon', in *Collected Works of Bernard Lonergan*, volume 4, *Collection*, edited by Frederick E Crowe and Robert M Doran (Toronto: University of Toronto Press, 1988), 200.
20. See Paul St Amour, 'Lonergan and Gilson on the Problem of Critical Realism', in *The Thomist*, 69 (2005): 557–92.
21. Bernard Lonergan, *Method in Theology* (Toronto: University of Toronto Press, 1990), 239.
22. *CWL* 3 *Insight*, 22.

thinkers as well as in contemporary analytic circles, to be more obscure than the naïve realism of common sense and of scholasticism, which while pre- or a-critical does not reject some role for human intelligence. Secondly, as one advances through the steps of the ascent, the distances between the viewpoints become greater. This happens to echo Plato's analogy of the line in *Republic*, Book VI. Plato specifies that the line depicting the operations and their objects, leading to the ultimate intuition of the One, is divided into thirds. The lower portion of sense and imagination takes up one third, and the higher portion takes up two-thirds. As one ascends the distances become greater, signifying the increasing significance of the operations and objects.

The climb to the second halfway house, the position of idealism, is more difficult. It is not simply a matter of refining one's empiricist claims and discovering new arguments in their defence. It involves the radical transformation of one's viewpoint and the repudiation of the empiricist position. It is a dialectical step, an intellectual conversion. In *Method in Theology* Lonergan distinguishes three types of conversion, religious, moral, and intellectual. In his account of intellectual conversion, he differentiates three basic philosophical horizons, and he points out the following about them: 'Empiricism, idealism, and realism name three totally different horizons with no common identical objects.'[23] Because the three horizons have no common objects, because each successive horizon repudiates central features of the previous horizon, there must be two dialectical moves necessary to reach the position of critical realism. However, Lonergan writes of intellectual conversion as a unitary achievement: 'Intellectual conversion is a radical clarification and, consequently, the elimination of an exceedingly stubborn and misleading myth concerning reality, objectivity, and human knowledge.'[24] It culminates in the adoption of the three-part basic position outlined in 'The Method of Metaphysics' in *Insight*.[25] But in light of the dialectical opposition of the three philosophic horizons of empiricism, idealism, and critical realism, this conversion can be understood to be a two-phase conversion, a conversion that has two distinct dialectical moments. The first moment is the leap from empiricism to idealism, and the second movement is the leap from idealism to critical realism. Both are necessary for the realisation of the horizon of critical realism. If one has not at least

23. Lonergan, *Method in Theology*, 239.
24. Lonergan, *Method in Theology*, 238.
25. *CWL* 3 *Insight*, 413.

visited the halfway house of idealism, one is not going to ascend to the summit.

We find in the works of Kierkegaard another thinker who dealt with conversion, but in different terms. In order to articulate the two dialectical moments of intellectual conversion, let us turn to his treatment, in *Fear and Trembling*, of how one becomes a person of faith. Kierkegaard often uses the term 'leap' when describing transitions from one standpoint to another, because such transitions involve nothing necessary or inevitable, conceptually or developmentally or historically.[26] He writes of leaps in thought as well as in existence. In the life of the intellect one encounters very definite limits and the next sphere cannot be reached without a leap.[27] In *Fear and Trembling*, the focus of Kierkegaard's pseudonym Johannes de Silentio is the dialectical leaps that are required to reach faith. This account provides rich insights not only into the nature of religious conversion but also into the nature of conversion in general.

The key to Kierkegaard's notion of conversion is the concept of *Gentagelse* (repetition), which he celebrates as his one original contribution to the history of metaphysics.[28] Repetition is the act of freedom through which one becomes oneself anew. The self facing the future of infinite possibility transcends the finite self it has already become in the past and becomes itself anew in the present moment. The moment is an act of decision, which requires intense self-conscious reflection and which is experienced in anxiety. The decision is constitutive of the self and the world. Through it one's thought and existence is transformed. Conversion, for Kierkegaard, is not to be thought of as a terminal achievement. The radical act of choice must be remade repeatedly in order to continue to exist as the newly transformed self. So the term 'repetition' is doubly significant: the act of repetition is a repetition of the self—the self is made anew; and the act of repetition must be ever repeated in the next moment.

In de Silentio's account there are two essential moments of transition one must engage in if one is to become a knight of faith: the act of infinite

26. Merold Westphal, *Becoming a Self* (West Lafayette, Indiana: Purdue University Press, 1996), 39.
27. Westphal, *Becoming a Self*, 70–71.
28. Søren Kierkegaard, *The Concept of Anxiety*, translated by Reidar Thomte (Princeton, New Jersey: Princeton University Press, 1980), 17–19. For an analysis of the concept of repetition, see Elizabeth A Morelli [Murray], 'The Existence of the Self Before God in Kierkegaard's *The Sickness Unto Death*', in *The Heythrop Journal*, 36 (1995): 15–29.

resignation and the act of accepting all again in faith. De Silentio describes what is required for the act of infinite resignation:

> In the first place, the knight will have the power to concentrate the whole substance of his life and the meaning of actuality into one single desire . . . In the next place, the knight will have the power to concentrate the conclusion of all his thinking into one act of consciousness . . . The knight then makes the movement . . . and, then, will recollect everything, but this recollection is precisely the pain, and yet in infinite resignation he is reconciled with existence.[29]

In concentrating all of one's desire into a single desire the self is able to renounce all of finitude, oneself and the world, with one act of total self-abnegation. In concentrating all of one's thought into one act of consciousness, the self attains the eternity of the philosopher. But this otherworldly suffering, no matter how dramatically embraced, is not faith; it is the last stage before faith. 'The act of resignation does not require faith, but to get the least little bit more than my eternal consciousness requires faith.'[30] One may ascend this far and live out one's life as a suffering ascetic: 'In infinite resignation there is peace and rest and comfort in the pain.'[31] In order to maintain oneself in this existence of the suffering ascetic, one must remember all one has renounced, one must remain acutely aware of one's desire and one's denial. The act of resignation must be made freely and repeatedly.

The second moment of conversion is also an act of freedom. It is the decision to accept back again finitude, all that one most deeply desires and had renounced, by virtue of faith. According to de Silentio this transition is made only by virtue of the fact that for God all things are possible. One can become a knight of infinite resignation through one's own strength, but to make the second move is not solely through one's own choice, although one's free act of choice is required. 'By faith I do not renounce anything; on the contrary, by faith I receive everything exactly in the sense in which it is said that one who has faith like a mustard seed can

29. Søren Kierkegaard, *Fear and Trembling*, edited and translated by Howard V Hong and Edna H Hong (Princeton, New Jersey: Princeton University Press, 1983), 43.
30. Kierkegaard, *Fear and Trembling*, 48.
31. Kierkegaard, *Fear and Trembling*, 45.

move mountains.'[32] Both movements require virtue. Infinite resignation requires strength, energy and spiritual freedom, a purely human courage, but the act of faith requires in addition a humble courage. As the act of resignation must be repeated, the act of freely accepting and returning to embrace the finite in faith must continually be made.[33] The two-phase dialectic of coming to faith, then, involves a moment of withdrawal and renunciation and a moment of return and acceptance.

The purpose here of recounting Kierkegaard's account of religious conversion is not to weigh the merits of his theology, but to glean from it both essential characteristics of conversion, and a model of a two-phased conversion. Lonergan's account of the nature of conversion in *Method in Theology* agrees essentially with Kierkegaard's account of repetition. He defines conversion as a free act of will, as a decision or a choice. He writes:

> It is a decision about whom and what you are for and, again, whom and what you are against. It is a decision illuminated by the manifold possibilities exhibited in dialectic. It is a fully conscious decision about one's horizon, one's outlook, one's worldview.[34]

As de Silentio sees the knight of faith as a rarity, because the required act of infinite resignation and the act of acceptance in faith are strenuous and rare, so Lonergan describes intellectual conversion as a 'high achievement'.[35] It is not simply a matter of drifting into some contemporary horizon. Through an exercise of vertical freedom, a rationally self-conscious and deliberate choice, one adopts a new horizon that is not consonant with the fundamental tenets of one's current horizon. A vertical exercise of freedom can serve to introduce a new horizon which is grounded in the potentialities of the previous horizon. The emergence of the variety of empiricisms, alluded to previously, illustrates such vertical yet consonant changes in horizons. But in the decision characteristic of intellectual conversion a horizon is adopted which is not consonant with the tenets of one's previous horizon. Rather, one decides to repudiate characteristic features of the old horizon. 'Such an about-face and new beginning is what

32. Kierkegaard, *Fear and Trembling*, 49.
33. Kierkegaard, *Fear and Trembling*, 37.
34. Lonergan, *Method in Theology*, 268.
35. Lonergan, *Method in Theology*, 269.

is meant by a conversion'[36] for Lonergan. Both Kierkegaard and Lonergan, then, view conversion as a dialectical act of freedom through which one transcends the self one has been and the horizon one has adopted, to find oneself in a radically new horizon. Finally, to be authentic in terms of one's intellectual life is to embrace the basic position on the nature of being, objectivity, and knowing. But this choice is not made once and for all. As Lonergan reminds us:

> Human authenticity is not some pure quality, some serene freedom from all oversights, all misunderstanding, all mistakes, all sins. Rather it consists in a withdrawal from unauthenticity, and the withdrawal is never a permanent achievement. It is ever precarious, ever to be achieved afresh.[37]

To underscore the key characteristics, then, Lonergan and Kierkegaard both view conversion as a matter of free, self-conscious decision, as involving a radical dialectical shift in horizon or orientation which repudiates one's former horizon or orientation, and as an act which must be repeated.

Is intellectual conversion a two-step process, a radical re-orientation that requires two dialectical moments? As noted previously Lonergan considers the basic philosophic horizons of empiricism, idealism, and critical realism to be three totally different positions having no common identical objects.[38] The radically different nature of these horizons means that to choose to move from one of them to another requires a vertical exercise of freedom, specifically, a conversional vertical exercise of freedom. We can distinguish two main moments of intellectual conversion: the first moment is the shift from empiricism to idealism, and the second moment is the shift from idealism to critical realism.

Before we examine the nature of these two moments, we should review what Lonergan means by empiricism, idealism, and critical realism. We should begin, though, by noting that Lonergan is, of course, simplifying the history of thought when he names just three major philosophic positions. As we have already seen, in his introduction to *Insight* he distinguishes materialism and naïve realism when locating the first halfway house. A

36. Lonergan, *Method in Theology*, 238.
37. Lonergan, *Method in Theology*, 252.
38. Lonergan, *Method in Theology*, 239.

plethora of empiricisms have emerged in the history of thought, from Empedocles to Hume to Daniel Dennett and the Churchlands, but for the sake of this exposition let us take Lonergan's lead and refer to empiricism as one possible philosophic standpoint. It is also a simplification to refer to *the* position of idealism, as though there is only one, where in reality there are a number of notable idealisms in the history of thought: Plato's naïve idealism, Berkeley's deistic idealism, Kant's critical idealism, Fichte's subjective idealism and Hegel's absolute idealism.[39] Bearing in mind this clarification, let us consider the three major positions to which Lonergan refers.

Critical realism is the horizon that affirms the basic tenets of the threefold position outlined in 'The Method of Metaphysics' in *Insight*:

> the real is the concrete universe of being and not a subdivision of the 'already out there now'; . . . the subject becomes known when it affirms itself intelligently and reasonable and so is not known yet in any prior 'existential' state; and . . . objectivity is . . . a consequence of intelligent inquiry and critical reflection, and not . . . a property of vital anticipation, extroversion, and satisfaction.[40]

The other two horizons fail in some way to grasp and affirm these three basic tenets. Empiricism assumes that the real is already constituted, outside of the subject, that knowing is a matter of looking or perceiving and forming beliefs, and that objectivity is only reached when one's opinions and beliefs are confirmed with the hard evidence of sense. If certain beliefs, such as belief in causality, cannot be confirmed in sense evidence, then knowledge of causality must be jettisoned, along with knowledge of God, of angels, of the human soul, and of anything that cannot be measured and tested. Idealism maintains the view that reality is already out there beyond the subject or, rather, that it may be but that we cannot experience it directly or know it—we can only think of it. Knowing is not immediate, as it is for the empiricist, but mediate. For Kant, for example, it is a matter of the constitution of phenomena through the imposition of *a priori* forms of sensibility and categories of understanding, through the transcendental synthesis of imagination and the guidance of principles of reason. Objectivity is achieved in morality on the basis of universal and

39. Lonergan, *Method in Theology*, 264.
40. *CWL* 3 *Insight*, 413.

necessary laws of reason, but our knowledge of fact is merely phenomenal. In summary, the horizon of empiricism is the view that we have objective knowledge of the real immediately through sense-perception. It is fundamentally naïve and extroverted. The horizon of idealism is the view that what we immediately experience as raw sense data has no meaning, that all meaning is constituted through the human mind. It is fundamentally constitutive and immanentist. The horizon of critical realism is both constitutive and attains objectivity.

Idealism, notably the critical idealism of Kant and the phenomenological immanentism of Husserl, maintains the basic empiricist identification of the real with an unknowable noumenal or transcendent realm. Despite this persistent residue of empiricism, the shift to the idealist standpoint marks a radical transformation. This radical shift to understanding the world as mediated and constituted by meaning is the first moment of intellectual conversion. It is a moment of withdrawal from the world as it has always been assumed to be. It attempts to suspend all commonsense and scientific presuppositions except, it should be noted, the fundamental ocular model of intentional operations.

There are obstacles standing in the way of any philosophic conversion. There is the anxiety one feels when confronted with a new horizon. Lonergan writes:

> When a person is confronted with a new philosophy that also involves or necessitates in him a conversion for its total acceptance, he will not and cannot attend simply to the philosophic arguments. His consciousness will be concerned to maintain itself, and he will trot out what Husserl and Heidegger will call his *Selbstverständlichkeiten*, his obvious, self-evident truths . . . [41]

In addition to the underlying dread of destroying one's successful synthesis in living, there is the theoretical assumption that the introduction of any new philosophic idea is simply a matter of argumentation—that no conversion is required, just sound reasoning. In fact to advert to such existential, subjective conditions of philosophic discourse is to engage in psychologism.

41. Bernard Lonergan, 'Lectures on Existentialism', in *CWL* 18 *Phenomenology and Logic*, 290–91.

In addition to the general obstacles to conversion, each of the two moments of intellectual conversion has its own set of difficulties and conditions conducive to its occurrence. Each moment also will be experienced differently depending upon the intellectual development, cultural milieu, and historical conditions of the subject. Accounts of experiences of radical intellectual shifts do not abound, as McShane suggests perhaps Maslow was correct in his pessimistic estimation that 'less than 1% of adults grow'.[42] One striking account of an experience of the first moment of intellectual conversion can be found in Fichte's letters:

> It is incredible how profoundly Kant's philosophy . . . has influenced the total system of one man's thinking and how decidedly Kant's philosophy has initiated a revolution in my total philosophic thought. Since I read the *Critique of Practical Reason*, I am living in a totally different world. The principles that I hitherto believed to be absolutely certain have been totally uprooted and destroyed . . . An inexhaustible joy fills me.[43]

What are the specific difficulties that obstruct the withdrawal to idealism?

The fundamental assumption of the empiricist horizon is the myth that knowing is like looking, that objectivity is seeing what is there, and that reality is what is already out there to be perceived. Lonergan describes this myth as exceedingly stubborn and misleading.[44] It is stubborn because we are not simply rational agents, but also we are animals having to survive in our habitats like all other animals. We are extroverted and this extroversion is a fact of our animal nature. The myth is misleading because it leads to an oversight of insight, to commonsense denigration of the merely theoretical, and to scientific reductionism. It leads to the truncation of the self as intelligent and reasonable. The difficulty of the first moment of intellectual conversion was not lost on Plato, who incorporated into his curriculum years of mathematical training for students in the Academy. In order even to begin the arduous, disorienting climb out of the darkness,

42. Philip Mc Shane, 'Features of Generalized Empirical Method and the Actual Context of Economics', in *Creativity and Method: Essays in Honor of Bernard Lonergan*, edited by Matthew Lamb (Milwaukee: Marquette University Press, 1981), 548.
43. At:<http://www.csudh.edu/phenom_studies/europ19/lect_2.html>. Accessed 1 June 2010.
44. Lonergan, *Method in Theology*, 238.

one must break the chains of sense, imagination, and accepted opinion. One must, as Lonergan puts it, cut the umbilical cord to the maternal imagination. Any moment of conversion entails anxiety, but there is a specific fear of idealism one may encounter in the first moment of intellectual conversion. Liddy recounts musing: 'Am I becoming an idealist? Does this insistence on the intellectual pattern of consciousness lose contact with reality? . . . [Am I] getting too wrapped up in my own "self" and never reaching reality "out there"?'[45] Lonergan wrote of the necessity of overcoming one's 'spontaneous estimate of the real, and the fear of idealism involved' in it.[46]

What are conditions that would be conducive to making the transition of the first moment of conversion? In order to perform any radical intellectual leap, it is best to adhere to Lonergan's transcendental precepts: Be attentive, Be intelligent, Be rational, Be responsible, and even Be loving. If one is not paying attention when one reads or otherwise encounters the thought of another, one will likely miss the clues, anomalies, and disturbing features that could spark one's interest. One must allow the questions that may disrupt one's horizon to arise, follow the reasoning and evidence to conclusions even if they conflict with one's cherished beliefs, and finally exercise openness and charity in considering the thought of others.

Specifically, the exigence that seems most operative in motivating one to make the first transition is that of the pure desire to know as wonder, as the spirit of inquiry. This normative exigence enables one to take the plunge, to let go of the familiar shore and head out into the sea of conscious intentionality. It delights in minor discoveries and rejoices in the *Ureinsicht* that grounds a whole new world. This spirit of adventure is sustained through moral virtues. Courage is required to overcome the fear of idealism, and a self-discipline or self-control can aid one in the solitary hours of intellectual pursuit. Fichte stipulates the moral prerequisite for intellectual conversion: 'All individuals must be educated into being persons, otherwise they would not be persons';[47] and 'the kind of philosophy one chooses thus depends on the kind of person one is . . .

---

45. Richard M Liddy, *Startling Strangeness: Reading Lonergan's* Insight (Lanham, Maryland: University of America Press, 2007), 206.
46. Bernard Lonergan, 'Consciousness and the Trinity', in *Collected Works of Bernard Lonergan*, volume 6, *Philosophical and Theological Papers 1958–1964*, edited by Robert C Croken, Frederick E Crowe and Robert M Doran (Toronto: University of Toronto Press, 1996), 130.
47. Johann Gottlieb Fichte, *Grundlage des Naturrechts nach Prinzipien der Wissenschaftslehre* (1796), *Samtliche Werke* III (Berlin: Walter de Gruyter, 1971), 51.

Someone whose character is naturally slack . . . will never be able to raise himself to the level of idealism.'[48]

In the first moment of intellectual conversion, then, one heeds the call of the unknown and bravely leaves the familiar 'real' world behind.

The second moment of intellectual conversion marks the transition from idealism to critical realism. There are even fewer accounts of the experience of this leap. Giovanni Sala provides one in the following:

> The surprising thing about this insight, which came to me at the end of a long search and in which the scales of intuitionism fell from my eyes, was that, in spite of all the complex particular forms and instances of human knowledge in all its various branches, the core of this doctrine proved to have a disarming simplicity: we know reality because and to the extent that we attentively observe the relevant data of experience, bring the data to an intelligible unity, and take the trouble of weighing the evidence for and against our interpretation of the data with intellectual honesty. Every human being who wants to know how it stands with reality spontaneously does precisely this! This same insight made it possible for me to see the chasm that intuitionism of every sort sets up between the cognitive acts which we de facto perform and the postulated intuition of the fact itself, whether it be Kant's merely sensible intuition or the neo-scholastic intellectual intuition.[49]

This dramatic account conveys both poles of the dialectical transformation that constitute the second moment of intellectual conversion, what is renounced and what is affirmed. Sala describes letting go of intuitionism, of both the empiricist kind found in the sophisticated naïve realism of neo-scholastics like Gilson and the idealist kind found in Kant's critical, transcendental philosophy. He also articulates the positive content of what is gained in this conversion, namely, the appropriation not only of

48. Johann Gottlieb Fichte, *Introductions to the 'Wissenschaftslehre' and Other Writings*, edited and translated by Daniel Breazeale (Indianapolis: Hackett Publishing Company, 1994), 20.

49. Giovanni Sala, *Lonergan and Kant: Five Essays on Human Knowledge*, translated by Joseph Spoerl, edited by Robert M Doran (Toronto: University of Toronto Press, 1994), xvi-xvii.

intelligence but also of reason's role in arriving at fact. The role of reason is suggested by Sala's reference to the process of weighing the evidence in coming to knowledge.

The second moment of intellectual conversion is an equally radical shift. It is effected through the *Ureinsicht* that the known is reached through a grasp of the virtually unconditioned and the act of judgement. It is the affirmation of the self's cognitional self-transcendence in the act of affirming what has been reflectively understood as virtually unconditioned. In the first moment of intellectual conversion, one withdraws into immanentism through renunciation of the familiar world of sense and imagination. In the second moment of intellectual conversion, one returns to objective reality (actually obtains it for the first time) through a transcendence of all subjective conditions. In the reflective insight into the conditions for something to be the case, and the reflective insight that those conditions have been met, one is carefully, reasonably, detaching the fact from its subjective grounds. In the judgement in which one affirms what is so absolute objectivity is attained; the fact is not relative to oneself. Lonergan writes: 'Objectivity is simply the consequence of authentic subjectivity, of genuine attention, genuine intelligence, genuine reasonableness, genuine responsibility.'[50]

This 'juridic' transformative moment has its own difficulties and conditions conducive to its occurrence. As is the case with the move to idealism, one must contend with the entrenched counter-positional myth. One may have already accepted the constitutive role of thought in experience, but, as Sala mentions, the confrontational model of knowing is still operative in Kantian idealist notions of intuition. This makes self-knowledge particularly problematic as the self-presence in reflective self-consciousness, if not delicately negotiated, leads conceptually to an infinite regress. A second obstacle is the modern ideal of knowledge as certain and necessary which is still operative in the idealist horizon. Necessity plays a role in the nature of the act of insight, and in the exigencies of syllogistic reasoning, but the knowledge attained in judgement of fact merely happens to be; it is contingent, historical, and may be revised. Adherence to the ideal of necessity in knowledge is so adamant, that the idealist would rather forego the possibility of arriving at knowledge than renounce this ideal. A third obstacle to the conversion to critical realism is the hubris of the idealist. As having attained the heights of theoretical ingenuity through clamber-

50. Lonergan, *Method in Theology*, 265.

ing up the scaffolding of esoteric terminology, it is most humbling to find that knowing what is objectively true is a matter of carrying out the everyday cognitional acts of every Tom, Dick, and Jane. A parallel is found in Kierkegaard's account of faith. After describing in the most heroic terms the feats of the knight of infinite resignation, he describes the knight of faith as unrecognisable in his ordinariness.

As in the case of the first moment of intellectual conversion, the second moment has conditions which make its occurrence more likely. Idealists, if not swept away with their own theory, can also heed the transcendental precepts. To leap beyond one's intellectual horizon requires the intelligence to understand the limitations and contradictions of one's viewpoint, and the reasonableness to accept the fact of performative contradiction. A normative exigence may also be at work. As the spirit of inquiry motivates the first moment, the exigence for rationality can motivate the second. It just may help one to move beyond obfuscation and indecision to affirmation of the fact and role of judgement in knowing. The transition to critical realism requires its own specific moral virtue, humility, or, in Kierkegaard's terms, a 'humble courage'. Beyond the transcendental ego of immanentism, I affirm myself as the concrete me of polymorphic consciousness. The self of critical realism is not only rational but also animal, and so engages in two forms of knowing which must be repeatedly distinguished, especially in one's philosophic pronouncements. Acknowledgment of the duality in knowing and the fact of human development leads one to admit the tension inherent in human existence. The real is not more or less than the horizon established by the set of judgements rationally affirmed. The paucity of the original judgements any one of us makes leads the critical realist to appreciate the value of collaboration, the fact of the reliance on belief, and the role of others in the self-correcting process of learning.

The critical realist, while critical of the naïve assumptions of the empiricist, and aware of the constitutive role of meaning, is thrust back into the objective world as just a single finite, polymorphic knower in a community of learners. While this may be a humbling transition from the idealist horizon, the critical realist must live with the tension of affirming that nevertheless he or she is a knower. As such, one bears the responsibility of an authority, and is not allowed the comfort of hiding behind one's ignorance. The critical realist occupies the precarious position beyond both the dogmatism of the empiricist and the relativism of the idealist.

In conclusion, our reflection on Lonergan's statements of his original aim in his major book *Insight* has led to examination of the role of conversion in the self-appropriation of rational self-consciousness. His images of rational self-consciousness as a peak above the clouds, and the half-way houses one encounters in the process of the ascent, have led us to consider the three basic philosophic horizons of empiricism, idealism and critical realism. In order to ascend to the peak of rational self-conscious appropriation of one's own rational self-consciousness, it is necessary to perform two dialectical transitions: the first is the move from empiricism to idealism; the second is the move from idealism to critical realism. We found that intellectual conversion is not a singular event in two senses. First, intellectual conversion has two moments, the moment of withdrawal to immanence and the moment of transcendence to objectivity. And secondly, intellectual conversion is not a final achievement. The horizon of critical realism must be gained and regained through rationally self-conscious and free commitment. To maintain, secure, and develop this horizon, the critical realist welcomes and relies upon collaboration within a community.

Chapter 3

Kant, *Insight* and the Life Context

William Mathews, SJ

> Plato's greatness lies in his fidelity to the social problem. His *Republic*, like Kant's *Kritik*, set a perfect question but utterly failed to answer it.[1]

The problem of the mind-world relation

After a number of years researching my intellectual biography of Bernard Lonergan,[2] building up a familiarity with the details of his life and works, I found myself eventually confronted with the question: what is the most important thing to understand about him?[3] The answer that came to me was his intellectual passion, the desire of his mind, that was omnipresent in his life and which found expression in his works. This in turn led to the title and sub-title of the book, *Lonergan's Quest: A Study of Desire in the Authoring of* Insight, and resulted in a major reorientation of my relation with the details of his life as I then understood it. That intellectual passion finds expression in and through the major problems which came to him and on which he worked. Not overnight, but only slowly did I come to identify in *Lonergan's Quest* a fourfold awakening of the desire of his mind. This left me with two problems. Firstly, there was the task of clearly focusing on the details of the four awakenings, each of which was con-

1. Bernard Lonergan, 'Essay on Fundamental Sociology,' 108, 1935 (Lonergan Research Institute Toronto, Archives File 713 (History)).
2. William A Mathews, *Lonergan's Quest: A Study of Desire in the Authoring of* Insight (Toronto: University of Toronto Press, 2005); hereafter *Lonergan's Quest.*
3. A more detailed account of this process can be found on my website page entitled 'Points for Discussion' at: <http://www.milltown-institute.ie/BillMathews/BillMathews.html>. Accessed I June 2010.

cerned with a major issue: the foundational problem of the subject-object relation in Kantian philosophy; the causes of the economic Depression; the metaphysics/dialectic of history; and the problem of a historically and culturally conscious method in theology.[4] Secondly, there was the interrelated task of understanding in that totality how his emergent intellectual desire became, in turn, constitutive of his emergent narrative selfhood, a topic to which I will return in the final section of this paper.

What is perhaps surprising from my present perspective is that what took the most work to uncover and assimilate in the four awakenings was how precisely the book *Insight* was addressing the central, and for Lonergan, the perfect question posed by Kantian philosophy. In my earlier readings of Lonergan, perhaps influenced by his essay, 'Cognitional Structure',[5] there had been a tendency to place an emphasis on the centrality of his insight into cognitional structure and the different levels of consciousness. Only with time, in the course of which I spent years meditating on his course notes on 'Intelligence and Reality,' which I consider to contain the real key that unlocks *Insight*,[6] did it begin to become clear to me that his insights into cognitional structure and the related levels of consciousness were a part of his response to a much greater problem. As the titles of Lonergan's courses, 'Intelligence and Reality' and his earlier 'Thought and Reality' make clear, his fundamental aim was not just to understand human intelligence, that is to say our thought processes or cognitional structure, in itself, but within the framework of the larger problem of the mind-world relation.

I also noted in the central foundational chapters of *Insight*, 9–13, two significant remarks. The first appears in Chapter 9: 'As yet, we are unprepared to answer the Kantian question that regards the constitution of the relation of the knowing subject and known object'.[7] The second appears in Chapter 13: 'The principal notion of objectivity solves the problem of

4. The four awakenings are introduced in *Lonergan's Quest,* 6–7.
5. Bernard Lonergan, 'Cognitional Structure', in *Collected Works of Bernard Lonergan,* volume 4, *Collection,* edited by Frederick E Crowe and Robert M Doran (Toronto: University of Toronto Press, 1988), 205–21 (hereafter *CWL* 4 *Collection*).
6. Bernard Lonergan, 'Intelligence and Reality,' 1951 (Lonergan Research Institute, Toronto LB 131.5)
7. *Collected Works of Bernard Lonergan,* volume 3, *Insight: A Study of Human Understanding,* edited by Frederick E Crowe and Robert M Doran (Toronto: University of Toronto Press, 1992), 300 (275). Page numbers in brackets, for *Insight* and other works, refer to the pagination of the original editions. Hereafter, the *Collected Works* edition of *Insight* shall be cited as *CWL* 3 *Insight.*

transcendence.'[8] The phrase, 'the problem of transcendence' occurs in Cassirer's discussion of objectivity in his *Substance and Function* which Lonergan had read.[9] I became convinced that these remarks articulated the problem that these central chapters were addressing and so provided a wider context for the insight into cognitional structure. I also became convinced that mastering the meaning of his remark about the principal notion of objectivity solving the problem of transcendence was central to the foundations of *Insight*. If one missed the point here one missed the real foundations and could end up distorting the entire intellectual vision of the book. Such was the challenge.

Mastering the meaning of the principal notion of objectivity involved in my own experience a fairly major intellectual conversion with which I struggled for many years and continue to struggle. As Liddy has written about his puzzlement about the where of an insight,[10] I have a decided memory of the strangeness I felt at certain points when I was struggling with the problem of the connection or relation between my so-called 'inner' thoughts and the 'outer' world. One of the dimensions had to do with the role of the imagination. Like Liddy I found that I just could not in any sense imagine 'the inner' and what the solution might be like. Resolving

---

8. *CWL* 3 *Insight,* 401 (377).
9. Ernst Cassirer, *Substance and Function* (Chicago: Open Court, 1923), 278; also of significance in this work is his treatment of things and mind (271). Lonergan's foundational work on the problem is in 'Thought and Reality,' the Second *Verbum* article, and the 'Intelligence and Reality' notes. Kantian influences on Lonergan include: 1926—Frick's *Logica*, the text book used by Whiteside, his first teacher of philosophy, which sums up the elements of Kant's philosophy and its Copernican revolution to which Lonergan refers in *CWL* 3 *Insight,* 438 (413) and *Method in Theology* (London: Darton, Longman & Todd, 1971), 96, 264. Frick refers to *Pascendi dominici Gregis,* Pio X 1906, para 7, which is on vital immanence; the criticism of Kant's philosophy of immanence would have been the dominant ecclesiastical position at the time. Stewart's *Plato's Doctrine of Ideas* read Plato from a Kantian perspective (6–7, 47, 58). Hoenen's 'On the Origins of the First Principles of Knowledge' (1933), which mentions Kant's name in the first two paragraphs, and his later 1938 articles, were a huge critique of Kant's theory of the immanence of the understanding. Lonergan's 1934 'Essay in Fundamental Sociology' contains the opening quote of the present essay. Keeler's book, *The Problem of Error from Plato to Kant: A Historical and Critical Study,* was reviewed by Lonergan in *Gregorianum* 16 (1935): 156–60 close to the time he was being influenced by Maréchal on judgement and Leeming's course on the *unicum esse* in Christ. While in Rome Lonergan also made notes on Kant's *Metaphysics of Morals* (Italian Translation) LRIT A 12, 11 pages, A 13, 5 pages. Finally, there is the influence of the neo-Kantian Cassirer.
10. Richard M Liddy, *Startling Strangeness: Reading Lonergan's* Insight (Lanham, Maryland: University of America Press, 2007), 204.

that confusion involved understanding that the conscious dimensions of real and verifiable conscious and intentional mental acts such as wondering and having insights are of the form of real but unimaginable awarenesses.

In Kant's *Critique* two interrelated components are involved in knowing something, sensible intuition and the employment of the concepts or categories of the understanding.[11] Those categories are not, for him, in any sense related to properties of what we know in the world. The laws that we employ are not in the world but in our minds. The link between the use of our sensible intuition which only makes objects in the world present to our senses and the categories of the understanding is given in the schematism of the categories. Finally, judgement for Kant, as for many logicians including Joseph, involves the 'is' of predication rather than of existence. Every judgement is of the form of an assertion that X *is* a property of Y. There follows what might be termed the philosophy of immanence, a philosophy in which in a particular sense the significance of our subjectivity is grossly inflated. All the significant categories and concepts needed to know anything are in us, not in any sense in the things which we claim to know but which for Kant are unknowable.

In *Substance and Function*, wrestling with the epistemological gap between Kant's inner and outer worlds, Cassirer writes:

> If we have once enclosed ourselves in the circle of 'self-consciousness,' no labor on the part of thought (which itself belongs wholly to this circle) can lead us out again. On the other hand, the criticism of knowledge reverses the problem; for it, the problem is not how we go from the 'subjective' to the 'objective,' but how we go from the 'objective' to the 'subjective'.[12]

Cassirer's remark articulates the two extremes of Kantian philosophy and recent scientific materialism. In the Kantian position there occurs an inflation of the subject, a sort of anthropocentricism run amok,

11. On the intuition of objects, A 10; the two sources of mind A 50, B 74; the concern with 'how subjective conditions of thought can have objective validity,' B 122, A 89–90; and Kant's account of the Copernican Revolution, B xvi–xvii.

12. Cassirer, *Substance and Function*, 278. See also 271 on the two distinct spheres of things and mind; 278 on the problem of transcendence; 297 on the epistemological gap where Cassirer, echoing Lonergan, remarks: 'we find there is no epistemological gap to be laboriously spanned by some authoritative decree'; and see 298 on the problem of the definition of an object.

which results in a loss of the sense of the reality of the world, which is considered unknowable in itself, merely our invention.[13] In scientific materialism there occurs an inflation of the object of knowledge or the world which results in the elimination of the subject of knowledge, in the taboo of subjectivity.[14] The subject disappears from view into a black hole. A lot of the latter can be found in Dennett and related philosophers of consciousness and scientists for whom the scientific observer is to be eliminated from our world view.

Not being very appreciative in general of philosophers, Francis Crick's statement of the problem also has its interest:

> The second philosophical conundrum that needs clarification concerns the reality of the outside world. Our brains have evolved mainly to deal with our body and its interactions with the world it senses to be around us. Is this world real? This is a venerable philosophical issue and I do not wish to be embroiled in the finely honed squabbles to which it has led. I merely state my own working hypotheses: that there is indeed an outside world, and that it is largely independent of our observing it. We can never fully know this outside world, but we can obtain approximate information about some aspects of its properties by using our senses and the operations of our brain. Nor, as we shall see, are we aware of everything that goes on in our brains, but only of some aspects of that activity. Moreover, both these processes—our interpretations of the nature of the outside world and of our own introspections—are open to error.[15]

Crick illustrates the dilemma of modern science as it backs itself into a cul-de-sac by equating mind and consciousness with brain processes.

A condition of possibility of engaging with the book *Insight* is that at some point one must allow oneself to be drawn, personally, into this prob-

13. For a contemporary expression of this position consult Michael Frayn, *The Human Touch: Our Part in the Creation of a Universe* (London: Faber, 2007).
14. For a refreshing critique of scientific materialism see B Alan Wallace, *The Taboo of Subjectivity: Toward a New Science of Consciousness* (New York: Oxford University Press, 2000).
15. Francis Crick, *The Astonishing Hypothesis: The Scientific Search for the Soul* (New York: Charles Scribner's Sons, 1994), 12.

lem of the relation between the subject and object of knowledge. How does one, on the one hand, escape from Kant's mental prison in which the mind is locked up within one's subjectivity without going to the other extreme by becoming a scientific materialist and eliminating one's subjectivity in preference for the object? At the centre of Lonergan's solution to this dilemma we find the significance he attributes to the pure desire to understand which is a central characteristic of human consciousness. That desire contains within the structure of its relations and temporality the surprising key to the prisons in which we find ourselves trapped by present thought about the mind-world relation and the reductionist position on what it means to be a human being to which Kant and scientific materialism commit us.

Because of this creative potential, in the aftermath of completing *Lonergan's Quest* I have found myself challenged to enlarge my understanding of the project, and this in two ways. To unlock the great contribution of Lonergan's insights there is a need to integrate Kant's problem and Lonergan's solution to it both into the narrative movement of our lives and related worlds from childhood to old age and into the related intersubjective dialogue of our lives with others. For our mind-world relations are not static and fixed but rather constantly changing throughout our lifetime from our elementary education as children, through our entry into high school and our movement into university, and into our subsequent adult working lives. There are the differing mind-world relations and contexts of the child, early, middle and late adult. Not only that, but there are the differing worlds within which our minds can journey, from the dramatic world of our situated historical existence in the presence of other selves or subjects, through the mathematical and scientific worlds that baffle and bewilder us with their technicalities and abstractions, to the world of the historian and interpreter of ancient cultures, and finally the world of the philosopher who attempts to make sense of or adds to the confusion and fragmentation of it all. So in the life of an individual the mind-world relation is not one-dimensional and is constantly changing through the learning and research process.

Is our journeying through our worlds that of Kantian solitary detached and unchanging observers? Might it involve an extremely intimate symbiosis by means of which our very interaction with our world brings our emergent selfhood into being? Might not the world in some strange way be immediately present in our minds and our minds have a related directing presence in our world? Might that engagement with our world be necessary for our selfhood to grow? Ought not self affirmation be understood as an invitation to learn how we learn through personal experience; an assimilation of an invariant norm of lifelong learning in us, a norm which articulates what it is to live authentically throughout one's life in one's worlds? Ought not that invitation, as presented by Lonergan, be addressed not just to the solitary reader but to a community in dialogue? Within the limits of the present paper I want to suggest an experiment by means of which we might explore these problems, not only in the manner of the personal invitation offered to the reader of *Insight*, but also in the context of the intersubjective educational process in which we are all involved in the presence of our dialogue relations with Others as well as with the topic being studied.

The direct and the introspective modes of knowing

From Lonergan's essay in 1943, 'The Forms of Inference,' it is clear that he wished to develop a science, with its related method, of the data of consciousness.[16] In the second *Verbum* article, which is centrally concerned with the problem of thought and reality, we find the remark: 'We know by what we are; we know we know by knowing what we are; and since even the knowing in "knowing what we are" is by what we are, rational reflection on ourselves is a duplication of ourselves.'[17] This quotation contains in a nutshell Lonergan's later solution to Kant's problem. The same mental operations: questioning, understanding and judging, are involved in spontaneously knowing facts in the world, and introspectively, in coming to know ourselves as the subjects of those mental operations. One and the same questioning wonder in us comes to know within its objective, that is to say what exists, the distinction between the subject and object of knowledge.

The methodology involved is more clearly articulated in his notes for his course 'Intelligence and Reality:

16. Bernard Lonergan, 'The Forms of Inference,' in *CWL* 4 *Collection,* 3–16. Also highly significant is Lonergan's fourfold use of the term 'insight' in the opening pages of that essay.
17. *Collected Works of Bernard Lonergan,* volume 2, *Verbum: Word and Idea in Aquinas,* edited by Frederick E Crowe and Robert M Doran (Toronto: University of Toronto Press, 1997), 99 (90) (hereafter *CWL* 2 *Verbum*). See also Mathews, *Lonergan's Quest,* 175.

> Direct und(erstanding) : sensible data : introspective und(erstanding) : data of concs(iousness) No difference qua understanding; Begin from experience of understanding; relate to inquiry, presentations, concepts, in process of maths, class(ical) phase, statist(ical) phase . . . identity of experimenter, experimented on, experimentation[18]

Surprising for those familiar with the empirical sciences and their insistence on the insignificance of the role of the experimenter is the comment about the identity of the experimenter, experimented on, and experimentation. But what is noteworthy about both quotes above is that in them introspection, with all its associated problems, enters into the problem in hand. In his writings other than dismissing the notion that introspection is a form of inward looking, Lonergan could be taken as assuming that what it means is self evident.

In the first or direct mode of knowing, through our interpersonal common sense and scientific questions, insights and judgements in relation to the situations, experiences and scientific data present to our senses, our knowledge expands and with it more and more of the world becomes known. Although Lonergan focuses on particular aspects of the direct mode of knowing, the mathematical and scientific, for most of us the direct mode of knowing is immersed in the details of the lifetime of our situated interpersonal, historical and cultural existence. Within that situatedness the intellectual pattern of experience emerges significantly within the educational process. The spontaneous use of our mental powers involved can be so taken for granted that most do not think about and are not interested in them. The suggestion that they are a source of a profound and mysterious question about what it means to be human can be met with hostility.

Engaging in the introspective mode of knowing involves breaking down such resistance. One way of addressing this might be to integrate it into the actual educational process. As B Allen Wallace remarks, at a 1994 conference sponsored by the Royal Society in London on 'Consciousness—

18. 'Intelligence and Reality,' 9, para 5 (Lonergan Research Institute, Toronto LB 131.5). In Thomas More Institute for Adult Education, *The Question as Commitment: A Symposium*, Thomas More Institute Papers, volume 17 (Montreal: Thomas More Institute, 1977), 33, Lonergan puts it: 'You have to become accustomed to insights by setting yourself problems. For example: why does taking a square root work? When you see why it works you'll have an insight.'

Its Place in Contemporary Science', when 'one participant suggested that research into consciousness must include the first-person perspective, a number of his colleagues expressed consternation'. It was better to maintain the taboo of subjectivity than open up that can of worms.[19] For Wallace our theories of introspection are currently at a rudimentary stage. As introspection deals with the unimaginable data of consciousness, I could not agree more with his remark. Associated with the introspective mode we find:

1. What is meant by introspection is anything but self-evident, as borne out by Lonergan's remark that you can't have insights into insights, which are unimaginable, but only into phantasms.[20] The awarenesses that comprise the data of consciousness are unimaginable. Insights are elusive which means, by definition, that they are difficult to find or catch, remember or recall. So if we don't go out of our way to notice them, they slip by and with them our sense of our concrete historically situated intellectual selfhood slips by.
2. Some of the most dramatic experiences of the awakening of an individual to a question or having an insight can occur in the classroom or in a conversation after class. A student can suddenly come alive in relation to a particular topic; equally, a teacher can, in the course of teaching, find him or herself challenged to understand better a topic which they are trying to present. All of these experiences are gold nuggets from the standpoint of self-affirmation but are usually quickly forgotten. So how might the intersubjective educational process itself become a vehicle of self-appropriation and of an understanding of the mind-world relation on a shared group level? Involved will be a use of an introspective method whose procedure and results are also open to intersubjective verification.
3. Ayn Rand distinguishes between the conscious, the subconscious and the unconscious in the process of writing:

   > When we speak, it feels as if the words come automatically—as if the words and the thoughts come simultaneously. Of course, they do not. If you observe children learning to

19. Wallace, *The Taboo of Subjectivity*, 75. This whole chapter is to the point.
20. See Frederick E Crowe, 'For a Phenomenology of Rational Consciousness', in *Method: Journal of Lonergan Studies* 18 (2000): 70–83; and 'The Puzzle of the Subject as Subject in Lonergan', in *International Philosophical Quarterly* 43 (2003): 195–200.

> speak, or yourself learning a foreign language, you discover that language is not innate and automatic, but an acquired skill. It is so well integrated at the adult level, however, that the transition from the thought you want to express to the words you use is automatic.[21]

Her distinction between the thought and the words that express it is spot on. But so also is her observation that it is in the learning process that we have a heightened conscious awareness of our mental operations. When we have acquired the insights and related linguistic skills the self awareness in their automatic use is of a low order and only becomes clear when things go wrong. This suggests that introspection will find its greatest rewards by attending to the learning process.

4. By the direct mode of knowing is meant the spontaneous and unanalysed performance and engagement of the mind with experiences, problems and situations in the world in the realms of common sense, science and history. The direct mode of knowing is a direct cultural insertion and engagement of minds with their given worlds. In this sense the richer the culture the richer will be the data of the introspective mode of analysis and the knowledge it can attain.
5. The direct mode of knowing is the data or source of the three basic, distinct but related questions of the introspective mode of analysis and knowing: What am I doing when I am knowing? Why is doing this knowing? And what do I know when I do it? This direct connection between the modes should never be severed; otherwise the project collapses. It follows that the introspective mode, far from being a withdrawal from the direct mode and its related cultural context, is itself conditioned in its performance by the richness of the achievements of the direct mode of knowing. The completeness of its analysis demands that all three questions and their relations be addressed.
6. Although related, the languages that are associated with the two modes should reflect more clearly the differences in the data they are addressing. The qualities of the data of consciousness, being of the form of different kinds of unimaginable awarenesses, are in a different dimension from those of the imaginable data of sense.

---

21. Ayn Rand, *The Art of Nonfiction: A Guide for Writers and Readers* (New York: Penguin, 2001), 58. See also the index under 'subconscious'.

7. 'The subjective is intrinsically open to intersubjective validation, if only we avail ourselves of a method and procedure for doing so.'[22] By this is meant that the unique conscious awareness experienced by the subject must not be considered as something private and incommunicable. Through the articulation of language the subject comes first to express and own what was tacit but also to communicate it to others who in turn can critique it as any other scientific theory might be critiqued.

8. Even those who think they take the introspective mode seriously can themselves suffer from degrees of blindness, truncation of the self and a large existential gap between what they are and what they think they are.[23] Practice makes perfect. The question has to be asked: what evidence is there in the community of Lonergan scholars that serious exploratory introspection of consciousness is happening? Liddy is one of the few who is making waves about the strangeness of it all. Might it be the case that many are living with the language with little engagement with what it is that the language is related to?

9. Contra Kant's immanence of the understanding, for Aristotle, Aquinas and Lonergan understanding involves an identification almost in the sense of a becoming of the object. Through our understanding objects in the world become immediately present to us. As the sounding of the bell causes hearing in us, so the intelligibility of the elements of the problem represented in the phantasm causes the act of insight. The intelligibility of the object is not passive but active, an agent cause of the insight. Our understanding is not immanent in us. Equally, our desire to know is not internally self-starting. It has to be called out of itself by problems in the world, all of which is at odds with Kant's immanentism. In this context ponder the significance of Crick's

---

22. Francisco J Varela and Jonathon Shear, 'First-Person Methodologies: What, Why, How?' in *The View from Within: First Person Approaches to the Study of Consciousness*, edited by Francisco J Varela and Jonathan Shear (Thorverton, UK: Imprint Academic, 1999), 2. The stance of Varela and Shear 'in regard to first-person methodologies is this: don't leave home without it, but do not forget to bring along third-person accounts as well' (2). They also acknowledge the need for second person mediation. See also Wallace, *The Taboo of Subjectivity*, especially chapter 4. On the opposite side see the influential Ray Jackendoff's *Language, Consciousness, Culture: Essays on Mental Structure* (Cambridge, MA: MIT Press, 2007), 78, where he holds that Crick's later scientific materialism, although 'distressing and alienating,' by now seems 'the only reasonable way to approach consciousness scientifically.'
23. Varela and Shear, *The View from Within*, 11–13.

remark in *What Mad Pursuit*: 'Rather than believe that Watson and Crick made the DNA structure, I would rather stress that the structure made Watson and Crick.'[24] Perhaps Crick did not appreciate just how profound that remark is.

10. There needs to be acknowledged the role of memory and description in the introspective mode. When one is composing an essay in a degree program or engaging in an experiment in a research laboratory the last thing one should do is start self reflective introspection. One simply does the work. The introspective reflection comes afterwards or outside of the direct mode work. Still, because our memory rapidly deteriorates with time, the time interval involved should be as short as possible. In the natural and life sciences a written record of the details of the experimentation is always kept. In line with this Perkins' approach to the study of consciousness almost identifies introspection with writing an actual account of one's thought processes as experienced in the course of the work.[25] Applying this to the key events in Lonergan's philosophy it would require that we keep a written record of our engagement with the invitation to the judgement of self-affirmation and the three related judgements of the principal notion of objectivity which could be read by another person. Otherwise it is most likely we give some form of notional assent to them as an idea or theory but don't do the real work involved. If one is not writing up one's experiences from the standpoint of introspection with respect to the direct mode of knowing, then one is not doing the introspective analysis.

---

24. Francis Crick, *What Mad Pursuit: A Personal View of Scientific Discovery* (Perseus Books, Alfred Sloan Foundation, 1988), 76.
25. For DN Perkins in *The Mind's Best Work* (Cambridge MA: Harvard University Press 1981), introspection is equated directly with *composing* a report on one's thought processes as involved in insight problems. See index under 'thinking: reports of, retrospective reporting.' In his web course on consciousness James Barr insists that the participants keep a journal; see <www.consciousness.arizona.edu>. Acccessed April 19 2010. In *Language, Consciousness and Culture,* Jackendoff considers the form of thought to be 'unavailable to consciousness', that is to say, to be '*in principle unconscious*' (104; emphasis original). One wonders if he has ever wrestled with a difficult crossword puzzle. The present view is that thought is characterised by an unimaginable conscious awareness.

Insight Chapter 17: from the subject-world relation to the intersubjective

So how might the previous methodology and related exercises be more directly incorporated into the intersubjective educational process itself? How, through that incorporation, might it better facilitate self-appropriation, with its problematic dimension of introspection, on an ongoing and group level? There are, I suggest, hints and pointers in Lonergan's treatment of truth, its expression and its subsequent reinterpretation in Chapter 17 of *Insight*; and in his treatment in Chapter 13 of the same work of the principal notion of objectivity with its three judgements, where he remarks on objects that are also subjects, that is to say knowers.

Consider then the problems involved in a creative individual expressing and communicating the content of his new insight to his contemporaries. The subjects of new and original insights, such as Socrates on virtue, Aristotle on the soul or psyche, Einstein on relativity, or Francis Crick on the genetic code, have to find some form of linguistic expression within the available social categories of communication. At least some of these instances, such as Einstein's theory, are paradigm shifts involving a rupture in the use of these categories. This observation points to the enormity of the problem of communicating new insights to others in terms of the current language use. Similarly the later teachers of the original insights of an author will themselves have to assimilate those insights and express them for their later audience. Consider in this context the following quotes:

> An expression is a verbal flow governed by a practical insight *F* that depends upon a principal insight *A* to be communicated, upon a grasp *B* of the anticipated audience's habitual intellectual development *C*, and upon a grasp *D* of the deficiencies in insight *E* that have to be overcome if the insight *A* is to be communicated.[26]

What is significant here is that the analysis is not trying to elicit an insight of one's own in response to some posed problem, as in the earlier quote from 'Intelligence and Reality' on method; rather here Lonergan is dealing with the problem of the communication of insights from the mind of one individual to that of another through the communication process. It could

26. *CWL* 3 *Insight*, 585 (562).

be a great scientific breakthrough such as Crick and Watson's discovery of the secrets of DNA or of the genetic code, or Mendel's discovery of the laws of genetics; more concretely, though, it occurs in the educational process all the time. The task is not just to solve the problem but to understand the insights of another person into the solution of the problem.

The teacher as a mediator through interpretation and communication of such past achievements for a later generation has, for Lonergan, to assess the state of intellectual development of his or her pupils and bring it into play in his or her communication. To him or her we can apply Lonergan's further remarks:

> By an interpretation will be meant a second expression addressed to a different audience. Hence, since it is an expression, it will be guided by a practical insight *F?* that depends upon a principal insight *A?* to be communicated, upon a grasp *B?* of the anticipated audience's habitual intellectual development *C?*, and upon a grasp *D?* of the deficiencies in insight *E?* that have to be overcome if the principal insight *A?* is to be communicated.[27]

What I would like to suggest is that in the actual performance of this task there is being generated an intersubjective community of learning that is sharing the experience of being awakened by certain questions that arose in the minds of others and of trying to assimilate the insights which have emerged in their response to them. From that interpretative perspective they have, as mediators/teachers, the challenge of re-expressing these insights in terms that are comprehensible to their contemporaries. The dynamic of this experience with its related intersubjective group could, I believe, be most useful in the movement towards self-affirmation.

The intersubjective significance of language and mind/insights

The emphasis placed on the relation between insights and their linguistic expression in intersubjective communication opens up a question about the relation between language and mental operations:

27. *CWL* 3 *Insight*, 585 (562).

> The interpenetration of knowledge and expression implies a solidarity, almost a fusion, of the development of knowledge and the development of language. Words are sensible: they support and heighten the resonance of human intersubjectivity; the mere presence of another releases in the dynamism of sensitive consciousness a modification of the flow of feelings and emotions, image and memories, attitudes and sentiments; but words possess their own retinues of associated representations and affects, and so the addition of speech to presence brings about a specialized, directed modification of intersubjective reaction and response. Still, beyond the psychology of words, there is their meaning. They belong together in typical patterns, and learning a language is a matter, first, of grasping such patterns and, secondly, of gradually allowing the insights by which the patterns are grasped to be short-circuited by a sensitive routine that permits the attention of intelligence to concentrate on higher-level controls.[28]

Significant here is the distinction between the psychology and the meaning of words. Speech adds something to physical presence, an intellectual presence between speaker and listener, of mind to mind.

Two dimensions of language stand out in this context. Firstly, there is the ordinary use of language in describing situations in our world. Through that use we can communicate with others about such situations. The language communicates to us what they are thinking about their worlds. Secondly, there is a use of language whose meaning directly discloses to us the mind of its author. It will refer, not to their weight or height but to their questions or problems, their state of confusion, their subsequent 'aha' experiences and the consequences thereof in relation to dealing with the problem, their false starts on a solution, their corrections to these false starts, and their eventual resolution of the problem. If we correctly understand the meaning of such language we will, by Aristotle's theorem of knowledge by identity, gain direct access to the mind, or more broadly, the mind-world relation of its author. When an author articulates their questions they are telling us something about their mental state. Their subsequent use of language articulates their thoughts about

28. *CWL* 3 *Insight*, 577 (554).

the problem they are exploring. In that context any time an author uses the word 'insight' in their text they are again telling us something about their mental, or more broadly, their mind-world relation or state. Both their insights and questions relate them to their worlds. It is also the case that significant changes in an author's language use are the expression of significant insights they have had but might not necessarily have identified. The emergence of the insight in response to the problem enables them to speak about it and suggest experiments and go on with things in a manner not previously possible.

All language, in its propositional dimension, is an expression of the thoughts thought by its author about the world of the direct or introspective mode. In this sense what I am writing at the moment is a verbal expression of what it is I am thinking. Correctly to understand the meaning of the propositions involved is to understand something about the thoughts thought by their author and their related world.[29]

An intersubjective educational experiment

In the light of the preceding suggestions consider the following thought experiment which incorporates the pedagogy of the early chapters in *Insight,* and its enlargement in accordance with the points arising in Chapter 17, into the life context of the educational process. You are a member of a group seminar taking a course in the lives of creative scientists, one segment of which deals with the life and work of Francis Crick and of his collaborator, James Watson.[30] The aim of the course will be to attempt to understand some of the essentials of Crick and Watson's personal views of scientific discovery, that is to say, to understand how creative science is done. From the perspective of the first quote above from Chapter 17 of *Insight*, the principal insights (A_i) which Crick and

29. This issue of the presence of the mind of an author to the mind of a reader is addressed by Martin Buber, *I and Thou* (Edinburgh: T & T Clark, 1958), 128, in terms of hearing the voice of the master when reading an ancient text. Hopefully it will evoke a certain amount of consternation in those who advocate the death of the author.

30. The actual content of this thought experiment is not written in stone. In a previous version of this paper read at the Boston Workshop in June 2007 I took as the seminar text Heidegger's letter to William Richardson. It would also be interesting to take some dramas such as Arthur Miller's *Death of a Salesman* or Ibsen's *A Doll's House* to facilitate an exploration of the dramatic pattern of experience with a group. I believe it is always possible to choose a suitable educational content for groups of different ages and educational stages.

Watson's verbal expressions are attempting to communicate are about their personal understanding of what goes on in the process of making discoveries in science. From the perspective of the interpretative work of the present group, the principal insights ($A_i?$) will be concerned with a reinterpretation of those insights in the light of their different cultural context which will, for instance, include a reading of Lonergan's book, *Insight*. In this the aim of the group, which could include Kantians and scientific materialists, is to understand the insights of another person. In this group dynamic the personal invitation to self-affirmation of *Insight* is also being extended from the individual to the group.

The chemistry of DNA has been studied since 1868. By the 1940s it was known that it was made up of individual units, called nucleotides, joined together to form long chains. Nucleotides were made up of an organic base, a sugar and a phosphorous group.[31] With Avery's identification of DNA as the source of the hereditary process, interest in it intensified. The discovery by Crick and Watson of the detailed structure of DNA occurred in 1953, their engagement with the problem taking place largely between the fall of 1951 and the publication of the paper expressing their solution to the problem in *Nature* on 25 April 1953. Watson's later account of the process of making the discovery, *The Double Helix: A Personal Account of the Discovery of the Structure of DNA*, drawing on extensive letters and journal entries he wrote during the research years, was published in 1968.[32] For present purposes it is worth noting as significant his remark to the effect that his *insight* into the DNA base pair structure was '*the insight that made it all come together*'.[33] Crick's later discovery of what is known as the genetic code was made in 1966. His personal account of how he made his two great scientific discoveries, *What Mad Pursuit*, was published in 1988.

The actual performance of making those discoveries amounts to what Lonergan would term the direct mode of operation of the mind. Its product is the published research paper on DNA or Crick's scheme for the genetic code in which no account of the mental processes involved in making the discoveries is necessary. The later personal account of how those

31. For details consult Jack J Pasternick, *An Introduction to Human Molecular Genetics: Mechanisms of Inherited Diseases* (Bethesda: Fitzgerald Science Press, 1999), 84.
32. James D Watson, *The Double Helix: A Personal Account of the Discovery of the Structure of DNA* (London: Weidenfeld and Nicolson, 1968).
33. James D Watson, *DNA: The Secret of Life* (London: Heinemann, 2003), 53; emphasis original.

discoveries were made amounts to a first person analysis with introspective overtones of the direct mode involved. In fact Francis Crick gives one of the most remarkable accounts of a moment of insight and its related flash of enlightenment in his description of the quest to discover the genetic code.[34] The content of the insight belongs to the direct mode but the description of the experience of the flash of enlightenment belongs to the introspective mode. The present experiment is transposing these accounts of their activities in their entirety into the framework of the analysis of the truth of an interpretation in Chapter 17 of *Insight*.

The basic reading for the seminar is Crick's memoir, *What Mad Pursuit*, complemented, where necessary by James Watson's *The Double Helix*.[35] By way of an introduction to the material the director invites the members of the group to read and familiarise themselves with the following points from the first of the three major research problems with which Crick engaged in his distinguished career. He also invites them to describe in their journals their learning experiences involved in reading themselves into this material.

Crick's first research problem: DNA and the hereditary code.

- What do you take to be the situated historical existence of Francis Crick, his selfhood in the world so to speak, family background, books that influenced him, persons that entered his life as a research scientist (*What Mad Pursuit*, Chapter 1)?
- How did Crick's two main research interests and three related core questions form in his life history? How was he influenced by the discovery of the genetic significance of DNA by Avery, the entry into his life of James Watson, Rosalind Franklin's A and B X-ray photographs, and the questions posed by Schrödinger in *What is Life*—in particular his speculation that the chromosomes and their genes might be of the form of an *aperiodic* crystal containing the hereditary code (*What Mad Pursuit*, Chapters 2–3)? What do you take to be the link between Schrödinger's speculations and those photographs?
- Outline the details of his apprenticeship to the problem of DNA, his mastery of the mathematics and techniques of X-ray crystallography,

34. Crick, *What Mad Pursuit*, 120, 140–41.
35. Further references will be made to Crick's second book, *The Astonishing Hypothesis*, and to Matt Ridley's *Francis Crick: Discoverer of the Genetic Code* (London: Harper/Atlas, 2006).

in particular how his research moved forward through setbacks (*What Mad Pursuit,* Chapters 4–5; *The Double Helix*, 46–113). Crick is of the opinion that making mistakes and learning from them is of the essence of scientific research.

- Discuss the phase of mastering the problem as problem prior to its resolution (*The Double Helix* 113–48). What sense do you make of the empirical data of the problem, the A and B forms of the x-ray crystallography photographs of DNA fibres? What was the most important theoretical discipline involved in understanding them? What was the main difference between the A and B form of the photographs (*The Double Helix*, 132; *What Mad Pursuit*, 73–74 on later refinements)? How does the final answer relate to the X-ray data, the helical problem, and the base pairs? How does it resolve Crick's baffling problem of the duplication of the hereditary material? Why did Crick not give his assent to the double helix as virtually unconditioned until the early 1980s?
- How do the final insights bring together in a synthesis all the elements of the problem, in particular the X-ray photograph data and the insights of Chargaff into the bases, as well as Schrödinger's problem of the transmission of the code from generation to generation (*The Double Helix,* 148–58)?
- What significance can you locate for the imagination, and related model building, in such breakthroughs or moments of insight? Into what images were they insights? How well do you yourself understand the content of those insights—what Lonergan names ideas? What aspects of those ideas are you comfortable with? What are simply beyond you—X-ray diffraction techniques and the related mathematics, for instance?
- Crick's caution re: the correctness of the solution, verification and judgement (*What Mad Pursuit,* 73–4).
- How do these questions enable you to identify in the individual the creative source of science?

In particular the course is interested in the question, what precisely might be the cognitive source and causes of Crick and Watson's unusual creativity? To the extent that for most this exercise will be a learning one there arises the possibility of an enhanced experience of the conscious dimension of one's mental processes in the course of reading the books of Crick and

Watson. In this context a basic strategy, insisted upon by the director, is that all class members familiarise themselves with Perkins' remarks on keeping a journal of the learning/discovery process[36] and adjust it to their experience, both of the set reading and of the class interaction. There is also the fact that one is being invited to understand, not a classical or a statistical law, but the mental processes of another person engaging in the creative process of doing science.

a. Learning some worldly/public facts about the life of Francis Crick

1. In order of significance, draw up a list of the persons involved with Crick and Watson in the course of their discovery of the structure of DNA. What locations were involved in the research? How was the problem prepared, historically, for them?
2. What was the public empirical data of the problem?
3. What books did Crick and Watson read? What good luck did they have?
4. Who were Crick's collaborators for his later work?
5. Write your reflections on the social and cultural context of a scientific research problem.
6. If you were to find out parallel facts about the life of some other person largely unknown, how would you go about it? Sometimes we get our facts wrong and have to correct them. What is involved in such a correction process?

b. Learning some facts about the intellectual life of Francis Crick

1. The awakening of intellectual desire to its path

On the basis of reading Chapters 2–3 of *What Mad Pursuit* write your reflections on how Crick came to make his decisions regarding his choice of a research career.

Or

Write your reflections on the basis of reading Chapters 3–6 of Watson's *The Double Helix* of how Watson came to make his decisions regarding his choice of a research career.

36. See n 25 above.

In this stage the group has been moved from questions about Crick and Watson's public personae to questions about their conscious mental life and its relation with the world. As you read the texts make notes in your journal on what impresses you about the content. How do you think their curiosity got started, purely internally or by means of some external stimulus in the world? What good luck and bad luck can you see in it? How would you describe the qualities of the self-awareness that accompanied this searching for and finding of a project in the world? What might Watson mean when he says: 'My interest in DNA had grown out of a *desire*, first picked up while a senior in college, to learn what a gene was'?[37] What do you think would satisfy the kind of desire he is taking about? Is the change involved just a change in him or a change in his relation to the data of the problem in the world? What might be meant by the notion of the awakening of such a desire to its path, by the beginning of a quest. This invitation to reflect on the beginning of a work, problem or quest puts before us the question about the genesis of our own interests.[38] So the next invitation is to write a few sentences in your journal about the awakenings of your own intellectual interests. At the conclusion of these writing exercises the group is invited to share and discuss the issues that are being opened up. What sort of knowledge is forthcoming about the genesis of Crick and Watson's questions; about the genesis of some interests and related questions of my own? What do you learn from the others from the group sharing? In these moves the solitary first person introspective method of *Insight* is being enlarged to include first, second and third person perspectives and their interactions.

2. The serving of the apprenticeship stage of the problem solving

On the basis of your reading of Chapters 3–5 of *What Mad Pursuit* and Chapters 7–17 of *The Double Helix* write some notes on how the problem grew for Crick and Watson.

37. Watson, *The Double Helix,* 28; emphasis mine.
38. Dennis Shasha and Cathy Lazere in *Out of Their Minds: The Lives and Discoveries of 15 Great Computer Scientists* (New York: Copernicus, 1995), 247, have some interesting remarks on how computer scientists find themselves choosing or being chosen by a problem to work on: 'Third, you have to be the right person for the problem. As Donald Knuth puts it, "It's not true that necessity is the only mother or father of invention . . . a person has to have the right background for the problem. I don't just go ahead working on every problem that I see. The ones I solve I say, oh, man, I have a unique background that might let me solve it—it's my destiny, my responsibility."'

As you read the account of how the problem expanded for Crick, and eventually Crick and Watson, make your own journal notes of what you consider important in it. What role do you find the data of the problem and the imagination of the researcher to play? What new and unexpected questions do you find emerging? What mistakes do you find emerging? What new insights emerge through the mistakes? When you have finished, make further notes on what you feel you have come to understand clearly in the account and what you have difficulty understanding. Can you identify in your own experience your own groping as an apprentice in the present course and its problem of the mind-world relation? Can you identify some misunderstanding you might have had about how scientific discoveries are made such that you now find you have to revise your understanding? Again, with the facilitation of the director, the group is invited to meet and share their journal entries and note what they learn from each other.

3. The mastery of the problem as problem

Read Chapters 18–26 of Watson's *The Double Helix.* What precise contribution to their understanding of the problem did the work of Chargaff make? What contribution did the tearing to shreds of Watson's scheme make (*The Double Helix,* 148)? The mastery stage of a problem arrives when an understanding of all the significant and relevant questions which must be addressed in order to solve it have emerged but a solution has not. At this stage one will be in a position to evaluate any proposed insights and their related ideas in terms of the manner in which they meet head on all of those relevant questions. Write some notes on what you think it was like for Watson to have mastered all the relevant questions but still not have a solution

4. The resolution of the problem

Chapters 26–28 of *The Double Helix* show us that the basic problem Watson has to resolve has to do with how the base pairs hold together the two intertwined helical strands of the molecule. From that perspective the group members are invited to write their own reflections on his remark that 'suddenly I became aware that an adenine-thymine pair held together by two hydrogen bonds was identical in shape to a guanine-cytosine pair held together by at least two hydrogen bonds',[39] and his later comment that this awareness involved '*the insight that made it all come together*'.[40] By this he implied that not only did it give the structure of DNA but also clues as to how DNA coded hereditary characteristics. What do you think he means by his sudden awareness and his use of the word 'insight'? Could the latter mean a gestalt shift, an intuition by another name, an immanent inner act of understanding, an act of understanding that is caused by the mind's apprehension of the structure of the solution to the problem in the imaginative presentations? Is that act of understanding just an unusually intense operation of the acts of our senses and imagination? Or is it a form of startlingly strange operation whose qualities are irreducibly beyond those of our senses and imagination? As colours activate our seeing and sounds our hearing, what in the world activates our insights? What activities in the world, previously impossible for us, does it now enable us to do? At this point a dialectical element can enter into the group's discussion.

For Lonergan it is the image, not as purely present to the senses or imagination, but as a symbol within the specific context of problem-solving, that represents and makes present to the intellect the key elements of the problem, that causes the insight. It follows that mistaken insights can be caused by getting the wrong or inadequate imaginative presentations of the problem.[41] The right image is necessary for the right insight. How, it might be asked, does this relate to Aristotle's theorem on the identity in act of what is understood in the image and the understanding itself? The

39. Watson, *The Double Helix*, 152.
40. Watson, DNA, 53; emphasis original.
41. For a wonderful parallel groping process with the imaginative presentations of a problem consult BL van der Waerden, 'Hamilton's Discovery of Quaternions', in *The Mathematics Magazine* 49, no 5 (November 1976): 227–34. Hamilton initially tried to enlarge the problem of the multiplication of numbers from complex (a+ib) to three dimensions: (a+ib+jc). After much frustration he found he could not work out relations between i and j and was getting nowhere. According to van der Waerden, Hamilton then had the insight which completely redirected his searching: 'and there dawned on me the notion that we must admit, in some sense, a fourth dimension of space for the purpose of calculating with triplets' (230). Instead of trying to multiply together numbers of the form: (a+ib+jc) he tried with (a+ib+jc+kd). Soon after, quite unexpectedly, while walking along the banks of the Royal Canal with his wife the insight came to him which found its expression in the equations: $i^2 = j^2 = k^2 = ijk = -1$. For some significant remarks on the profound significance of insights in mathematics consult Robert Kanigel, *The Man Who Knew Infinity: A Life of the Genius Ramanujan* (London: Abacus 1999), 225–27; on the source of mathematical creativity in desire, see 230.

conclusion would be that the intelligible structure of DNA as represented in the elements of the image becomes immediately present to and acts directly on the understanding. What is understood is what the image represents. Nothing comes between them. What significance do you think this has for our understanding of the mind-world relation? How does it relate to Kant and to scientific materialism? How does it relate to your own experience in learning? Again your responses to the material are to be noted in your journal and brought to the group sharing. What do you learn from the group sharing?

5. Verification/falsification/assent. Is it correct?

Comment on the attitude of Crick, Wilkins and others to the final structure of DNA proposed by Watson. Although initially some were struck by the beauty of the structure, unlike the media presenters, they also approached it with a critical hardnosed attitude concerned with testing how it stood up to all the known relevant questions. Why was Francis Crick so cautious about accepting the solution (*What Mad Pursuit,* 73–74)? What finally convinced him that the solution was not just plausible or very plausible but *virtually* certain? What significance do you think that assent has for the structure of the mind-world relation? It seems that it was only when Crick gave his assent that he was confident that he knew some fact in the world. It seems that facts, what exists rather than what we think is the case, are made known to us through our critical acts of assent. A further dialectic of realisms can enter the group at this point. Make appropriate notes in your journal.

Does Lonergan's principal notion of objectivity solve the problem of transcendence?

> In knowledge considered developmentally, first there is had material objectivity, next normative, thirdly absolute, and fourthly consequent objectivity. For first we sense, or experience, next we inquire and reflect, thirdly, we judge, and fourthly through several judgements we contemplate the field of existence.[42]

42. Lonergan, 'Consciousness of Christ,' point 8 (Lonergan Course Notes 1952: LRIT LB 138). These notes, written after Chapter 13 of *Insight,* replace 'experiential' with

In order to understand Lonergan's solution to Kant's problem in terms of the three judgements of the principal notion of objectivity a number of things are necessary. Most notably, I believe the problem needs, as the above quotation suggests, to be approached genetically. This requires that we read Chapter 13 backwards, from experiential (material), normative and absolute to the principal (consequent) notion and fill out all the relevant details with respect to each of the three judgements. Experiential objectivity requires that the data relevant to each of the problems to which the judgements are resolutions be clearly identified and acknowledged. Normative objectivity requires that the questions for intelligence specifically arising from those data must be identified. Absolute objectivity requires that the final solution is invulnerable to further relevant questions. The principal notion of objectivity requires that a specific plurality of judgements is made in and through which the distinction within being of the subject and object of knowledge is established. What light on this project of understanding the problem of the transcendence of mind does our engagement with Crick and Watson shed?

Since, spontaneously, we know by what we are, first of all we have to come to know something in the world. In Crick's case it was the unknown chemical structure of DNA. Experiential objectivity required that their spirit of inquiry establish a genuine intellectual relation with the data of the DNA fibres and the X-ray photographs taken by Rosalind Franklin at King's College in which the unknown which they wished to discover lay concealed. Secondly, normative objectivity required that in their pursuit of the unknown they allow all the relevant questions in the problem to surface and be resolved. Those questions, which were evoked by the data, had been prepared by Avery's determination of DNA as the hereditary source, the heuristic of Schrödinger with its anticipation of an aperiodic molecule containing a code, and the introduction of helices by Pauling. In the course of the investigation the insights of Chargaff proved essential in clarifying the questions about the base structures. As the problem unfolded the issues which a solution had to resolve became clear. Thirdly, absolute objectivity required that the final insights address all the relevant questions in the inquiry and, through assent, lead to a known fact in the world. At the term of the discovery process, acknowledging that all the relevant questions had been addressed, and for Crick this did not come until the early 1980s, it was concluded that the factual nature of that struc-

'material', and 'principal' with 'consequent', and reverse *Insight*'s order of treatment. See Mathews, *Lonergan's Quest,* 305, for the context.

ture in the world, which is independent of the subjectivity of any researcher, had been established. This kind of investigation can be carried out with little or no reference to the mental powers of the investigators involved in it. In the process of coming to know some fact in the world rarely does the question of how we come to know the fact surface with any great seriousness and is usually assumed by scientific materialists and others to be of no real significance.

Secondly, we know that we know by knowing what we are. Crick and Watson in their memoirs show how this further question does not arise in the abstract, but is provoked by the very personal experience of engaging in scientific research and making specific discoveries. But whereas the experiential objectivity of the direct mode involved a correct intellectual relation with a datum in the world, DNA crystals, around which a cluster of questions arises, in the present mode the data were the coincident and correlative data of consciousness of the subjectivity of the scientific researcher. There is an inevitable conscious awareness involved in doing research and experiential objectivity demands that intellectually, we establish a correct questioning relation with it. When Crick and Watson describe how their personal interest in the problem of DNA arose, we note how experiential objectivity required that their desire to understand establish a correct intellectual relation with that datum. The same applies to Crick's description of being in a fog when problem solving or not even being able to imagine the shape of the solution they were seeking. He is again talking about an identifiable but unimaginable conscious awareness in his subjective experience. When Watson remarks that he suddenly became aware of an identity in the shape of an adenine-thymine and a guanine-cytosine pair, he is describing a change in awareness of himself that is coincident with a change in his awareness of a relation in the world. When he remarks that it was the related insight that made the final solution possible, he is showing how through the conscious and subjective event of a significant insight some key relation among data in the world became known.[43] Finally, there are Crick's remarks about the process of

43. Crick's account of their discovery that he and Sydney Brenner were barking up the wrong tree in their choice of a messenger enzyme in their pursuit of the genetic code is one of the most dramatic accounts of the startling flash of enlightenment that is a characteristic of all really creative discoveries in science and mathematics (*What Mad Pursuit,* 120, 140–41). As the lives of Darwin, Einstein, Ramanujan, Hamilton and Poincare illustrate, until you have had the key insight you do not yet have a theory. The theory is formulated out of the insight's content. If the insight makes known some sought-after quality of the object to be explained, the fact still remains that as insight it

arriving at a virtually certain assent in relation to the structure of DNA. The content of the assent given was about a hypothesis concerning a fact in the world; the coincident act of assent was a conscious activity of the scientific subject. Coinciding with the event of the assent the fact became known and the subject, Crick, experienced himself as a knower.

As the destination of the direct mode was the discovery of the molecular structure of DNA, so that of the introspective mode is of an assent to a patterned process of related mental activities constitutive of the subject who engages in scientific research. In the lives of Crick and Watson we can identify clear instances of being in the tension of inquiry, of the emergence of new insights and their ideas, of testing them and rejecting many, and finally, finding that a particular set of insights resists their every effort to find a fatal flaw in it. But, as Crick has pointed out, we can be just as much open to error in our introspections, so they too must be put to the test of critical analysis. At this point Lonergan would point out that any attempt to critique this understanding of the discovery process duplicates the process which one is attempting to understand and so constitutes a further key element of the evidence in the investigation.

Now what needs to be clearly drawn out is that at the heart of both enterprises, the spontaneous doing of research science, and the reflective movement of writing a personal account of the experience, is one and the same questioning activity, what Lonergan terms the pure desire to know. In the first or direct or spontaneous mode the research scientist comes to know scientific facts in the world: the structure of DNA, the genetic code and so forth. In the second or reflective or introspective mode one comes to know how one comes to know those facts. In the first mode one comes to know objects of knowledge in the world; in the second one comes to an understanding of a patterned process of distinct kinds of mental operations constitutive of the subject who knows them. That questioning activity finds its destination in a set of related judgements:

- The chemical structure of DNA is a double helix with a determinate pitch and base properties which code hereditary characteristics.
- Reflecting questioningly on that process of making the discovery I came to identify myself in it performing a set of mental operations, questioning, imagining, experimenting, having insights, leading to

---

is a property, not of DNA or the genetic code, but of Crick and Watson, the discoverers.

further experiments until the final moment when it all clicked into place.

- The same operations of questioning, understanding and judging were also involved in my efforts to understand the discovery process in doing science.
- The term of that process was a judgement about what it is for a human being to make scientific discoveries; I affirmed myself as the subject who knows.
- As characterised by wonder or curiosity, insights, judgements, I made the further judgement that I am not DNA.
- At the same time, through the theorem of the identity of the knower and known, I came to affirm that there is a wonderful and strangely intimate relation between my knowing and what I come to know in the world.

In these judgements the distinction and relation between the subject and object of knowledge within being, that is to say the objective of the pure desire to know, is made. Involved are two distinct but intimately connected realms of data: the world accessible to our senses and imagination, and the related world of the conscious intellectual activities that are called into existence through our coming to know the world. Also significant is the fact that both the object and the subject are known by means of the same operations of mind but operating on different fields of data: sensible and imaginable data in coming to know the object; conscious and unimaginable data in coming to know the subject. A most important feature of the pure desire to know is that in either of the domains we have investigated there is no epistemological gap between it and the data. In a certain sense it could be argued that the data can in some instances directly provoke our wonder. But because in the direct mode of problem solving all the attention is focused on the problem in the world, the very existence and qualities of the desire of the mind can go unnoticed. Only through the introspective mode, which in Lonergan's understanding goes hand and hand with the direct mode, does the existence and mode of operation of the pure desire to know as a notion of being, of everything that there is, become known.

In this Lonergan's solution dismisses the Kantian chasm of inner acts and outer phenomenon to replace it with something entirely different. Within the one universe that comes to be known through our pure desire to know, he distinguishes between objects, facts, situations and other selves in our world, all of which come to be known by us in the direct mode, and the subject whose very intellectual powers are activated by our coming to know these objects, facts, situations, and other selves. Both are known in essentially the same way and so there is no chasm. There is, however, a fundamental gulf between the data of sense which are imaginable and the data of consciousness which are not.

Crick, Watson and others remarked that they found something beautiful about the structure of DNA and the manner in which it coded the hereditary material.[44] I would like to suggest that there is also something very beautiful about what Lonergan terms the pure desire in us to know, from whose probing no corner of the universe is safe, even itself. There is also something very beautiful about the intimacy of its relation with the world which it strives to understand and know. There is no aspect of the empirical world, from the big bang, quarks, protons and neutrons, atoms, through the whole chain of being up to the human with its languages, social structures, cultures, and histories with which it cannot, potentially, enter into a questioning and wondering relation. The desire of the mind scrutinises all aspects of the data of the problem in a most intimate way. Equally, the unknown structure of DNA in the elements of the phantasm actually acts directly on our understanding, our insights. In the act of assent, facts, what exists in the universe, become immediately present to us. This beautiful intimacy of mind and world seems the sort of thing that Paul Davies and Werner Heisenberg are seeking to understand.[45]

Appropriating the emerging concrete intelligible unity of the self

> 'By the "self" is meant a concrete and intelligible unity-identity-whole.'[46]
> 'The being of the subject is becoming.'[47]

If the previous section was concerned with understanding the core significance of the desire of the mind for resolving Kant's perfect question about the mind-world relation, the present section will end by drawing

44. Watson, *The Double Helix*, 148, 167, 171; Crick, *What Mad Pursuit*, 76, 79.
45. Paul Davies, *The Goldilocks Enigma* (London: Penguin, 2006), 262–63; on Heisenberg consult *Manas*, 29, no 40 (October 6, 1976): 1.
46. *CWL* 3 *Insight*, 343 (319).
47. Bernard Lonergan, 'Existenz and Aggiornamento,' in *CWL* 4 *Collection*, 223.

attention to its equally profound significance for our understanding of what Lonergan at different times names the self or subject. In *Insight* the (intellectual) self is defined as a concrete intelligible unity present in the unity of consciousness although the nature of the intelligible unity is never specified.[48] It follows that in the judgement of self affirmation one does not know this concrete historically situated self, but only the invariant core cognitional processes by means of which in and through their situated historical existence the unity of the emergent intellectual self or subject will come into existence. A further quote makes this point clearer:

> Still, if the unity of consciousness would have to be postulated on the hypothesis that it were not given, it remains that it is given. By this, of course, I do not mean that it is the object of some inward look. What is meant is that a single agent is involved in many acts, that it is an abstraction to speak of the acts as conscious, that, concretely, consciousness pertains to the acting agent.[49]

'Existenz and Aggiornnamento' approaches the topic in terms of the being of the subject (of a world) as becoming. If the subject becomes, then the implication is that the subject-world relation grows with that becoming; but again the details are thin. An assimilation of the presence of the pure desire to know of the human mind throughout the lifetime of the self or subject will, it is proposed, greatly illuminate these points.

---

48. In later writings, Lonergan adds human historicity to human nature. See, for example, his treatment of historicity in 'Natural Right and Historical Mindedness', in *A Third Collection: Papers by Bernard JF Lonergan,* edited by Frederick E Crowe (London: Darton, Longman and Todd, 1985), 170–71. See also the following statement from c 1976: 'Similarly, the structure of our knowing and doing expresses the conditions of being an authentic person; but this structure is a matter of being attentive, being intelligent, being reasonable, being responsible; accordingly, there are four basic precepts that are independent of cultural differences. Moreover, since the actuation of the structure arises under social conditions and within cultural traditions, to the four may be added a fifth, Acknowledge your historicity.' ('Questionnaire on Philosophy: Response', in *Collected Works of Bernard Lonergan,* volume 17, *Philosophical and Theological Papers 1965-1980,* edited by Robert C Croken and Robert M Doran (Toronto: University of Toronto Press, 2004), 378.
49. *CWL* 3 *Insight*, 350 (326).

> A distinction needs to be drawn between experiencing the totality of consciousness and intentional activities throughout a life time, and understanding in that experience some form of intelligible unity. It is also clearly the case that there is no possibility that we might, towards the end of our lives, remember every question we asked, insight we experienced and word that we spoke. Still, Aristotle in his analysis of the action line in a plot makes a helpful suggestion. Out of the myriad of actions that happen in a lifetime there are those which stand out from the rest such that if any of them did not occur in the life the action line would be significantly different.[50]

Ira Progoff refers to these as stepping-stones, the serendipitous sequence of events in which, from a later time in life, we can see the movement of the self or subject from an origin to their present perspective. Stepping-stones in general are events, situations, circumstances, largely serendipitous, by means of which some kind of direction, not necessarily well understood at the time, emerges in a life story. Stepping-stones are also those events which, if they were taken out of the life, would change it in a quite drastic manner. Only with hindsight can they be clearly identified because sometimes when they occur other events might be competing with them for our attention. In time the impact of those other events diminishes. Earlier, we noted Watson's remark: 'My interest in DNA grew out of a desire, first picked up while a senior in college, to learn what a gene was'.[51] Later he would write: 'It was Wilkins who had first excited me about X-ray work on DNA' at a small scientific meeting in Naples.[52] If the desire started something, his encounter with Wilkins moved it forward. His meeting with Francis Crick in Cambridge was a further stepping-stone on the way. His intellectual journey is moving through those events.

From this perspective I would like to pose the question: from a reading of Crick's *What Mad Pursuit,* can the stepping-stones of his intellectual desire be identified? Can we identify moments such that if they were removed from his life then we would find ourselves dealing with a substantially different concrete and intelligible unity-identity-whole, that is to say

50. Aristotle, *Poetics*, Chapter 8, 1451^{a} especially 30–35.

51. Watson, *The Double Helix*, 28.

52. Watson, *The Double Helix*, 28.

a different person. I suggest the following written in the first person to indicate Crick as their subject.

The stepping-stones of Francis Crick's intellectual desire[53]

1. After the war, at the age of thirty, with a mind that wanted to turn to new problems, to fundamental research, inspired by a lot of background reading, including Schrödinger's *What is Life*? I narrowed down my interests to two main areas: the borderline between the living and the non-living, and the workings of the brain but decided for molecular rather than neurobiology.
2. After two years working at Strangeways, Mellanby cleared the way for me to join Max Perutz and John Kendrew at the Cavendish in 1949 which opened the door into the future life which I truly desired.
3. At the Cavendish, much to the annoyance of Bragg, I became an expert in the technique and mathematics of X-ray crystallography, skills that would become essential for me later.
4. This in turn led me into the field of Pauling's Alpha helix, discovered in 1948, published in spring 1951. Helices were from now on in the air and I became quite familiar with the field.
5. In 1951, quite by chance, James Watson came to work at the Cavendish. Although neither of us were commissioned to work on DNA, our desire to understand it became such that it was to become our joint passion. Without him, I doubt I would have taken up this pursuit in such an enthusiastic manner, if at all.
6. Between 1951 and 1953 our familiarity with every aspect of the problem, the A and B X-ray photographs, the problem of the number of helical strands, the water content, and Chargaff's base structure, grew through many many setbacks.
7. In April 1953 we came up with a solution to the chemical structure of DNA in which Watson's insight into the complementarity of the base structure suggested a copying process and made it all possible.

53. The significance in Crick's stepping-stones of the decisions made about what truths to pursue in his research makes clear that it is in the notion or pursuit of value in a human life that the ultimate unity of the self or subject is to be understood. This is tacit in my present treatment.

8. After all the fuss about the Double Helix discovery settled down there came clearly into view the next problem: what did it do—how did it influence the rest of the cell? Involved was an understanding of how the four DNA bases, C, T, A and G coded onto the twenty amino acids which, in turn, were the constituents of the proteins in the cells.
9. I wrote a response to Gammow's theory in 1956 but as time went by various theoretical approaches to the problem were tried and failed.
10. There followed the task of fingerprinting proteins, of showing experimentally that the sequence of bases in a stretch of nucleic acid was in step with the sequences of amino acids that it coded.
11. DNA makes RNA makes protein but the PaJaMo experiment and its description by François Jacob showed how we had been barking up the wrong tree. Once this key insight had been obtained, the rest followed automatically. The memory of the sudden flash of enlightenment that was involved in it remained with me for the rest of my life.
12. At the 1961 Biochemical Congress at Moscow I came across the experimental work of Marshall Niremberg and was electrified by his epoch-making discovery. The path to the solution became clear and there was now no looking back.
13. By 1966 I was in a position to summarize the work of a host of collaborators into the genetic code which I consider has the same importance for biology as the periodic table has for chemistry.
14. The questions of biology which interested me for all these years being resolved, I now had to think about what to do with the rest of my life. I decided that my main long-term interest was in the problem of neurobiology and the associated field of consciousness.
15. After a sabbatical in the Salk in 1976, the president offered me a chair. Since 1985/6, with Christof Koch, I worked on the problem of the neural correlates of visual consciousness. It was a strange new field, with no real success, but the desire to understand remained alive in me to the end.

The stepping-stones of the desire of the mind are the events around which, singly or in clusters, the broad detailed chapters in the intellectual life story of the desire of the mind form. If any of them were removed then the life story that would follow would differ in some substantially significant manner. What the stepping-stones suggest is that there is a direction in the opening up of the desire of the mind in a life story. It is also the case that that narrative structure is of the form of a work of art that is inherently irreducible to some scientific law. In this sense the desire of the mind has the form of a quest structure through which an ever expanding but always incomplete intellectual vision comes to be articulated. There is always more to our desiring than can ever be achieved. In this tension between dynamism and inevitable incompleteness there is manifested the form of a potential infinity within the finitude of the human being.

As with Crick and Watson so in authoring *Lonergan's Quest* I was drawn into the question—what, concretely, in the life of Lonergan does the desire in him (which is the source of all intellectual creativity in science and the drama of common sense interpersonal living) do? But as you proceed to show what it does, how it awakens to a problem, searches for clues, solves this element and that element of the problem until it all clicks into place, inevitably the question arises, what is this real, conscious, but unimaginable desire like? To do this involves finding oneself being opened up, paradoxically, to an infinity in the finitude of a human being. This leads to the question: how well can I understand this desire in another person, and in myself?

How you answer these questions has huge anthropological implications, implications in the realm of what meaning and destiny you assign to a human being. Religiously it is the same desire in us that desires, when religiously awakened, to understand God—how could it be any different? What kind of a desire in us does it take to understand God—the same kind of a desire that understands other human beings and everything else? Our efforts to understand the Others in our lives are pointers towards the ultimate and transcendent destination of the desire of our minds and hearts. What does a desire in us have to be like if its ultimate destiny is, in some sense, to understand God? And I don't here necessarily mean understand God in this life. The answer must of course be: something exceptionally and unimaginably strange, in a sense quite unlike anything else in the universe, even though that desire can in a sense measure everything in the universe. In *Verbum* Lonergan, with reference to Aquinas, states that the wisdom sought by intellectual light is 'the most convincing sample in us of the stuff of which the author of the universe and of our minds consists' and 'is acquired gradually'.[54] Can we ever get to the bottom of such a desire, tame it with the apparatus of an explanatory theory? The longer I struggled with the challenge of understanding this

54. *CWL* 2 *Verbum*, 100 (90).

desire of the mind in Lonergan's story and the more I became familiar with its irreducible and ungraspable strangeness the more fascinating did it become. That was the basic lesson learnt on my journey and I treasure it.

Chapter 4

Consciousness in Lonergan and Wojtyla

Robin Koning, SJ

Introduction

In his encyclical *Fides et Ratio*, Pope John Paul II manifested a suspicion of philosophies of subjectivity. Modern philosophical research, he says, has abandoned 'the investigation of being' and 'concentrated instead upon human knowing', leading to agnosticism, relativism, and scepticism.[1] Further on, he makes the same point, giving an example of a false, but widely-accepted, conviction:

> An example of this is the deep-seated distrust of reason which has surfaced in the most recent developments of much of philosophical research, to the point where there is talk at times of 'the end of metaphysics'. Philosophy is expected to rest content with more modest tasks such as the simple interpretation of facts or an enquiry into restricted fields of human knowing or its structures.[2]

At the time this encyclical was published, some students of Bernard Lonergan's work wondered whether such criticism applied also to Lonergan's philosophy, since it invites readers, by paying attention to the workings of their own minds, to discover the structure of their knowing. It is clear from the above quotations, though, that it is not theories of human knowing in themselves which are the problem, but rather theories which abandon the investigation of being or suggest the end of metaphysics, that is,

1. John Paul II, *Fides Et Ratio* (Libreria Editrice Vaticana, 1998) # 5; at <http://www.vatican.va/edocs/ENG0216/_INDEX.HTM>. Accessed 8 December 2007.
2. John Paul II, *Fides Et Ratio* # 55.

those which enter the human mind never to emerge. This charge certainly cannot be laid against Lonergan, whose monumental work *Insight*, while beginning with cognitional structure, moves on to epistemology and then to metaphysics. Moreover, as Neil Ormerod has noted, *Fides et Ratio* itself draws on the realm of interiority in at least four places, despite its explicit disavowal of such approaches.[3]

This appeal to subjectivity is in keeping with the tenor of Karol Wojtyla's philosophical writings before he became Pope John Paul II. There, in works such as *The Acting Person*,[4] we find him, like Lonergan, drawing on human experience and analyses of consciousness and subjectivity. Also like Lonergan, while grounding his study in Thomas' metaphysics, he seeks to develop it into a more mature expression, at the level of our times, especially by taking seriously the contemporary turn to the subject while avoiding the turn to subjectivism. Both approach their studies phenomenologically, focusing attention on the concrete experience of the human subject.[5] For Lonergan, the focus in *Insight* was primarily on ourselves as knowers—people who move from experience to understanding to judgement under the dynamism of our desire to know. Wojtyla, as the title of his work *The Acting Person* suggests, was more concerned about how people act in the world—with people deciding and carrying out their decisions at what Lonergan would call the fourth level of consciousness, the existential level. Finally, both Wojtyla and Lonergan invited their readers to a performative engagement with what they were reading, inviting them to confirm what the writer is saying in their own experience.[6]

---

3. Neil Ormerod, 'Faith and Reason: Perspectives from Macintyre and Lonergan', in *Heythrop Journal* 46 (2005): 15. Ormerod notes that the encyclical appeals to the human heart's quest for meaning (# 4), to the wonder awakened in humans (# 4), to the truth present deep within the human person (# 15), and to the human desire for knowledge, yearning for infinite riches beyond itself (# 17).
4. Karol Wojtyla, *The Acting Person*, translated by Andrzej Potocki (Dordrecht, Holland: D Reidel Pub Co, 1979).
5. Wojtyla writes that he 'owes everything to the systems of metaphysics, of anthropology, and of Aristotelian-Thomistic ethics on the one hand, and to phenomenology, above all in Scheler's interpretation, and through Scheler's critique, also to Kant, on the other hand' (Wojtyla, *Acting Person*, xiv).
6. *Collected Works of Bernard Lonergan*, volume 3, *Insight: A Study of Human Understanding*, edited by Frederick E Crowe and Robert M Doran (Toronto: University of Toronto Press, 1992), 11 (hereafter *CWL* 3 *Insight*). Buttliglione notes the same invitation to the reader's own experience in *The Acting Person* when he describes it as 'an articulated discourse on the fundamental structure of the experience of life which

There are, therefore, many points of contact between these two writers, in methodology as well as in content in some areas.[7] In this paper, I will focus on one area closely associated with the issue of subjectivity I began with, and that is the nature of consciousness. We should note from the start a lack of equivalence here, in that consciousness was a lifelong study of Lonergan's[8] whereas in *The Acting Person,* Wojtyla deals with consciousness simply as an introduction to the heart of his work, which is, as the title suggests, the human person in action.[9] Hence we would expect, as we shall in fact see, that Lonergan's account of consciousness has reached a clarity around important distinctions which is not always

---

solicits every person to reflect on his own self to confirm and to enrich the author's reflection. The philosopher limits himself to interpreting, to bringing to a higher degree of consciousness, what happens in common experience' (Rocco Buttiglione, *Karol Wojtyla: The Thought of the Man Who Became Pope John Paul II*, translated by Paolo Guietti and Francesca Murphy (Grand Rapids, Michigan: Eerdmans, 1997), 122).

7. A number of works have treated of connections between the thought of Lonergan and Wojtyla/John Paul II. See, for example, Ormerod, 'Faith and Reason'; Vincent G Potter, 'Philosophical Correlations among K Wojtyla, CS Peirce, and B Lonergan', in *The Thought of Pope John Paul II: A Collection of Essays and Studies*, edited by John M McDermott (Roma: Editrice Pontificia Universita Gregoriana, 1993), 205–12; Giovanni Sala, 'The Encyclical Letter of Pope John Paul II, Fides Et Ratio: A Service to Truth', in *Lonergan Workshop* 17 (2002): 197-208. I should also note an unpublished paper written by my colleague, Meredith Secomb, entitled 'The Person: Karol Wojtyla/ Pope John Paul II and Some Comparisons with Bernard Lonergan', which was a valuable starting point for my own reflections for this paper.

8. Bernard JF Lonergan, *Method in Theology* (London: Darton, Longman & Todd, 1972), 6–20; Bernard JF Lonergan, 'Christ as Subject: A Reply' and 'Cognitional Structure', in *Collected Works of Bernard Lonergan*, volume 4, *Collection*, edited by Frederick E Crowe and Robert M Doran (Toronto: University of Toronto Press, 1988), 153–84, 205–21; *CWL* 3 *Insight*, 344–52; Bernard JF Lonergan 'Consciousness and the Trinity', in *Collected Works of Bernard Lonergan*, volume 6, *Philosophical and Theological Papers 1958-1964*, edited by Robert C Croken, Frederick E Crowe and Robert M Doran (Toronto: University of Toronto Press, 1996), 122–41; Bernard JF Lonergan, *Collected Works of Bernard Lonergan*, volume 7, *The Ontological and Psychological Constitution of Christ*, translated by Michael G Shields (Toronto: University of Toronto Press, 2002), 157–89; Bernard JF Lonergan, *Collected Works of Bernard Lonergan*, volume 12, *The Triune God: Systematics*, edited by Robert M Doran and H Daniel Monsour (Toronto: University of Toronto Press, 2007), 314–17, 378–81 (hereafter *CWL* 12 *Triune God*).

9. 'I do not intend to enter here into an analysis of consciousness as such and in itself' (*Acting Person*, 29). Likewise, a few pages later, Wojtyla says: 'Obviously the aim of our present discussion is not to elaborate a complete and finished theory of consciousness' (33). See also *Acting Person*, 304 n 17.

found in Wojtyla's work. However, I shall show that in key regards they share common ground.

Lonergan on consciousness

In the chapter on 'The Self-Affirmation of the Knower' in *Insight,* Lonergan begins by making clear what consciousness does *not* mean for him. Firstly, and critically, 'consciousness is not to be thought of as some sort of inward look'.[10] This is the mistake of those who presume that knowing is a sort of looking, and that consciousness, being a sort of knowing, must therefore be a sort of looking. Secondly, an act does not become conscious by being inquired into or understood or judged to have occurred.[11] Thirdly, an act does not become conscious by being done deliberately, with full determination of the will. Fourthly, consciousness is not the account we give of it. It is the given we seek to understand and to give an account of. 'Consciousness as given is neither formulated nor affirmed . . . To formulate it does not make one more conscious . . . To affirm it does not make one more conscious.'[12] Moreover, in 'Cognitional Structure', Lonergan adds to these points, and in a way summarises them, by saying that consciousness is not self-knowledge. Knowing is a structured whole of experience, understanding and judging. Therefore, self-knowledge—knowing my knowing—is a reduplication of that structure. It is 'experience, understanding, and judgement with respect to experience, understanding, and judgment'.[13] From this it follows that cognitional activities may be conscious without being known.

With those guideposts as to what Lonergan does not mean by consciousness, let's look at what he says positively about it. In *Insight* he speaks of it as 'an awareness immanent in cognitional acts'.[14] It is an awareness—an experience. It is connected with cognitional acts—we do not have this experience independent of such cognitional acts as seeing, hearing, inquiring, understanding, conceiving, judging. It is not another act alongside these, and it does not require another act—it is immanent in these very acts. It is self-presence; in consciousness, I am present to myself in my various operations; I experience myself operating; I am aware of

10. *CWL* 3 *Insight*, 344.
11. *CWL* 3 *Insight*, 345.
12. *CWL* 3 *Insight*, 350.
13. Lonergan, 'Cognitional Structure', 208.
14. Lonergan, 'Cognitional Structure', 208.

myself operating.[15] In later writings, Lonergan will make clear that consciousness is the awareness immanent not just in strictly cognitional acts, but in all the operations of intentional consciousness, including those on the fourth level of deliberation.[16]

In 'Cognitional Structure', Lonergan develops his analysis of consciousness by averting to the distinction often made between external and internal experience. External experience is of what we sense—sights, sounds, smells, tastes, texture, heat—while internal experience 'is of oneself and one's apprehensive and appetitive activities'.[17] He points out that when we speak of internal and external, we are applying spatial categories to experience, which is not spatial. This distinction at the level of spatial metaphor points to different sorts of presence. Material presence—the presence of this page before the reader—involves no knowing. Intentional presence, however, involves knowing, and there are two kinds of intentional presence:

> There is the presence of the object to the subject, of the spectacle to the spectator; there is also the presence of the subject to himself, and this is not the presence of another object dividing his attention, of another spectacle distracting the spectator; it is presence in, as it were, another dimension, presence concomitant and correlative and opposite to the presence of the object. Objects are present by being attended to; but subjects are present as subjects, not by being attended to, but by attending. As the parade of objects marches by, spectators do not have to slip into the parade to become present to themselves; they have to be present to themselves for anything to be present to them; and they are present to themselves by the same watching that, as it were, at its other pole makes the parade present to them.[18]

15. Lonergan, *Method*, 8.
16. See, for example, *Method,* 9–11.
17. Lonergan, 'Cognitional Structure', 209.
18. Lonergan, 'Cognitional Structure', 210. *Method in Theology*, 6–8, follows the same basic analysis of consciousness. My operations of seeing, tasting, inquiring, imaging, understanding, judging and so on are shown both to be intentional, having objects, and to be the operations of an operator who is conscious. Such operations are not performed in dreamless sleep or when one is in a coma. Lonergan's discussion here also distinguishes the presence of the object from that of the subject.

Thus, I will not discover myself *as subject* by introspection—by trying to reach back and uncover my subjectivity. This is the sort of inward look that Lonergan distinguishes from consciousness. By attempting to 'look at' or attend to the subject in any way, I find only the subject *as object*; the subject as subject is the 'I' who is doing the finding.

Lonergan's teasing out of the difference between external and internal experience is a helpful place to draw to a close this brief introduction to his view of consciousness, and to move into Wojtyla's account in *The Acting Person,* for that work begins with a similar treatment of experience in its inner and outer modes.

Wojtyla on consciousness

a. Experience

In his introduction to *The Acting Person,*[19] Wojtyla speaks of the duality of our experience—the way in which my 'experience of anything outside of [myself] is always associated with the experience of' myself; I never experience 'anything external without having at the same time the experience of' myself.[20] This experience of myself is unique: 'no external relation to any other human being can take the place of the experiential relation that the subject has to himself'.[21] Thus there is an 'essential disparity' between any experience of others, however close they may be to me, and

19. The major commentaries in English on *The Acting Person* can be found in relevant sections of the following works: Buttiglione, *Karol Wojtyla,* 117–76; Robert F Harvanek, 'The Philosophical Foundations of the Thought of John Paul II', in *The Thought of Pope John Paul II: A Collection of Essays and Studies,* edited by John M McDermott (Roma: Editrice Pontificia Universita Gregoriana, 1993), 1–21; Jaroslaw Kupczak, *Destined for Liberty: The Human Person in the Philosophy of Karol Wojtyla/John Paul II* (Washington, DC: Catholic University of America Press, 2000), 66–141; John H Nota, 'Phenomenological Experience in Karol Wojtyla', in *The Thought of Pope John Paul II,* 197–203; Andrzej Poltawski, 'Ethical Action and Consciousness: Philosophical and Psychiatric Perspectives, in *Analecta Husserliana* VII (1978): 115–50; Kenneth L Schmitz, *At the Center of the Human Drama: The Philosophy of Karol Wojtyla/Pope John Paul II* (Washington, DC: Catholic University of America Press, 1993), 58–89; George Weigel, *Witness to Hope: The Biography of Pope John Paul II* (New York: Cliff St Books, 1999), 172–76; George Huntston Williams, *The Mind of John Paul II: Origins of His Thought and Action* (New York: The Seabury Press, 1981), 186–218; Andrew N Woznicki, *A Christian Humanism: Karol Wojtyla's Existential Personalism* (New Britain, Connecticut: Mariel Publications, 1980).
20. Wojtyla, *Acting Person*, 3.
21. Wojtyla, *Acting Person*, 6.

'that unique experience—the experience of the man who is myself'.[22] This same point is made in terms of inner and outer aspects of experience. It is only in relation to myself that I can have experience from the inside (inner experience). All other people 'are included in experience had from the outside, termed "outer experience"'.[23] In relation to others, I can only have experience in its outer form—they are part of my 'outerness', not my 'innerness'. While something of my experience of myself can be communicated to others, 'the inner experience itself is untransferable by and out of the ego'.[24]

Surprisingly, perhaps, Wojtyla does not directly link this account of inner experience with consciousness in the way Lonergan does. For Lonergan, as we have seen, consciousness is precisely this 'inner experience' that one has of one self and of one's conscious acts. But the identification of inner experience with consciousness is implied by Wojtyla in at least two ways. Firstly, he notes that this experience of myself is continuous, but that it is interrupted by sleep, that is, when one is not conscious.[25] Secondly, Wojtyla discerns the roots of the major divorce between philosophies of being and philosophies of consciousness, between the objective and the subjective, in this disparity in the experience of man between inner aspect and outerness. There is a 'duality in the data', a 'double aspect of experience'.[26] But both are aspects of experience, both are part of the data, and indeed Wojtyla notes that the inner and outer forms of experience complement and compensate for each other. Rather than attributing 'absolute significance' to one or other aspect, leading to the one-sidedness evident in some philosophies of being, which highlight the objective side, and in some philosophies of consciousness, which highlight the subjective side, we need to acknowledge their mutual relatedness.[27] From this it is clear that philosophies which focus attention on the inner form of experience are seen by Wojtyla to be philosophies of consciousness, suggesting

---

22. Wojtyla, *Acting Person*, 6.
23. Wojtyla, *Acting Person*, 7.
24. Wojtyla, *Acting Person*, 7. This inner form of experience will later be spoken of as 'immanent experience' (18).
25. Wojtyla, *Acting Person,* 3. Lonergan would differentiate dreamless sleep from dream states in which a 'fragmentary and incoherent' form of consciousness is present (see Lonergan, *Method*, 9).
26. Wojtyla, *Acting Person*, 19. Note the parallel with Lonergan's distinction between the data of sense and the data of consciousness (*CWL* 3 *Insight*, 299–300).
27. Wojtyla, *Acting Person*, 19.

an identification between what he describes as consciousness and what he describes as the inner experience of oneself.

One point in which Lonergan's definition of consciousness might contribute to the point Wojtyla is trying to make here is in freeing him from the need to hold that experience is always experience of an object. At times, this presumption leads him to suggest that the key distinction between inner and outer experience is that they are experiences of different *objects*. Thus he can speak of my experience of myself in terms of a relation 'in which I am both the subject and the object';[28] of other people being 'objects of experience . . . in a different manner than I am for myself';[29] and about everyone being the object of his or her own unique experience.[30] In each case, it is clear that Wojtyla is speaking of what he has called our 'inner experience' of ourselves, an experience which is concomitant with our experience of anything outside of ourselves. Thus, he seems to be using 'object of experience' to mean 'that which is experienced'. Furthermore, he never breaks free of the limitations of the spatial metaphor of inner and outer, so that experiences are seen to be different, not because of some differentiation within the subject, but because of the location of their objects. The fundamental difference for Wojtyla is between my experience of myself in my innerness and my experience of anything else external to me.

We saw above how Lonergan transcended the spatial metaphor by elaborating its basic point as a concern about different kinds of presence. As there, so here the basic distinction for him is not between different kinds of objects, a distinction ultimately based on whether those objects are internal or external to the subject. Rather, he distinguishes between different kinds of experience of the subject. Concomitant with my experience of objects is my experience of myself as a subject. 'For whether we are reflecting upon ourselves or are concerned with entirely other things that we are apprehending or desiring, we are present to ourselves in either case.'[31] I can in fact be the object of my own experience; I can hear myself, see myself (at least in part), touch myself. In so doing, *as an object* of my experience, I am no different from other objects I experience. The key distinction is not between my experience of myself as an object and my experience of other objects. Rather, it is between my experience of anything, including myself and my acts, as an object, and my concomitant

28. Wojtyla, *Acting Person,* 4.
29. Wojtyla, *Acting Person,* 5.
30. Wojtyla, *Acting Person,* 6.
31. *CWL* 12 *Triune God,* 379.

experience of myself as a subject. I experience myself as a subject in all my operations, whether the object of those operations is myself or another. This would seem to be the distinction Wojtyla is attempting to make in his treatment of experience. We now turn to his treatment of consciousness proper.

b. Consciousness as reflective

In dealing with consciousness, Wojtyla begins by distinguishing between conscious acting and the consciousness of acting.[32] Humans not only act consciously but are also conscious that they are acting and that they are acting consciously.[33] To speak of conscious acting is to speak of a sort of acting which is according to the will, which is voluntary.[34] Traditionally, the human act has been seen as conscious in this sense, so that for an act to be human, it needed to be willed, to be voluntary.[35] In this view, consciousness was merged in the dynamism of the will, thus preventing us from coming to a more developed understanding of consciousness itself. In the Scholastic approach, for example, consciousness was not so much explicitly treated as simply implied in rationality and, 'as it were, hidden' there.[36] While Wojtyla does not wish to attribute absolute significance to consciousness, a path which could lead to idealism,[37] he *does* want to examine consciousness *as such*, consciousness in what he calls a 'substantival and subjective sense'.[38] By this, he does not mean that consciousness itself is a substance in the sense of 'a separate and self-contained reality', and certainly not 'an independent, self-contained subject', since it is the human person of whom we predicate a state of consciousness, not consciousness itself.[39] But Wojtyla does wish to 'exhibit consciousness as an *intrinsic and constitutive aspect of the dynamic structure*, that is, *of the acting person*'.[40]

32. Wojtyla, *Acting Person*, 29.
33. Wojtyla, *Acting Person*, 28.
34. Wojtyla, *Acting Person*, 28–29.
35. Wojtyla, *Acting Person*, 30.
36. Wojtyla, *Acting Person*, 30.
37. Wojtyla, *Acting Person*, 33.
38. Wojtyla, *Acting Person*, 30.
39. Wojtyla, *Acting Person*, 33–34. Indeed, this section of his argument is entitled 'Consciousness Is not an Autonomous Subject'.
40. Wojtyla, *Acting Person*, 31; emphasis original.

Thus his work will focus not on conscious acting but on the consciousness of acting 'and consequently on the consciousness of the acting person'.[41]

At this point, Wojtyla makes a statement about his approach to consciousness which suggests both some similarity and some difference between his approach and that of Lonergan:

> [M]an not only acts consciously, but he is also aware of both the fact that he is acting and the fact that it is he who is acting—hence he has the awareness of the action as well as of the person in their dynamic interrelation. His awareness is simultaneous with conscious acting and, so to speak, accompanies it. But it is also present before and after. It has its own continuity and its own identity separate from the continuity and identity of any particular action. Every action finds consciousness, if one may say so, already there; it develops and comes to pass in the presence of consciousness, leaving behind little trace of its passage. Consciousness accompanies and reflects or mirrors the action when it is born and while it is being performed; once the action is accomplished consciousness still continues to reflect it, though of course it no longer accompanies it. The accompanying presence of consciousness is decisive in making man aware of his acting rather than in making his action conscious. Again, it is its presence that makes him act as a person and experience his acting as an action, the role of the aspect of consciousness being manifested most appropriately in the latter.[42]

Much of this account resonates with Lonergan's treatment of consciousness. Most importantly, consciousness is spoken of as awareness—an awareness that accompanies any action of the subject, and that includes awareness both of the action and of the person who is the subject of the action.[43] In the middle of this passage, though, is a statement which has no obvious parallel in Lonergan's thought on consciousness. This is the statement about consciousness as reflecting or mirroring action. What this means precisely is not easy to discern, but we shall note a few points which

41. Wojtyla, *Acting Person*, 29.

42. Wojtyla, *Acting Person*, 31.

43. A little further on, 'being aware' is said to be the 'specific character' of conscious acts (see Wojtyla, *Acting Person*, 34).

are clear. Before discussing these, though, we might clarify a term which is central to Wojtyla's discussion here, namely 'cognition', along with its associated adjectives, 'cognitional' and 'cognitive', since it is in contradistinction to cognition that Wojtyla defines reflective consciousness.

Cognition for Wojtyla is not simply about thinking or understanding, but includes experience. He speaks of the 'experience of man' as a 'great cognitive process', and states that being 'in a direct cognitive relation' with a subject is to be 'the object of experience' for that subject.[44] He also speaks of 'experiential acts' as 'direct cognitive encounters with reality'.[45] Moreover, in the Preface, he parallels cognition and thinking with 'observing, interpreting, speculating [and] reasoning'.[46] Cognition, indeed, seems to refer to any engagement of the subject with reality; it is cognitively (though not only cognitively) 'that man enters into the world of other men and objects and even discovers himself there as one of them'.[47]

Wojtyla makes a number of major points about reflective consciousness. Firstly, if it is by cognition that the person enters into the world of other people and objects, we might say that reflective consciousness is the way in which the world enters into us. Consciousness is a reflection of what happens in me and of my acting, of what I do and how I do it, of everything I meet with in my external relations by means of my doings. All of this is mirrored in consciousness. In this sense, it can be said that consciousness contains the whole person and the world accessible to the concrete person.[48]

Secondly, all of this is contained in consciousness in its own manner, that is, in a non-intentional manner. Cognitive acts are intentional. They seek to apprehend the elements of the object and to objectify it; in this way, comprehension and knowledge contribute to the formation of the object. But acts of consciousness 'are not essentially intentional by nature'.[49] Schmitz notes Wojtyla's denial that intentionality is 'the hallmark

44. Wojtyla, *Acting Person*, 3, 4.
45. Wojtyla, *Acting Person*, 7.
46. Wojtyla, *Acting Person*, vii.
47. Wojtyla, *Acting Person*, 34. Wojtyla does speak at one point of cognitive acts as 'acts of comprehension and knowledge' (32). But the context of this comment does not make clear if he intends this to be a definition of cognitive acts or if he is delimiting the meaning of the term in a particular discussion. Schmitz also understands Wojtyla's use of cognition to include any activity directed to something beyond the subject (Schmitz, *At the Center of the Human Drama*, 70).
48. Wojtyla, *Acting Person*, 31.
49. Wojtyla, *Acting Person*, 32.

of consciousness' and claims that it represents a key way in which Wojtyla distances himself from some aspects of phenomenology, and indeed much of contemporary philosophy, which tends to have an 'almost exclusive emphasis on intentionality'; instead, Wojtyla sees cognition, which is intentional, as serving consciousness, which is non-intentional.[50]

Thirdly, this non-intentional nature of consciousness is described as reflecting or mirroring. Unlike cognition, consciousness as such is not involved in the active constitution of the object; it is 'restricted to mirroring what has already been cognized'.[51] Thus it is only after an object has been constituted by intentional cognition that it becomes available to consciousness. Consciousness is 'the derivative of the whole actively cognitive process and of the cognitive attitude to the external reality'.[52] While it is true that Wojtyla talks of consciousness in the text above as already present before any action, and as then accompanying and reflecting the action, it would seem that any new element to come into consciousness does so only as a result of first being cognised; reflective consciousness has something to reflect once the subject engages with an object in some way. Moreover, while cognition actively engages with reality—Wojtyla speaks of the 'actively cognitive process'—reflective consciousness does not. Its role would seem to be passive or, perhaps better, receptive. Even where consciousness is described as 'penetrating and illuminating' the subject's cognitive possessions, Wojtyla distinguishes this from 'the active understanding of objects' which is the work of cognition.[53]

Fourthly, reflective consciousness has to do with 'images' of reality in the mind, a point emphasised by the use of the term 'mirroring'. In one of the few examples he gives in this work, Wojtyla speaks of a mountain landscape 'in my experience' and the same landscape 'reflected in my consciousness'.[54] More generally, he writes:

50. Schmitz, *At the Center of the Human Drama*, 69–70.
51. Wojtyla, *Acting Person*, 32; Wojtyla immediately continues that consciousness is 'so to speak, the understanding of what has been constituted and comprehended' (33). Here, 'the understanding' cannot refer to the act of understanding, for Wojtyla is keen to distinguish reflective consciousness from 'the active understanding of objects' (35). Perhaps he means that once an object has been comprehended, that understanding is reflected in consciousness and remains there.
52. Wojtyla, *Acting Person*, 33.
53. Wojtyla, *Acting Person*, 33
54. Wojtyla, *Acting Person*, 43.

> Indeed, it is not only cognitively that man enters into the world of other men and objects and even discovers himself there as one of them: he has also as his possession all this world in the image mirrored by consciousness, which is a factor in his innermost, most personal life . . . This reflection . . . carries within itself a faithful image of the action as well as of the person.[55]

It is hard to fathom what Wojtyla precisely means by this mirrored image. It may be that what he intends when he speaks of reflective consciousness in this way is that presence of the object to the subject of which Lonergan speaks when he says that 'by seeing, there becomes present what is seen, by hearing there becomes present what is heard, by imagining there becomes present what is imagined'.[56] If this is the case, then the seeing, hearing, imagining and so on represent what Wojtyla means by speaking of active cognition, while the becoming present to the subject of what is seen, heard and imagined represent what Wojtyla means by the reflection of these things in consciousness. Hence Lonergan's use of the passive 'becomes present' parallels Wojtyla's insistence that reflective consciousness is not part of the active cognition and constitution of the object.[57]

For Lonergan, of course, becoming aware of the object in our operations is precisely what is meant by intentionality, and his statement that 'by seeing there becomes present what is seen' is an elaboration of what it means to say that operations intend objects.[58] Wojtyla, however, prefers to save the term 'intentional' for the active outward-moving engagement with reality. His insistence that consciousness is non-intentional, however, would seem to be compromised by his mention in a number of places of 'acts of consciousness'.[59] In fact, he seeks to clarify this point in a note. While emphasising that he rejects the intentional character of consciousness and its acts, he says that, along with the phenomenological tradition which has influenced him, he does not deny that consciousness is always consciousness *of* something. But this acceptance is qualified. For

55. Wojtyla, *Acting Person*, 34.
56. Lonergan, *Method*, 7.
57. This view is perhaps supported by Poltawski's identification of reflective consciousness with Henri Ey's 'stage of the lived and spoken present' ('Ethical Action and Consciousness', 145).
58. Lonergan notes elsewhere that 'that which is known is in the knower with an intentional existence' (*CWL* 12 *Triune God*, 505).
59. See, for example, *Acting Person*, 32.

as soon as he says this, he notes the importance of asking why and in what way consciousness is always the consciousness of something. To answer this, he seeks to clarify the concepts of act and of intentionality:

We thus regard as *acts* in the strict sense of the word only the manifestation of the real powers of the person. Thus when following the manner of speaking widely accepted in phenomenology we refer to 'acts of consciousness,' the reader has to remember that we are using the phrase only figuratively, for its convenience and not its adequacy. Similarly we understand 'intention' as an active directing upon the object; thus strictly speaking consciousness, as here conceived, has no intentionality and so the term, as we use it, has only a secondary and derived meaning owing to the intentional acts of knowledge or self-knowledge as real faculties.[60]

Wojtyla's need to clarify these points suggests that he is aware that his talk of reflective consciousness as non-intentional and as not involving attention to an object is somewhat problematic. If I am dealing with images in my mind, these are also objects, even if they are not external to the subject. Likewise he speaks of consciousness as 'penetrating and illuminating' what has become my 'cognitive possession,' 'keeping objects and their cognitive meanings "in the light"'.[61] Furthermore we find Wojtyla speaking of consciousness allowing us 'to have an inner view of our actions (immanent perception)'.[62] Penetrating, illuminating, and keeping objects in the light are all operations presuming an object. In the light of this description of reflective consciousness, the claim that it is not intentional only makes sense if Wojtyla is defining an object as that which is external to the subject. In this case, we return again to the distinction we noted in his treatment of experience, and the concern expressed there that he allows the spatial metaphor to dominate and to take on a significance it cannot bear. The key distinction for Lonergan is not the location of some image or object but what is happening in the experience of the subject. Each of the subject's operations is both intentional and conscious—intentional in

60. Wojtyla, *Acting Person*, 304; emphasis original.

61. Wojtyla, *Acting Person*, 33. Schmitz sees this reflective function in terms of what traditional philosophy would call immanence, 'that interior 'light' which belongs to consciousness as such, the proper sphere of its activity by which the mind appropriates its received contents according to its own immaterial mode' (*At the Center of the Human Drama*, 72). If this is true, the question of intentionality remains, since the appropriation of contents is still an operation on objects. Poltawski sees reflective consciousness in terms of 'Ethical Action and Consciousness'.

62. Wojtyla, *Acting Person*, 42; emphasis original.

that the object becomes present to me; conscious in that, in operating, I am present to myself operating.[63]

This idea of consciousness as self-presence is not absent from Wojtyla's work, but comes into play when he speaks of the second function of consciousness. Before moving on to that aspect of consciousness, though, we need to see how Wojtyla distinguishes consciousness from self-knowledge. We have seen how Lonergan makes this distinction. For him, consciousness stands at the level of experience—it is my experience of myself as subject as I experience, understand, and judge. Self-knowledge, on the other hand, involves the same process as any other knowledge—the dynamic movement of inquiry drawing us from experience to understanding and on to judgement. In self-knowledge, the data is that of consciousness—my experience of my own intentional consciousness as I experience, understand and judge. Thus I come to know myself by inquiring into this data of consciousness—by understanding my experience of experiencing, understanding, and judging, and then making a judgement about my understanding of my experience of experiencing, understanding, and judging.

The Acting Person also distinguishes self-knowledge from consciousness. As we have already noted, consciousness for Wojtyla is not involved in the objectification or the constitution of the object; that is the work of cognition. So too with that form of knowledge which is self-knowledge, in which the subject matter is the ego:

> self-knowledge consists in the understanding of one's own self and is concerned with a kind of cognitive insight into the object that I am for myself . . . At this point self-knowledge and consciousness come closest together, but, at the same time, they deviate from each other, since consciousness, for all the intimacy of its subjective union with the ego, does not objectivize the ego . . . This function is performed by acts of self-knowledge themselves. It is to them that every man owes the objectivizing contact with himself and his actions.[64]

63. Lonergan, *Method*, 7–8.

64. Wojtyla, *Acting Person*, 36. The ego for Wojtyla is 'the subject having the experience of his own subjectiveness and in this aspect it also means the person' (*Acting Person*, 304 n 17).

Another way of putting this is that in self-knowledge, the subject becomes the object of knowledge.[65] Because of this distinctiveness of the data, self-knowledge is distinguished from any other sort of knowledge.[66] Moreover, since consciousness is so intimately connected to the subject,[67] it too becomes an object of self-knowledge. 'Self-knowledge has as its object not only the person and the action, but also the person as being *aware* of himself and *aware* of his action. This awareness is objectivized by self-knowledge.'[68]

Hence we find a similar insistence on the difference between self-knowledge and consciousness in Lonergan and Wojtyla. With Lonergan, the more detailed delineation of the structure of human knowing enables an articulation which can situate consciousness at the level of experience and self-knowledge as the whole process which begins with this experience and seeks to understand and come to judgement about that understanding.

c. *Consciousness as reflexive*

It would seem that Lonergan's definition of consciousness as self-presence is what Wojtyla means when he speaks of reflexive consciousness. While he sees this reflexive function as complementing the reflective function, he also sees it as more important. Reflexiveness 'endows consciousness with the ultimate reason for its presence in the specific structure of the acting person'.[69] It represents the 'essential function' of consciousness—'to form man's experience and thus to allow him to experience in a special way his own subjectiveness'.[70]

This experience of subjectiveness is the key to understanding what Wojtyla means by the reflexive function. 'Consciousness allows us not only to have an inner view of our actions (immanent perception) . . . but also to *experience these actions as actions and as our own*'.[71] Consciousness allowing an inner view of our actions refers to reflective consciousness. Consciousness allowing us to experience them as actions and as our ac-

65. Wojtyla, *Acting Person*, 37.
66. Wojtyla, *Acting Person*, 35–36.
67. Wojtyla, *Acting Person*, 36.
68. Wojtyla, *Acting Person*, 37.
69. Wojtyla, *Acting Person*, 42.
70. Wojtyla, *Acting Person*, 42.
71. Wojtyla, *Acting Person*, 42; emphasis original.

tions refers to reflexive consciousness. It is the experiential nature of this reflexiveness which distinguishes it from both reflective consciousness and the sort of reflection proper to cognitional acts. Thought is reflective when we turn back to a previous act to grasp it more fully. This sort of reflection is important in the development of understanding and knowledge. But when it comes to experience, both this kind of intellectual reflection and the reflective function of consciousness are insufficient. Here we need reflexive consciousness, which is 'a special turning back upon the subject, and it is to this turn that we owe, along with experience, the emphasized subjectiveness of the experiencing ego'.[72]

Wojtyla therefore distinguishes three things. Firstly, there is being the subject. Secondly, there is being cognised or objectivised as the subject—this is self-knowledge as discussed above. Thirdly, there is experiencing oneself 'as the subject of one's own acts and experiences';[73] this is the reflexive dimension of consciousness. It is this experience of myself as the distinctive subject which allows me to use the pronoun 'I'.[74] 'I' always denotes a concrete person. Thus I am able to move beyond an ontological definition of myself as 'an autonomous, self-centered individual being' to the concrete person who is this distinctive subject—from an ontic subjectiveness to an experienced subjectiveness.[75]

It is clear from this outline that Wojtyla means by reflexive consciousness what Lonergan means by consciousness *tout court*. One problem in making this identification, though, is Wojtyla's talk of reflexive consciousness as 'a special turning back upon the subject'.[76] This would seem to go against the grain of much else that Wojtyla says about this reflexivity, and certainly goes against what Lonergan means by consciousness. For the talk of turning back on the subject suggests a move away from the *experience* of myself as subject immanent in my attention to an object and towards an introspective attention to myself as subject. If this is what Wojtyla means, then, as Lonergan has pointed out, such an introspective turn will only attain the subject as object, while the subject as subject steers the turn and continues to elude introspection. Turning back on the subject loses the subjectivity of the subject.[77]

72. Wojtyla, *Acting Person*, 44.
73. Wojtyla, *Acting Person*, 44.
74. Wojtyla, *Acting Person*, 45.
75. Wojtyla, *Acting Person*, 45.
76. Wojtyla, *Acting Person*, 44.
77. It is this sense of reflexiveness which Lonergan distinguishes from consciousness in a

Certainly Wojtyla's expression of this point in terms of 'turning back on the subject' is unfortunate. A close reading, however, shows that his fundamental intention is to highlight the experiential and subjective nature of what he calls reflexive consciousness; describing this as a turning back is one attempt to express this reality. This is evident in the following statement taken from his initial introduction of the concept of reflexive consciousness.

> This state of consciousness points not only to the mirroring and all that is reflected or mirrored at any given moment, but also to experience, in which the subjectiveness of man, as the subject having the experience, gains a special (because experiential) prominence. It is in this sense that the *reflexive trait* or *reflexiveness* of consciousness denotes that consciousness, so to speak, turns back naturally upon the subject, if thereby the subjectiveness of the subject is brought into prominence in experience.[78]

Here, the phrase 'in this sense' highlights that it is the experiential and subjective dimension, emphasised in the first sentence, which controls the meaning of 'turning back to the subject'. Moreover, the phrase 'so to speak' suggests that this expression is not to be taken literally but is an attempt to formulate an insight which is not easily expressed. The purely experiential nature of reflexive consciousness is to the fore throughout the discussion. Indeed, the heading of one subsection dealing with the two functions of consciousness is simply 'Mirroring and Experience'.[79] The reflective function is mirroring, the reflexive function is simply 'experience'. Likewise, where Wojtyla speaks of reflexiveness in terms of the person being directed 'inwards', he maintains that this direction inwards is, 'to some extent, identical with experience'.[80] As he says, 'owing to my consciousness in its reflexive function I . . . experience my ego, I have the experience of myself as the concrete subject of the ego's very subjectiveness, . . . the subjectiveness that makes of every concrete human being the unique, individual ego'.[81]

---

footnote in 'Christ as Subject' ('Christ as Subject', 166 n 14).

78. Wojtyla, *Acting Person*, 43.
79. Wojtyla, *Acting Person*, 54.
80. Wojtyla, *Acting Person*, 46.
81. Wojtyla, *Acting Person*, 46.

Finally, we might note that, in his analysis of consciousness, Wojtyla, like Lonergan, is concerned to take subjectivity seriously without falling into subjectivism. He speaks of showing the subjectivity of the human person as 'fundamental [to] the realistic position of [his] study.'[82] It is this subjectivity which grounds objectivity. Experience of action, of the interrelation of person and action, and of the moral value germinating there—these are all 'data that hold their objectivity . . . only and exclusively in the subjectivity of man.'[83] Thus, at the same time as he argues for attention to subjectivity and against subjectivism, Wojtyla also speaks against 'a narrow and one-sided objectivism.'[84] Here we find strong resonances with Lonergan's claim that genuine objectivity is the fruit of authentic subjectivity.[85]

Conclusion

This last point, about an authentic approach to subjectivity freeing us from the dead-ends of both subjectivism and narrow objectivism, reminds us of the critical issues involved in any account of consciousness. This paper has sought to show some fundamental convergence in the views of Lonergan and Wojtyla on consciousness, especially that which Wojtyla calls reflexive consciousness, and on the related question of the dual nature of experience. It has also pointed out divergences, and ways in which Lonergan's more clearly articulated distinctions can enhance the basic points Wojtyla wishes to make. The importance of proposing a coherent account of consciousness which takes subjectivity seriously, while not being lost in subjectivism, is evident from the ways in which these two thinkers have used their accounts—Lonergan, to offer insight into the consciousness of Christ and into the psychological analogy for the Trinity; and Wojtyla, to ground his account of human action, which influences his later papal writings, particularly his theological anthropology and his theology of the body.

I noted earlier a small number of works relating the thought of Lonergan to that of Wojtyla/John Paul II. These sorts of works not only shed light on the both thinkers; they also contribute to wider dialogue within the church. Robert Doran lists what he considers will be 'the most

82. Wojtyla, *Acting Person*, 57.
83. Wojtyla, *Acting Person*, 58.
84. Wojtyla, *Acting Person*, 58.
85. Lonergan, *Method*, 292.

influential Catholic theological achievements of our time'.[86] He notes Lonergan's account of 'the transcendental aspirations of the human spirit'; von Balthasar's presentation of 'the aesthetic and dramatic theological categories'; and the concern for transformative praxis which has entered into church teaching on structures of sin and the option for the poor. I agree with Doran that these elements, and some integration of their emphases, are crucial for further advances in systematic theology. I would suggest, however, that a further element needs to be included here, namely John Paul II's seminal contribution, which continues to generate considerable interest in the academy, particularly in the *Communio* circles and John Paul II Institutes. It is a body of work which needs to continue to be engaged and to be counted as a fourth permanent achievement of twentieth century theology. Hopefully the sort of conversation between Lonergan and Wojtyla represented by this paper may contribute to that ongoing engagement.

86. Robert M Doran, *What Is Systematic Theology?* (Toronto: University of Toronto Press, 2005), 86–88.

Chapter 5

Be Attentive: Theological Method and the Christian Phenomenon

Anthony J Kelly, CSsR

At the heart of Lonergan's achievement is his brilliant phenomenology of insight. He shows us how we are all brilliant, at least for a moment, when we have an insight, but the brilliance tends to wane when we wish to explain it or present its meaning—as this presentation will undoubtedly show. Not so Lonergan, as we all know who have been reading his works and learning from them over these many years. His special achievement is how he elaborated the metaphysical and theological implications of that original phenomenological moment of insight. It led to an affirmation of God as 'Infinite Insight' and, on our finite level, of our participation in that insight in our every act of knowing. His further insight into the dynamics of self-transcending consciousness gave rise to his account of the framework of eight-fold collaborative creativity known to us *Method in Theology*.

A question arising—and returning

Over thirty years ago, I wrote a fundamentally appreciative article entitled, 'Is Lonergan's *Method* Adequate to Christian Theology?'.[1] It appeared in *The Thomist*, and in an irenically edited version in *Theology Digest*.[2] Part of the context of my query was that the works of Hans Urs von Balthasar were beginning to appear in the English-speaking world at the time. The great Swiss theologian's treatment of revelation caused me to ask, in the

1. Anthony J Kelly, CSsR, 'Is Lonergan's *Method* Adequate to Christian Mystery?', in *The Thomist* 39 (1975): 437–70.
2. Anthony J Kelly, CSsR, 'Lonergan's *Method* and Christian Mystery', in *Theology Digest* 24.2 (1976).

course of the article, whether the great Canadian thinker had allowed sufficiently for the phenomenon of Christian revelation, Christ himself. Was faith in Christ just a specification of a general category of religion? Was Christ himself simply the 'outward word' clarifying the prior 'inner word' of the Spirit?[3] Did Lonergan's inspiring phenomenology of religious love need a stronger connection with the phenomenality of the *donum* of Christ incarnate? In short, was Lonergan's method really adequate to Christian theology? I concluded that a further refinement was called for.

Twenty years or so later, based on his splendid doctoral thesis, Neil Ormerod published his *Meaning, Method and Revelation: The Meaning and Function of Revelation in Bernard Lonergan's* Method in Theology.[4] He engaged with my questions and, while appreciating the legitimacy of my query, argued that I had too abstract a notion of the reality of conversion at the heart of theological method.[5] Point well made, and taken—after all, I never doubted that Bernard Lonergan, a Jesuit priest theologian of great authenticity, would ever have meant to locate Christ at the periphery of his theological method.

But the question keeps returning; and today, as Ormerod already had pointed out,[6] Robert Doran, no less, is prepared to speak of another kind of conversion that would enable, say, von Balthasar's phenomenological theology of the paschal mystery to figure in the foundations of theology. This Lonergan-Doran-von Balthasar context was constructively elaborated by Anne Hunt in her exploration of how the classic tradition of the psychological analogy could be related to the Trinitarian self-revelation of God in the death and resurrection of Christ.[7]

In the spirit of the first of Lonergan's transcendental precepts, 'Be Attentive',[8] (and in the course of writing a book on the phenomenon of the

3. See Bernard Lonergan, *Method in Theology* (London: Darton, Longman and Todd, 1971), 112–19.
4. Neil Ormerod, *Method, Meaning and Revelation: The Meaning and Function of Revelation in Bernard Lonergan's* Method in Theology (Lanham: University Press of America, 2000).
5. Ormerod, *Method, Meaning and Revelation*, 4, 9, 97, 211–19, 225.
6. See Ormerod, *Method, Meaning and Revelation*: 'Kelly's criticisms of Lonergan's *Method* are, in many ways, truly perceptive, especially in the ways in which they anticipate the extension of Lonergan's methodology as they would later occur in the work of Robert Doran' (216).
7. Anne Hunt, 'Psychological Analogy and Paschal Mystery in Trinitarian Theology', in *Theological Studies* 59 (1998): 197–218.
8. Lonergan, *Method*, 18, 136–37, 231–32.

Resurrection and theology[9]), I have been wondering whether a more supple and inclusive approach to phenomenology might be useful in appropriating the Lonergan inheritance more fully, and thereby in extending his method into the specificity of Christian theology. Needless to say, in my own books and articles, and in the course of supervising numerous doctoral theses, I have found Lonergan's method marvellously productive.[10] But a question niggled. Despite the limits of this presentation, I hope to suggest a productive talking point on the topic of Lonergan, phenomenology and Christian revelation.

Lonergan and von Balthasar: polar opposites?

Given the range and erudition of the writings of von Balthasar, I feel a considerable sympathy for the aesthetic phenomenology of his approach. One had to admire his extraordinary grasp of the Christian revelatory event as it is disclosed to faith. In his exploration of the multi-faceted phenomenality of the gift of God in Christ, this great Swiss theologian, like Karl Barth before him, evokes the transcendent 'objectivity' of revelatory event as the self-disclosure of the divine subject. His emphasis is on the uniqueness of the Christian phenomenon, even while situating it with unmatched erudition within the history of religious and philosophical thought. Though his vast *oeuvre* is a commanding elaboration of theological meaning, it contains mythic-dramatic elements that have caused some unease, especially his highly dramatic and seemingly untraditional treat-

9. Since the present paper was presented, this book has been published as Anthony J Kelly, *The Resurrection Effect: Transforming Christian Life and Thought* (Maryknoll, NY: Orbis, 2008).
10. Some examples of my application of Lonergan's method are to be found in the following: *The Trinity of Love: A Christian Theology of God* (Wilmington, Del: Michael Glazier, 1989); *A New Imagining: Towards an Australian Spirituality* (Melbourne: Collins Dove, 1991); *An Expanding Theology: Faith in a World of Connections* (Sydney: EJ Dwyer, 1993); with Francis J Moloney, *Experiencing God in the Johannine Writings* (New York: Paulist Publications, 2003); *Eschatology and Hope* (Orbis: Maryknoll, NY: 2006); 'The Historical Jesus and Human Subjectivity', in *Australian Lonergan Workshop II*, edited by Matthew C Ogilvie and William J Dannaher (Drummoyne: Novum Organum Press, 2003), 151–79; 'Dimensions of Meaning: Theology and Exegesis', in *Transcending Boundaries. Contemporary Readings of the New Testament*, edited by Rekha M Chennattu and Mary M Coloe (Rome: LAS, 2005), 41–56; 'Dimensions of Adult Religious Education', in *International Handbook of Religious, Moral and Spiritual Dimensions in Education*, edited by Marian de Souza et al (Dordrecht, The Netherlands: Springer, 2007), 815–29.

ment of Holy Saturday in the *triduum paschale*.[11] Still, his overall sense of the paschal form of divine revelation is a valuable orientation in current Trinitarian theology as Anne Hunt has shown. The problem of a fruitful alignment of the methods of Lonergan and von Balthasar has been perceptively addressed by Robert Doran.[12] The two methods are ostensibly polar opposites. Where von Balthasar speaks of the particularity of the Christian event in terms of God's self-disclosive act, Lonergan grounds his theological method in the self-transcending subject. His terms and categories appear to go from the general (shared by all searchers for meaning, truth and goodness) to the particular—expressed in the 'outward' word of revelation in Christian tradition.[13] Lonergan is the master of meaning in all its stages, dimensions, carriers, modes and so on. But von Balthasar concentrates on the luminous particularity of biblical events. From that point, his thinking unfolds through a variety of concentric circles spiralling off from the aesthetically-given and dramatically-enacted revelatory event. However, Doran does not see the two as polar opposites; and I agree. For example, I have made extensive use of many of Lonergan's categories in the course of my own recent work, especially in my forthcoming book on the phenomenon of the resurrection, by suggesting how the phenomenon of the resurrection is productive of different dimensions of meaning. In his theological method, Lonergan has little to say about revelation, and even less about the resurrection. Although my presentation of the resurrection as the heart of revelation is more easily aligned to von Balthasar's approach, it has nonetheless been notably strengthened by Lonergan's method. Let me give a brief indication: Doran relates von Balthasar's aesthetics to Lonergan's method by exploiting the categories of 'potential [elemental] meaning' and 'conversion'—specifically, 'psychic' conversion.[14] I would suggest that the phenomenon, however actual as an event, is always the elemental site of 'potential meaning', and, indeed, of a limitless potential of meaning.[15] From the shock and confusion of the earliest witnesses (eg Lk 24:4–9, 37), through to the risen Jesus himself exegeting the scriptures in the midst of his disciples (Lk 24:44–47), to the

11. Alyssa L Pitstick, *Light in Darkness: Hans Urs Von Balthasar and the Catholic Doctrine of Christ's Descent into Hell* (Grand Rapids, MI: Eerdmans, 2007).
12. Robert Doran, SJ, 'Lonergan and Balthasar: Methodological Considerations', in *Theological Studies* 58 (1997): 61–84.
13. Lonergan, *Method*, 112–13.
14. Doran, 'Lonergan and Balthasar', 78–83.
15. See Lonergan, *Method*, 63, 67, 74.

creation of the New Testament itself and the development of the sacramental forms of the liturgy, and on to the efforts of theology in every age to grasp and explore the significance of all this for thought and praxis, the phenomenon of the resurrection has been a elemental site of 'potential' meaning. Moreover, even though I appreciate Doran's specification of 'psychic' conversion on the level of imagination and affect, as supplementary to the religious, moral and intellectual aspects of conversion shaping the very foundations of theological thinking, my emphasis has been more on receptivity to the resurrection-event. It entails a phase of what we might term 'phenomenological conversion'—not only to the phenomenon of consciousness itself as Lonergan has so compellingly presented it, but to the resurrection as the focal phenomenon of Christian faith in its 'saturating' effect on that consciousness. It provokes its own kind of conversion and a self-engagement governed by what is given in the resurrection of the Crucified. Embedded in Lonergan's account of the dynamics of conscious self-transcendence are the 'transcendental precepts, Be attentive, Be intelligent, Be reasonable, Be responsible'.[16] In this respect, I have endeavoured to stress the necessity of the first, 'Be attentive'—so that attentiveness is focused on what most demands attention—an event that is not the product of our knowledge and choice, but one that dismantles and abolishes the horizon of what our previous knowing and choosing presupposed. The Christ-event introduces a new horizon in which the transformative act of God's love affects every dimension of our consciousness, to transvalue our values and engender new dimensions of meaning, in our understanding of God, our selves, and our world.[17]

In fact, Wittgenstein surmised that '. . . only *love* can believe the Resurrection. Or: It is *love* that believes the Resurrection'.[18] The wave of such love—as Wittgenstein implicitly understands it, or as Lonergan explicitly describes it, causes a far more profound disturbance to habitual ways of theological thinking than simply calling for some new kind of phenomenological method. It raises the question of where theology situates itself—in the Areopagus of modern culture and in the lecture rooms of the university? In places of grief, failure and disgrace? In the hospices of the dying or in the studios of artists? In the world's immense regions of

16. Lonergan, *Method*, 53.
17. Here, I am deliberately rephrasing Lonergan's beautiful description of the gift of radical love. See Lonergan, *Method*, 106.
18. Ludwig Wittgenstein, *Culture and Value*, edited by GH von Wright in collaboration with Heikki Nyman, translated by Peter Winch (Oxford: Basil Blackwell, 1980), 33.

poverty and in the exuberantly religious Southern hemisphere; or in the post-Christian world of the West? The theologian may work in any or all of these situations, for each is an aspect of what pluriform reality of what we commonly we term 'the post-modern world'.

Lonergan's 'phenomenological' transposition

Let me backtrack a little, first to Lonergan's transposition of the Thomist system. It is fair to say that Lonergan transposed to a considerable extent the main points of Aquinas' metaphysically modulated systematic approach into a more critically grounded phenomenology—especially the questions of God, Trinity, the soul, the faculties of intellect and will, grace and so on. Lonergan put his finger on that weak point in the Aristotelian inheritance which certainly carried over into later Thomist commentators. What was the specific act on the part of the human mind that could affirm God as Be-ing? Impressed by the fertility of the notion of God as limitless act of Being present and operative in all beings, the temptation (notably for Gilson[19]) was to think of being as somehow intuited in every existent. Others, following the Anselmian tradition, considered that infinity of the divine being was so evident in itself that it had to entail actual existence: the ontological argument. Lonergan's monumental response was to point out that all being, and above all infinite Being, could only be affirmed in that full complement of cognitive activities that terminated in the act of judging. The pivotal phenomenon was insight—insight into all data, and the insight that arose when all conditions for making a judgment of existence were fulfilled. Chapter 19 of *Insight* takes us further, to present God as 'infinite insight', the luminous unconditioned rapture in which all that God is, in himself and for all creation, is affirmed, and as grounding all our knowing. *Esse intentionale*, instead of being a mode of being, for Lonergan became the dynamic site of the disclosure of Infinite Being as pure Insight. Despite the exquisite intricacy of his argument in this complex chapter, Lonergan shows himself throughout as phenomenologist of human consciousness.

In Aquinas' universe of being emanating from subsistent 'To Be', the nature of human being was specified by a being-open-to Being, that is, as through a spiritual soul, with its spiritual faculties of intellect and will.

19. For example, Etienne Gilson, *The Unity of Philosophical Experience* (London: Sheed and Ward, 1938), 320–27.

These were strengthened and elevated by the whole panoply of virtues, theological and moral, and moved to higher orders of activity through the gifts of the Spirit. Again, Lonergan the phenomenologist took the core of this and anchored it in the phenomenon of consciousness. The human being was not primarily a spiritual soul, but a self-transcending subject.

He went further. Where Thomas spoke of the state of grace as an entitative habit inhering in the essence of the soul, Lonergan the phenomenologist gives us a particularly moving account of grace as a state of being in love with God, a gift of love that worked at the peak of all our conscious self-transcending activity, sublating all our human loves.

Again, Thomas, in the vast systematic range of his thought, drew on the Old and the New Testaments, the different senses of scripture, the Patristic tradition, the dogmatic pronouncements of the Magisterium, along with what was to be learned from Greek philosophy. For his part, Lonergan shaped all this into a refined and articulated historical process, brimming with its own phenomenological evidences. For example, the differentiations of consciousness, stages, dimensions and carriers of meaning, all signal a phenomenological sensibility pervading his theological method.

Finally in this comparison, there is the rather large consideration of scholastic *ratio*—often too neatly translated as 'reason'. It was elaborated in all kinds of contexts—demonstrations of God's existence, the intelligibility of naming God, the role of analogy, and the always intriguing dimension of knowledge by way of connaturality. Lonergan not only brings considerable precision into all this, but also gives a special drama into the workings of reason, through his phenomenology of consciousness, self-transcendence, horizons and different kind of conversion—intellectual, moral, religious . . . and 'psychic' (through his endorsement of Doran's suggestion).

The Christian element

Clearly, Lonergan, in all these matters, proceeded with a phenomenological sensitivity. Moreover, he insisted, at least in a general sense, it be kept in play. For the self-transcendence of authentic consciousness self-destructs if it is deaf to the primary imperative—Be Attentive! Still, Lonergan acknowledged quite early the weakness of chapter 19 of *Insight* on the God-Question, and came to see the need for an inclusion of what we can call a phenomenology of religious experience.[20] There are more phenomena than those of an intellectual kind. But when pressed further, he took a further step to acknowledge 'a specific element proper to Christianity':

> If I have concluded that there is a common element to all the religions of mankind, I must now add that there is *a specific element proper to Christianity*. Christianity involves not only the inward gift of being in love with God but also the *outward expression of God's love in Christ Jesus* dying and rising again. In the paschal mystery the love that is given inwardly is *focused and inflamed*, and that focusing unites Christians not only with Christ but also with one another.[21]

Some pages later, he speaks of the '*objective manifestation of God's love in Christ Jesus*',[22] and the '*intersubjective component*' that creates a Christian difference.[23] Which brings us to the question: can Christ, the intense focus of Christian experience, the 'outward expression' of God's love, its 'objective manifestation', and 'inter-subjective component' be more fully developed? Can such a development meet Rahner's requirement that the mystery of God's self-communication in Christ determine the method more specifically and concretely determine the method of theology?[24] Is von Balthasar right in insisting that the transcendent, objective form of revelation displace the primacy of the subject—any subject, even a self-transcending subject, as he writes, 'Christianity is destroyed if it lets itself be reduced to transcendental presuppositions of man's self-understanding whether in thought or in life, in knowledge or in action'.[25] This is to say that theology operates with a kind of 'reverse intentionality': God's self-transcending self-revelation displaces and radically re-orders the self-transcending capacities of the human subject.

---

20. Bernard Lonergan, *Philosophy of God, and Theology: The Relationship between Philosophy of God and the Functional Specialty, Systematics* (London: Darton, Longman and Todd, 1973), 21–44.
21. Lonergan, *Philosophy of God*, 10; emphasis original.
22. Lonergan, *Philosophy of God*, 20; emphasis original.
23. Lonergan, *Philosophy of God*, 67; emphasis original.
24. K Rahner, 'Kritische Bemerkungen zu BJF Lonergan's Aufsatz: Functional Specialties in Theology', in *Gregorianum* 51/3 (1970): 537–40; 'Reflections on Methodology in Theology', in *Theological Investigations*, volume 2 (London: Darton, Longman and Todd, 1974), 69–114.
25. Hans Urs von Balthasar, *Love Alone* (New York: Herder and Herder, 1969), 43.

A phenomenological contribution

In this regard, a phenomenology of the Christ-event can contribute to a more adequate theological method. Husserl, long recognised as a seminal figure in the development of phenomenological methods, sought to recall an abstract and ego-centred philosophy to return to 'the things themselves' (*zu den Sachen selbst*). A new centre of gravity had to be established to serve the genuineness of thinking. It would contest the negative bias inherent in the pretensions and projections of the omni-competent thinking subject. In the Enlightenment setting, the self is the starting point; and the 'given', the data, tend to be a mirror-image of the rationalistic ego, an 'idolic' projection. But when the given phenomenon begins to be appreciated in its own right and in the conditions of its appearance, the intentionality of the all-competent rational subject is reversed. The centre of gravity shifts. A critical and even contemplative reverence for the given phenomenon becomes primary, thus allowing it first of all to be received on its own terms. In this sense, what is given to consciousness may be metaphorically described in Marion's terms as 'iconic', for it shines with light from beyond the limited world of our habitual vision, even as it allows an endless play of perspectives.

The 'idolic' mode of thinking stands in contrast to this 'iconic' mode of disciplined receptivity to what is given. Grammatically speaking, this idolic form privileges the nominative case—as when 'I' am always the subject of the sentence; or the accusative—as it affects 'me'; or the ablative—it is what is done 'by me'. By contrast, the iconic character of the phenomenon, in resistance to any reduction to a pre-established, all-governing ego, privileges the dative case.[26] It is what is given, in its own terms, 'to me'. In its uniqueness, it presents a surplus and an excess of significance in the face of all abstract ideas, systems and methods. 'I' am not the all-comprehending ego, but the one to whom things have been given, appearing in their arresting and particular otherness.

There are resonances here with the Scholastic adage, *quidquid reciptur recipitur per modum recipientis*, for the degree of receptivity allows for different modes and capacities. There are different attitudes, moods, preoccupations and perspectives. This plurality of possibilities affects not only an endless variety of individuals, but also cultures, societies, historical

---

26. See Ian Leask, 'The Dative Subject and the "Principle of Principles"', in *Givenness and God: Questions of Jean-Luc Marion,* edited by Ian Leask and Eion Cassidy (New York: Fordham University Press, 2005), 182–89.

epochs and the church itself. Differing or contrasting modes of receptivity can conflict. The viewpoint of a reductively secular method constricts everything within its own self-limited horizon. To such an outlook, the Christian revelation, for example, is an impossibility, or at best a mythic expression of something more real and familiar. Such an attitude is diametrically opposed to that of faith. For the Christian believer, the mystery of Christ is the focal (and 'inflaming') phenomenon. Its significance affects every aspect of one's interpretation of the world.

Newman's words are vivid: referring to the prodigality of God's self-giving, he writes:

> We all confess that He is infinite . . . but, we ask, what is infinity? . . . the outward exhibition of infinitude is mystery; and the mysteries of nature and of grace are nothing else than the mode in which His infinitude encounters us and is brought home to our minds. Men confess that He is infinite, yet they start and object, as soon as his infinitude comes in contact with their imagination and acts upon their reason. They cannot bear the fullness, the superabundance, the inexhaustible flowing forth, and 'vehement rushing', and encompassing flood of the divine attributes. They restrain and limit them to their own comprehension, they measure them by their own standard, they fashion them by their own model.[27]

The phenomenological attitude involves being receptive 'to the superabundance, the inexhaustible flowing forth' of the gift of God, beyond the limits of human comprehension.

27. John Henry Newman, *Discourses Addressed to Mixed Congregations* (London: Burns and Oates, 1881), 309. For further citation and insightful commentary, see Mark A Mcintosh, *Discernment and Truth: The Spirituality and Theology of Knowledge* (New York, NY: The Crossroad Publishing Company, 2004), 184–86.

Marion's 'saturated phenomena'

Here, the writings of Jean-Luc Marion[28] and his followers are a special resource.[29] The overflowing or 'saturated' significance of the phenomenon imposes itself on the subject. It is given to such an extent that the subject is more like a witness to an event rather than an agent of its construction.[30] To make this point, Marion coins a word to highlight the passivity and receptivity of the subject in regard to what is given, namely, *l'adonné*, 'the one to whom it is given', the recipient of the self-giving in question.

As implied already, 'Grace', the gift of God in all its forms, is most expressed in the grammar of the dative case. The gift is given to the believer; it is not simply 'there' to be inspected or possessed, as something taken

28. Marion's phenomenology, along with the general turn in this direction, follows the direction of Husserl's original efforts to return to 'to the things themselves', *zu den Sachen selbst* (Husserl). Along with Husserl and Heidegger and most others, he is engaged in a critical reversal of Descartes' egological subjectivism. However, Marion considers that neither of these two sufficiently breaks free from the limits of the imposition of the ego or the self in their concerns to respect the 'given-ness' of the phenomena. They are still considered too much as projections of the self, either as objects constituted by consciousness or in terms of being. His emphasis, therefore, can be termed 'donatology', that is, a critical receptivity to what is given, beyond the limits prescribed by the imposition of the self. See Robyn Horner, *Rethinking God as Gift: Marion, Derrida and the Limits of Phenomenology* (New York: Fordham University Press, 2001).
29. A critically elaborated account of the radically 'given' quality of what is disclosed is found in his influential trilogy, *Reduction and Givenness: Investigations of Husserl, Heidegger, and Phenomenology*, translated by Thomas A Carlson (Evanston, IL: Northwestern University Press, 1998); *Being Given: Toward a Phenomenology of Givenness*, translated by Jeffrey L Kosky (Stanford, CA: Stanford University Press, 2002); *In Excess: Studies of Saturated Phenomena*, translated by Robyn Horner and Vincent Barraud (New York: Fordham University Press, 2002). For further elaboration and background, see *God Without Being: Hors-Texte*, translated by Thomas A Carlson (Chicago, IL: Chicago University Press, 1991); 'Le possible et la révélation', in *Eros and Eris: Contribution to a Hermeneutical Phenomenology: Liber Amicorum for Adriann Peperzak*, edited by P van Tongeren, P Sars, C Bremmer and K Boey (Dordrecht: Kluwer Academic, 1992), 217–31; 'The Saturated Phenomenon', in *Philosophy Today* 40 (1996): 103–24; 'They Recognised Him; and He Became Invisible to Them', in *Modern Theology* 18 (2002): 145–52; *Le phénomène érotique: Six Meditations* (Paris: Grasset, 2003). I am much indebted to Shane Mackinlay, *Interpreting Excess: The Implicit Hermeneutics of Jean-Luc Marion's Saturated Phenomena* (Leuven: Katholieke Universiteit Leuven. Hoger Instituut voor Wijsbegeerte, 2004); also his 'Phenomenality in the Middle: Marion, Romano, and the Hermeneutics of the Event', in *Givenness and God: Questions of Jean-Luc Marion*, edited by Ian Leask and Eion Cassidy (New York: Fordham University Press, 2005), 167–81.
30. Marion, *Being Given*, 216.

for granted. It gives itself, communicates itself, to the subject, and re-constitutes it in a new awareness: 'for those who are in Christ, there is a new creation' (2 Cor 5:17). In this instance, as in others more generally, what is given is primary—not the preconditions laid down by our rational capacities. In this regard, true thinking must be aware of the modes of givenness at its foundations. It is less thinking 'about' something, and more thinking from *within* what is given, by responding to it, and by allowing it to appear in its arresting 'other-ness'. This phenomenological return or 're-duction' to the given provokes a kind of conversion in the theologian's method and style. Theology understands itself first of all as a 'theology of disclosure', beholden, humbly and reverently, to what is given. It is marked by contemplative receptivity to the data of faith. I suggest, therefore, that some currents of contemporary phenomenology can be a rich resource for theological method—especially as it regards the culminating gift of God's self-giving in Christ.

Understandably, there will be some theological uneasiness over such an approach. On the one hand, is there not a danger of collapsing everything into a fideistic subjectivism? On the other, some may be rightly wary of a revelational objectivism that overwhelms the role of the believing and thinking subject. Admittedly, a disclosive theology inverts habitual patterns of intentionality with its presumption of the subject being already self-constituted, already 'given to itself', before anything is given or appears to it. In contrast, a phenomenological style puts the emphasis on the self-giving 'other'. As a result, any activity on the part of the subject is conceived in terms of receptivity and responsiveness. The rational ego no longer occupies centre-stage. The subject is not a detached monad projecting itself onto what is other.[31] For the subject, literally, is the one who is 'subjected' to what is overwhelmingly other, and made a witness to it by being stripped of all pretensions to comprehend or constitute what is given.[32] In this receptive posture, the subject becomes a luminous indicator of what is given, to function as a screen on which the phenomenon is registered in its originality.[33] In this manner, the subject is reconstituted, as it were, by being drawn into the saturated field of the phenomenon. Its role is to disclose the 'visibility' of what has been given from beyond its vision.

31. Marion, *Being Given*, 261.
32. Marion, *Being Given*, 216–17.
33. Marion, *Being Given*, 264–65.

Take, for example, the phenomenon of one's own birth. A response of gratitude is called forth, and indeed an endless effort of interpretation of the personal and communal meaning of such an unobjectifiable event.[34] It provokes an exploration of both the past that preceded it, of the present as it occurs, and of the future it gives rise to—even though the event of my 'being born' fits into no prior project on my part—and perhaps not on the part of my parents!

Marion refers to five especially saturated phenomena: an event, a painting, the flesh, the face, and, in a way that tends to combine all four, revelation.[35] Put briefly in Christian terms, I am affected by a world-shaping event. As a recipient of revelation, I am beholden to a light and a beauty not of this world. As celebrating the Eucharist, I live a new sense of embodied existence. In faith, I am confronted by one who sees me, and indeed sees through me. As caught up in the wonder of the sheer givenness of the universe, I come to appreciate what God's self-revelation might mean. All five such instances have this in common, namely, a primordial self-giving.[36] None of them is constituted by the subject, but each appears in its original and self-imposing impact. Thus, the subject comes to itself in a new consciousness only through self-giving otherness of the phenomenon concerned.

Though Janicaud, for example, objected to an unwarranted intrusion of theological perspectives into phenomenological methods,[37] that is not our problem. In fact, Marion has conveniently posed the question:

> Could not theology, in virtue of its own demands, and solely in view of formulating them, suggest certain modifications of method and operations to phenomenology? . . . Could not theology's demands allow phenomenology to transgress its own limits, so as finally to attain the free possibility at which, from its origin, it claims to aim?[38]

I think so.[39] Theology can be only enriched by a more phenomenological method. And, in its turn, it can enrich that method with possibilities

34. Marion, *Being Given,* 289; see also Marion, *In Excess*, 33, 42.
35. Marion, *Being Given*, 234–36.
36. Marion, *Being Given,* 5.
37. Dominique Janicaud et al, *Phenomenology and 'The Theological Turn': The French Debate*, translated by Bernard G Prusak (New York: Fordham University Press, 2000).
38. Marion, 'Le possible et la révélation', 228.
39. For a critical appreciation of Marion's contribution, see Brian Robinette, 'A Gift to

deriving from attentiveness to the singularity of positive revelation.[40] Still, the general phenomenological principle stands. The saturated phenomenon shows itself by giving itself, and in a more intense and saturated manner in the case of theology.[41]

What then, in the case of Lonergan? Do I need say more than to stress the necessity of taking the Lonerganian precept more seriously: 'Be attentive'—be receptive; be open to the unutterably given; be contemplatively aware in praise and thanksgiving . . . All this before the other dynamics of self-transcendence take over. Before theology deals with the data of Christian doctrine, it must be contemplatively alive to the donum, given in the 'saturated phenomenon' of the Christ-event.

Conclusion

These brief remarks indicate a kind of benign dialectic in progress, even in the writings of Lonergan himself:

- between an intentionality analysis of the self -transcending subject on the one hand, and, on the other, a phenomenological receptivity to God's self-communication in Christ;
- between a phenomenology that pivots on the experience of insight, and one that is governed by the concrete actuality of God's self-revelation in Christ (even if, in most cases, it shows little awareness of the phenomenon of insight);
- between the horizon of intellectual conversion, and that of 'psychic' or phenomenological conversion in regard to the mode of given-ness proper to God's self-giving revelation;
- between the self-transcending self and the self-giving quality of the Other;
- between proceeding from the generalised to the particular, and proceeding from the privileged particular to its universal significance;
- between the horizon of Being, and the personal disclosures of Love;
- between incarnation as one carrier of meaning, and the Incarnation as *the* carrier of meaning;

Theology? Jean-Luc Marion's "Saturated Phenomenon" in Christological Perspective', in *Heythrop Journal* 48/1 (January, 2007): 86–108.

40. Marion, 'Le possible et la révélation', 231; *Being Given*, 242.

41. Marion, *Being Given*, 367.

- between doctrinal forms and revelational experience;
- between the pure desire to know, and the senses inherent in connatural knowledge—or 'emotional intelligence' if you wish;
- between revelation inspiring 'a tradition of rationality',[42] and revelation as first demanding a specific form of phenomenology.

In all this, Lonergan calls us to the practice of a more thorough-going intentionality analysis of the Christian phenomenon. To address this task is to appreciate more fully the fertility of the inheritance he has left us in his seminal writings.

42. Ormerod, *Meaning, Method and Revelation*, 217–19.

Chapter 6

Contingent Predication and the Four-Point Hypothesis

Neil Ormerod

Lonergan often commented on the need for a closer relationship between systematic theology and the philosophy of God.[1] We can see for example how a Thomistic philosophy of God underpins Lonergan's account of Thomas' position on grace and freedom. One cannot understand the relationship between grace and freedom without some account of the relationship between creator and creation, which Lonergan formulated in terms of a theorem on divine transcendence.[2] In this paper I would like to explore further the relationship between systematic theology and the philosophy of God by a consideration of Lonergan's notion of contingent predication, and how his position on contingent predication underpins his so-called 'four point hypothesis'. This hypothesis is to be found in *De Deo Trino*, recently available in English translation. By comparing Lonergan's account with that of Karl Rahner, I will argue that Lonergan's position is a major advance on a position that has become standard among Catholic theologians. I shall also comment on recent discussions in the journal *Theological Studies* on the four-point hypothesis, particularly the criticisms levelled by Charles Hefling against the hypothesis.[3]

1. Most notably in Bernard JF Lonergan, *Philosophy of God, and Theology: The Relationship between the Philosophy of God and the Functional Specialty, Systematics* (Philadelphia: Westminster Press, 1974).
2. *Collected Works of Bernard Lonergan*, volume 1, *Grace and Freedom: Operative Grace in the Thought of St. Thomas Aquinas*, edited by Frederick E Crowe and Robert M Doran (Toronto: University of Toronto Press, 2000); (hereafter *CWL* 1 *Grace and Freedom*).
3. Robert M Doran, 'The Starting Point of Systematic Theology', in *Theological Studies* 67 (2006): 750–76; Charles C Hefling, 'On the (Economic) Trinity: An Argument in Conversation with Robert Doran', in *Theological Studies* 68 (2007): 642–60; Robert

Contingent predication and the four-point hypothesis

I shall begin my account with Chapter 19 of *Insight* on 'General transcendent knowledge' where Lonergan establishes the existence of God and seeks to explicate the properties of divinity through a discussion of various 'points'. Having developed his eighteenth 'point' about God he spells out five corollaries which detail the conclusions of his notion of 'contingent predication'.[4] These deal with the issue of how necessary being (that is, God) relates to contingent being, without change in that necessary being. It affirms the efficacy of the divine will, while still maintaining the contingency of creation. Further God can eternally will temporal events without either making God temporal or those events eternal. These two tightly argued pages spell out the implication of the theorem on divine transcendence that Lonergan first identifies in his doctoral thesis, published as *Grace and Freedom*.[5] Overall Lonergan is up-dating the classical Thomistic position that the relationship between the creature and God is a real relation, while the relationship between God and the creature is a logical one, or a relation of reason.[6] While countless modern authors have been critical of this position, most notably those adopting a process account,[7] the alternative of stating a real relation between God and the creature is to diminish divine transcendence and bring into question the eschatological triumph of good over evil.[8]

The other significant element in *Insight* that I wish to highlight is Lonergan's comments in the Epilogue of that work. After discussing the limitations of a metaphysics of proportionate being, that is, being proportionate to human experience, Lonergan notes that 'the theologian is under no necessity of reducing to the metaphysical elements, which suffice for

---

M Doran, 'Addressing the Four-Point Hypothesis', in *Theological Studies* 68 (2007): 674–82.

4. *Collected Works of Bernard Lonergan*, volume 3, *Insight: A Study of Human Understanding*, edited by Frederick E Crowe and Robert M Doran (Toronto: University of Toronto Press, 1992), 684–85 (hereafter *CWL* 3 *Insight*).
5. *CWL* 1 *Grace and Freedom*.
6. The relation of the creature to God is a real relation because it is constitutive of the reality of the creature; the relation of God to the creature is a logical one, or a relation of reason, because it is not constitutive of God's reality, that is, God would still be the same God whether or not the relation with the creature exists.
7. For example Charles Hartshorne, *Aquinas to Whitehead: Seven Centuries of Metaphysics of Religion* (Milwaukee: Marquette University Publications, 1976).
8. Neil Ormerod, 'Chance and Necessity, Providence and God' in *Irish Theological Quarterly* 70 (2005): 263–78.

an account of this world, such supernatural realities as the incarnation, the indwelling of the Holy Spirit, and the beatific vision'.[9] Here Lonergan is questioning the suitability of metaphysical elements such as potency, form and act in dealing with these strictly supernatural realities. While he does not mention them by name, it is likely he has in mind accounts such as those of Maurice de la Taille, with his notion of actuated act,[10] and Karl Rahner, with his notion of quasi-formal causality.[11] However, in this largely philosophical work Lonergan does not enter into further discussion of how these supernatural realities might be properly dealt with by theologians.

However, we can see Lonergan working through these questions in his work on the ontological and psychological constitution of Christ, recently made available in English translation.[12] The question Lonergan is seeking to understand is how a divine person, notably the Logos, or second person of the Trinity, can be incarnate in the contingent reality of a human being, Jesus of Nazareth. Significantly his solution will involve utilising the philosophical notion of contingent prediction. Whereas the notion of contingent predication refers to the divine nature as a whole, Lonergan extends his analysis to the individual divine persons as follows: 'Proper contingent truths predicated of a divine person add to the subsistent relation only a relation of reason in the divine person, but imply an appropriate created term outside God that is really related to the divine subsistent relation'.[13]

The logic of Lonergan's position is as follows. In order to understand how there can be a real relation between a created reality and any of the divine persons, we must understand it analogously to the real relation between the creature and God since 'a divine subsistent reality [such as the

9. *CWL* 3 *Insight*, 756.
10. Maurice de la Taille, 'Actuation créée par acte incréé: Lumière de gloire, grace sanctifiante, union hypostatique', in *Recherches de science religieuse* 18 (1928): 253–68. Lonergan provides an explicit critique of de la Taille's position in Bernard JF Lonergan, *De Verbo Incarnato* (Rome: Gregorian University Press, 1960), 343–44.
11. See Karl Rahner, 'Some Implications of the Scholastic Concept of Uncreated Grace', in *Theological Investigations*, volume 1 (London: Darton, Longman & Todd, 1961), 297–346. Also Karl Rahner, *Foundations of Christian Faith: An Introduction to the Idea of Christianity* (New York: Crossroad, 1982), 120–22.
12. *Collected Works of Bernard Lonergan*, volume 7, *The Ontological and Psychological Constitution of Christ*, edited by Frederick E Crowe and Robert M Doran, translated by Michael G Shields (Toronto: University of Toronto Press, 2002); (hereafter *CWL* 7 *Ontological and Psychological Constitution*).
13. *CWL* 7 *Ontological and Psychological Constitution*, 97.

Logos] is really identical with the immutable divine essence'.[14] All that is needed for the truth of the relation is an 'appropriate created term outside God' which exists if (and only if) God wills to create such a term. Thus the mystery of a created participation of the divine nature, such as the Incarnation, is an extension of the mystery of creation itself. Created participations of the divine nature 'extend' the relationship between creator and creature by drawing the creature into the inner Trinitarian relations.

While this is as far as Lonergan goes in this Christological text, the door is open for a vast extension of the argument to all four Trinitarian relations. Lonergan takes this step in his Trinitarian work *De Deo Trino: Pars Systematica*,[15] recently made available in English translation.[16] Here we find Lonergan's first (and perhaps only)[17] exposition of the 'four point hypothesis'.

> There are four real divine relations, really identical with the divine substance, and therefore there are four special modes that ground the external imitation of the divine substance. Next, there are four absolutely supernatural realities, which are never found uninformed, namely, the secondary act of existence of the Incarnation, sanctifying grace, the habit of charity, and the light of glory. It would not be inappropriate, therefore, to say that the secondary act of existence of the Incarnation is a created participation of paternity, and so has a special relation to the Son; that sanctifying grace is a [created] participation of active spiration, and so has a special relation to the Holy Spirit; that the habit of charity is a [created] participation of passive spiration, and so has a special relation to the Father and the Son; and that the light of glory is a [created] participation of sonship, and so in a most perfect way brings the children of adoption back to the Father.[18]

14. *CWL 7 Ontological and Psychological Constitution*, 97.
15. Bernard Lonergan, *De Deo Trino, Pars Systematica* (Rome: Gregorian University Press, 1964).
16. *Collected Works of Bernard Lonergan*, volume 12, *The Triune God: Systematics*, edited by Robert Doran and Daniel Monsour, translated by Michael Shields (Toronto: University of Toronto Press, 2007); (hereafter *CWL* 12 *Triune God*).
17. This point is made by Hefling, 'Conversation with Robert Doran', 645.
18. *CWL* 12 *Triune God*, 471–73.

It is worth spelling out the logic of this account further to clarify what is going on in Lonergan's position. The four 'absolutely supernatural realities' which he speaks of are created realities, the 'appropriate created term outside God' which transform the natural realities they inhabit. They are a created participation of the divine nature. Lonergan is here maintaining a strict distinction between the divine and the created.[19] The supernatural life in us is not some fusion of the divine and the human, as is perhaps suggested by Rahner's category of quasi-formal causality. Rather, it is a created term which nonetheless produces a supernatural participation in the divine life. This position, which is already present in Lonergan earlier writings on grace, is largely a matter of ruling out all alternatives to arrive at this position. There Lonergan describes supernatural grace as a 'created, proportionate, and remote principle whereby there are in the creature operations by which God is attained as he is in himself'.[20] Further it is a created term which corresponds to one of the four divine relations. Thus for example the relation, paternity, has as its term the Son. So, the created participation of the divine relation of paternity defines the secondary act of existence of the Incarnation. Similarly, the relation of active spiration by Father and Son has as its term the Holy Spirit (the *filioque*). Thus the created participation in active spiration in us is the indwelling of the Holy Spirit.[21]

There are still some important issues in this schematisation of these mysteries of faith. One is the reality of the distinction between sanctifying grace and the habit of charity, which has been a matter of dispute between Thomistic and Franciscan schools of theology. The more probing question

19. This distincton is blurred for example in Eastern accounts of the 'uncreated energies' of God; for a treatment of this position see George Maloney, *A Theology Of 'Uncreated Energies'* (Milwaukee: Marquette University Press, 1978).
20. An outline of *De ente supernaturali: supplementum schematicum* taken from J Michael Stebbins, *The Divine Initiative: Grace, World-Order, and Human Freedom in the Early Writings of Bernard Lonergan*, Lonergan Studies (Toronto: University of Toronto Press, 1995), xiii. Stebbins notes how 'minimal' this definition is (49), adding that 'no matter how earnestly we pose the further question of how a simple, infinite, and absolutely necessary being can communicate itself to a being that is composite, finite and contingent, nothing short of the beatific vision can provide an answer' (51).
21. There is also a shift in language from Lonergan's earlier language of 'communications' of the divine nature and the later language of 'participations' in the divine nature. The shift is important in freeing up the possibilities. There are only two communications of the divine nature: the Father communicates divinity to the Son and the Father and Son communicate it to the Spirit. The language of participations gives Lonergan extra room to move and then to consider the four relations, not just the two processions.

is how one can make the shift from the technical metaphysical language of acts and habits to the interior language demanded of the third stage of meaning, that is, what is the difference between these two in the language of interiority, of consciousness? This question has been taken up by Robert Doran in a recent article in *Theological Studies*.[22] I have also written a more detailed comparison between Lonergan's schematisation and the more well-known position of Karl Rahner in a recent issue of that journal.[23] Here I shall push that question further before returning to the question of the distinction between sanctifying grace and the habit of charity.

Rahner and quasi-formal causality

Rahner develops a parallel account to Lonergan's in his discussion of Christology.[24] There Rahner also places the divine self-communication within a context of an understanding of creation. However, Rahner's starting point is not creation as a relation between creator and creature, but creation as an act of efficient causality whereby God creates that which is not God.[25] This conception then leads Rahner to ask whether there is the possibility that God can create Godself in the other, in that which of itself is not God. This has parallels with Lonergan's notion of a created participation of the divine nature. If this is a possibility, then the normal form of creation, whereby God creates that which is not God, must be viewed as a deficient mode of creation, lacking as it does the full possibility of creation, whereby God creates Godself in the other.[26] For Rahner such a possibility cannot come about through efficient causality. For it to be realised another type of causality must be involved, and so Rahner evokes the notion of a quasi-formal causality, which is originally derived from Aquinas' speculations on the beatific vision.[27] Here, however, Rahner presses it into service to help us understand both grace and incarnation. He argues that through quasi-formal causality God is able to create Godself in the created order, which is then an instance of the fullness of creation, as distinct from the deficient form of creation resulting from an exercise of efficient causality.

22. Doran, 'The Starting Point of Systematic Theology'.
23. Neil Ormerod, 'Two Points or Four?—Rahner and Lonergan on Trinity, Incarnation, Grace, and Beatific Vision', in *Theological Studies* 68 (2007): 661–73.
24. See his treatment in Rahner, *Foundations*, 176–203.
25. Rahner, *Foundations*, 121.
26. Rahner, *Foundations*, 120–22.
27. Rahner 'Some Implications of the Scholastic Concept of Uncreated Grace'.

The difficulties with such an approach can be gauged from a consideration of Aquinas' account of the beatific vision which is undoubtedly one of the longest articles in the *Summa*.[28] He not only considers sixteen distinct objections, he also cites six sources of authority for his position, where normally one suffices. The difficulty, of which Aquinas is more than aware, is that simple discussion of an act of formal causality would imply a breakdown in the distinction between creator and creature, compromising the divine transcendence and threatening to obliterate the creature, hence, the importance of the qualified 'quasi', 'as if.' Aquinas is finding some analogy between the process of imparting the divine 'form' and the beatific vision. However, he is not intending to compromise the divine transcendence in any way. Unfortunately this is less clear in Rahner who goes on to speak of the divine changing 'in the other' through the incarnation.[29] This notion of changing 'in the other' comes close to the process notions of antecedent and subsequent natures of God, though it has a more restrictive range, than of the supernatural actions of God in the created order. Certainly we get a sense of Rahner's position compromising the divine transcendence, at least in the supernatural order.

Here we can identify one advantage of Lonergan's approach using the notion of contingent predication. Lonergan develops the notion of contingent predication in order to give an account of the relationship between the necessary being of God and the contingent being of creation which does not compromise the divine transcendence. While various theologians, particularly in the process school of thought, are making moves in this direction, I think they are based on an inadequate way of raising the question. They ask, 'How is the transcendent God close to the created order?' Posed in this way divine immanence is conceived in almost local terms, as closeness 'in space and time'. Once this imagined closeness dominates our thinking it is difficult not to then have God's being affected by the created order. However, if we pose the question as, 'How is the created order close to God?', then the answer can be found in divine acts of knowledge and love, which are creative of that order. This shifts us from some imagined local closeness to an intentional closeness which in no way compromises the divine transcendence. Lonergan's notion of contingent predication, for understanding the relationship between creature and creator, and its analogous extension to supernatural participations of the divine life, completely avoid the problem of some imagined closeness

28. *Summa Theologiae*, Suppl III q92, a1.
29. Rahner, *Foundations*, 219–23.

which would compromise the divine transcendence. Here good philosophy assists in the development of good systematics.

Sanctifying grace and the habit of charity

I would now like to turn my attention briefly to another issue raised by Lonergan's four-point hypothesis. It concerns the distinction between sanctifying grace and the habit of charity. This question has been the subject of disputation between two Lonergan scholars, Charles Hefling and Robert Doran, in the 2007 issue of *Theological Studies*.[30] Hefling has taken issue with Doran on the four-point hypothesis, arguing that Lonergan more frequently speaks of a three-fold participation of the divine nature,[31] and that while the distinction between sanctifying grace and the habit of charity made some sense in the metaphysical realm of theory, it is no longer tenable in a transition to the realm of interiority. While I am not in a position to resolve this dispute, I would like to raise some questions and make some points in relation to it.

Firstly, Hefling notes some of Lonergan's comments about the process of such a transition from the realm of theory to the realm of interiority in both *Second Collection* and *Method in Theology*. Lonergan notes that not all aspects of the traditional scholastic theology will have permanent validity. Hefling points out that, in Lonergan's summary efforts to outline a transition to interiority in relation to a theology of grace, Lonergan shifts from speaking about 'a metaphysical psychology in terms of the essence of the soul, its potencies, habits and acts' to an account that speaks of 'acts'[32] since, as Hefling quotes from *Second Collection*, in studying the human subject one must 'prescind from the soul, its essence, its potencies, its habits, for none of these is given in consciousness'.[33] Hefling concludes that 'conscious acts, precisely as conscious, survive the transition to a methodical theology of grace. The potencies and the essence of the soul do not'.[34] If Hefling is correct then the distinction between sanctifying grace

30. See Charles C Hefling, 'On the (Economic) Trinity: An Argument in Conversation with Robert Doran', in *Theological Studies*, 68 (2007): 642–60 and RM Doran, 'Addressing the Four-Point Hypothesis', in *Theological Studies*, 68 (2007): 674–82.
31. This is evident, for example, in the quote above from the Epilogue of *Insight* which only mentions three instances of supernatural participation of the divine nature.
32. Bernard JF Lonergan, *Method in Theology* (London: DLT, 1972), 288–89.
33. Bernard JF Lonergan, *A Second Collection*, edited by William F Ryan and Bernard Tyrrell (Toronto: University of Toronto Press, 1996), 73.
34. Hefling, 'Conversation with Robert Doran', 650.

and the habit of charity may not survive the transition into a methodical theology based on interiority.

If I understand Hefling correctly here then I think he is overstating his case. If all we can speak about are conscious acts, then what are we to make of talk about the detached disinterested desire to know that features so prominently in *Insight*? Similarly in *Method in Theology* Lonergan argues that 'other-worldly love, not as this or that act, not as a series of acts, but as a dynamic state whence proceed the acts, that constitutes in a methodical theology what in a theoretical theology is named sanctifying grace'.[35] If only the acts survive a transition to methodical theology, then Hefling's strictures would appear to rule out speaking of sanctifying grace as well, since Lonergan does not speak of it as an act but a state.

Secondly, I would suggest an analogy which might be helpful in identifying the distinction between sanctifying grace and the habit of charity. In *Insight* Lonergan speaks of the desire to know, as a dynamic state which underpins all our acts of knowing, but he also speaks of a scientific habit of enquiry. The desire to know is a constitutive element in human consciousness, but the scientific habit of enquiry is not general or even common. It requires a specific commitment and personal discipline. Clearly the desire to know is the remote principle of the scientific habit, but of itself is not identical with the scientific habit. Do we have a similarity here with the distinction between sanctifying grace and the habit of charity? Hefling does affirm some distinction, but refers to the classical distinction between grace as operative and cooperative. In that case it is the one grace which is both operative and cooperative. But the cooperation may be intermittent and spasmodic, just as commonsense is intermittently touched by the desire to know, or it may be committed and systematic, as we find in a scientific habit of mind. What grounds the transition from the intermittent and spasmodic to the committed and disciplined habit, keeping in mind that 'cooperation' is present in both?

Thirdly, I would like to suggest some hints, more from the level of doctrines than systematics, which may further reinforce the possibility of a real distinction between sanctifying grace and the habit of charity. The first hint is the classical distinction between mortal and venial sin. Mortal sin breaks the bond of sanctifying grace, while venial sin does not. Could we construe venial sin in terms of a failure in the habit of charity? Indeed the very distinction between mortal and venial sins would seem to imply

35. Lonergan, *Method*, 289.

some such distinction within the life of grace. The second hint can be found in the Johannine discourses on the work of the Father (and the Son), for example John 4:34–38, 5:17–47. Jesus proclaims that his 'food is to do the will of the one who sent him and to complete his work' (4:34). Moreover, 'My Father goes on working and I am at work too' (5:17). The Son 'can only do what he sees the Father doing and whatever the Father does, the Son does too' (5:19). This 'work' closely links Father and Son. It is not an inner state *per se* but an orientation to a 'work' or mission, the mission of the Son which is to do the work of the Father. Perhaps in these hints we can grasp why there might be a relationship between passive spiration (and hence a relationship to the Father and the Son) and the habit of charity, though a more modern theological language might speak of the mission of the building of the Kingdom. If such a position is valid, it allows for an important and overlooked theological distinction between the mission of the Son, which is constituted by his sending in the incarnation, and the work of the Son (and the Father) which is constituted by the work of building up the Kingdom of God. This would be an interesting theological outcome of the present debate.

Conclusion

The four-point hypothesis is a significant theological suggestion that requires further exploration and testing to either uncover its faults or exploit its fruitfulness. Clearly, as I have argued in the present paper, the seeds of the position lie in Lonergan's philosophical account of contingent predication as propounded in *Insight*. As I have shown elsewhere, Lonergan's position has advantages over the more commonplace Rahnerian position based on the two processions.[36] Most of those advantages would survive in the suggestion of Hefling that we focus on a three-fold participation which would eliminate reference to passive spiration. The real challenge, as Doran acknowledges in his response to Hefling, is to provide a convincing account, from the realm of interiority, for grounding the distinction between sanctifying grace and the habit of charity.

36. Ormerod, 'Two Points or Four?'

Chapter 7

Hearing the Call of God: A Study Informed by Hans Urs von Balthasar and Bernard Lonergan

Meredith Secomb

Introduction

Hans Urs von Balthasar and Bernard Lonergan were both followers of St Ignatius of Loyola.[1] Balthasar's dramatic experience of calling[2] differs considerably from Lonergan's early spiritual life, which Frederick Crowe referred to as 'quite arid'.[3] Nevertheless, they both embraced the Ignatian

1. When Balthasar left the Society of Jesus to found the Community of St John with Adrienne von Speyr, it was not because he rejected its charism but because he had heard another call and in following it believed he was being utterly true to the spirit of Ignatius. Balthasar considered the Order to be his 'beloved homeland' for which see Hans Urs von Balthasar, *A First Glance at Adrienne von Speyr* (San Francisco: Ignatius Press, 1981), 43. Balthasar subsequently sought readmission after 1985 and negotiations were proceeding smoothly until, in 1988, his death intervened, for which see Werner Löser, 'The Ignatian Exercises in the Work of Hans Urs Von Balthasar' (Frankfurt am Main: Philosophich-Theologische Hochschule Sankt Georgen, 1999); available from <http://www.sankt-georgen.de/leseraum/loeser3.html>. Accessed 13 July 2007.
2. For Balthasar's likening of his experience of call to being 'struck by lightning', see Hans Urs von Balthasar, 'Pourquoi je me suis fait prêtre. Témoignages recueillis par Jorge et Ramón Sans Vila', cited in Peter Henrici, 'Hans Urs von Balthasar: A Sketch of His Life', in *Hans Urs von Balthasar: His Life and Work*, edited by David L Schindler (San Francisco: Ignatius Press, 1991), 11.
3. Lonergan had mentioned to Frederick Crowe that he learnt how to pray through suffering various injustices, and that prior to that time he experienced little affectivity in prayer, for which see Gordon Rixon, 'Bernard Lonergan and Mysticism', in *Theological Studies* 62 (2001): 480. Information about Lonergan's Jesuit formation was obtained from conversations between Frederick Crowe and Gordon Rixon, for which see Rixon, 'Lonergan and Mysticism', 480, n 3. Frederick Crowe, as a Jesuit student, sat under Lonergan's teaching and retreat giving.

emphasis on hearing the Call of Christ, as it is presented in the Second Week of the *Spiritual Exercises*.[4] Their considerations of the call yield complementary emphases. In this paper I reflect on those emphases and, with Lonergan's help, on the dynamics of consciousness operative in hearing and responding to God's call.

The call of God: scripture and the saints

Scripture attests to the fact that throughout the ages God has called men and women to accomplish great missions. God called, for example, Moses, David, the prophets, John the Baptist, the disciples, Paul, and continues to call men and women in every age to a specific life task. I will refer to this type of call as the 'call-writ-large'. There are others, however, for whom the 'call' is to live in the presence of God, accomplishing the will of God in the present moment. With Paul, such people simply desire in all that they do to be 'led by the Spirit of God' (Rom 8:14). Mary, the mother of Christ, exemplifies this type of call, as did Brother Lawrence, Pierre de Caussade, and Thérèse of Lisieux.[5] I will refer to this type of call as the 'call-writ-small'. I am interested in identifying the dynamics of consciousness that constitute both the call-writ-large and the call-writ-small. Both Balthasar and Lonergan can contribute to that understanding. Both were Jesuits and so we start with hearing the call of God in St Ignatius of Loyola (1491–1556).

The call in St Ignatius of Loyola

St Ignatius of Loyola tells us that we are 'created to praise, reverence, and serve God our Lord' and by this means to save our souls.[6] As well as prayer, Ignatius emphasises service. He does not, however, propose any kind of service. Rather, he proposes the kind that God uniquely wills for each individual.

4. For one presentation of the exercises, see *The Spiritual Exercises of St Ignatius: A Literal Translation and a Contemporary Reading*, edited by David L Fleming (St Louis: Institute of Jesuit Sources, 1978).
5. See Jean-Pierre de Caussade, *Abandonment to Divine Providence* (New York: Image Books, 1966); Brother Lawrence, *The Practice of the Presence of God* (London: Burns & Oates, 1977); St Thérèse of Lisieux, *Story of a Soul: The Autobiography of St Thérèse of Lisieux* (Washington: ICS Publications, 1976).
6. *Spiritual Exercises*, n 22.

Ignatius developed a series of meditations on the life of Jesus Christ with a view to helping a retreatant make a choice between two or more possible decisions. There are three possible times or ways in which such a choice can be made.[7] The first time is exemplified by the experiences of St Matthew and St Paul when, 'without doubting, or being able to doubt', they followed what they were shown.[8] The second time is 'when enough light and knowledge is received by experience of consolations and desolations, and by the experience of the discernment of various spirits'.[9] The third time is 'quiet, when the soul is not acted on by various spirits, and uses its natural powers freely and tranquilly'.[10] Nevertheless, it, too, includes the non-discursive aspect of putting oneself in the imagined situation and of engaging in a 'sort of make-believe or even play-acting experiment'.[11]

Ignatius considers that the second mode will be the norm and that within that mode there are two essential dimensions for the decision-making that leads to the choice between the various available options. The first is the foundational experience of the consolation-without-previous-cause, which is the reference point for the discerning of different interior movements.[12] Using this experience as a criterion, the retreatant then employs Ignatius' second foundational element of the *Exercises*, the 'Rules for Discernment of Spirits'. The Rules teach retreatants how to discern between the different 'spirits' moving them.[13] Retreatants need to learn to pay attention to the movements of their consciousness as they reflect on possible choice options. Ignatius was ahead of his time in being alert to the movements of consciousness, a theme that Bernard Lonergan picks up, as we will see later.[14]

Hans Urs von Balthasar noted that Ignatius effected a 'revolution' in the thinking of the Middle Ages which had, prior to Ignatius, adopted a

7. *Spiritual Exercises*, nn 175–77.
8. *Spiritual Exercises* n 175. See Mt 9:9, Acts 9:4–8.
9. *Spiritual Exercises*, n 176.
10. *Spiritual Exercises*, n 177.
11. See Karl Rahner, 'The Logic of Concrete Individual Knowledge in Ignatius Loyola', in *The Dynamic Element in the Church* (London: Burns & Oates, 1964), 161 n 43.
12. Rahner, 'The Logic of Concrete Individual Knowledge', 131.
13. For the 'Rules of Discernment of Spirits', see *Spiritual Exercises*, nn 313–36. For the observation that Ignatius considered these Rules to be 'his own special discovery', see Rahner, 'Logic', 95. Ignatius refers to 'good spirits' and 'evil spirits'. We now recognise that the psyche also provides motives for action; it is not merely a matter of God or the devil.
14. See especially in Bernard JF Lonergan, 'Bernard Lonergan to Thomas O'Malley November 8, 1978', in *Method: Journal of Lonergan Studies* 20 (2002): 81.

'universal concept' of perfection.[15] Ignatius taught that perfection is not a matter of striving to achieve merit according to a particular set of rules of behaviour but, rather, a matter of finding one's unique calling.[16] It is to Balthasar's reflections on 'the call' that we now turn.

Hans urs von Balthasar: the call-writ-large

Hans Urs von Balthasar addressed the issue of God's call extensively in the dramatic component of his trilogy,[17] and in his study on the various states of the Christian life.[18] For Balthasar, we find fulfilment when we find our unique 'idea' in Christ.[19] This 'idea' issues in mission and to the extent to which individuals, in prayer and with an attitude of receptivity and surrender, pursue God's will and unique calling in service to others, to that extent individuals participate in the personhood of Jesus Christ. The call is always an historical event in the 'here-and-now' and not a 'general, diffused sound' that could be overlooked.[20] It is situated at a specific time and place and Balthasar exemplifies the point with scripture: 'It comes to the prophets as they are guarding their flocks, to the apostles as they are mending their nets, to Levi as he is collecting taxes'.[21] The call occurs, in other words, in the midst of the pursuit of everyday activities.

Balthasar speaks of responding to God's call, of finding our mission, of discovering our 'role', all of which contribute to our fulfilment.[22] In this regard, he refers to a state of life and to what Mark McIntosh has called 'patterns of meaning' or 'contours' within our life that correspond with those of Jesus Christ's life.[23] To speak in this way is to speak of a landscape,

15. See Hans Urs von Balthasar, *The Christian State of Life*, translated by Sr Mary Frances McCarthy (San Francisco: Ignatius Press, 1983), 391 (hereafter *State of Life*).
16. Balthasar, *State of Life*, 391.
17. Hans Urs von Balthasar's trilogy comprises three parts: *The Glory of the Lord, Theo-Drama* and *Theo-Logic*. For a reflection on biblical examples of call, see especially Hans Urs von Balthasar, *Theo-Drama: Theological Dramatic Theory*, volume III, Dramatis Personae: *Persons in Christ* (San Francisco: Ignatius Press, 1992), 263–71 (hereafter *TD* accompanied by the appropriate volume number).
18. For an extended discussion of call, see Balthasar, *State of Life*, 391–504.
19. Hans Urs von Balthasar, *Theo-Drama: Theological Dramatic Theory*, volume II, Dramatis Personae: *Man in God* (San Francisco: Ignatius Press, 1990), 302–3.
20. Balthasar, *State of Life*, 403.
21. Balthasar, *State of Life*, 403.
22. See especially the first three volumes of Balthasar's *Theo-Drama*.
23. Mark A McIntosh, *Mystical Theology: The Integrity of Spirituality and Theology* (Oxford: Blackwell, 1998), 102. McIntosh (101–12) provides an interesting reflection

of a 'macro' approach to one's life. It is to speak of making major choices that affect the overall direction one's life will take in relationship to the world. It is an emphasis that focuses on what we could call an awareness of the call-writ-large in the human person.

Bernard Lonergan: the call-writ-small

Bernard Lonergan was also aware of the importance of the call to a specific expression of God's will for the life of an individual. In a retreat given to Jesuit students, shortly after ordination, Lonergan observed that we must make 'our end' not an 'abstract' but a 'concrete ideal'.[24] He conceives the goal as one of the 'realization of my concrete, whole, coherent, unified and harmonized ideal' in the circumstances of my vocation.[25] Lonergan invited the students to consider two factors in determining their vocation. First, he recommended that they reflect on their capacities, shortcomings, and the feeling of dissatisfaction that accompanies the effort of self-transcendence, a feeling he referred to as a 'divine discontent'.[26] Secondly, he recommended they reflect on the needs of the existing circumstances. Together, these dimensions would help them in determining the 'concrete ideal' to which they were called.[27]

This might seem like an emphasis on the call-writ-large that we found typifies Balthasar's approach. However, Lonergan gives a different perspective to Balthasar, stressing moment-by-moment aspects of daily living that Balthasar overlooks. While Lonergan recognised the importance of such traditional practices as 'penance, mortification and reformation of life',[28] he advised retreatants that the attempt to 'speak or think with God' was more important for meditation.[29] To speak or think

---

on Balthasar's contribution to the development of a Trinitarian mystical theology.

24. Lonergan, cited in Rixon, 'Lonergan and Mysticism', 481–82. Rixon draws on the retreat notes made by a retreat participant, Michael Lapierre. Others at the retreat were Frederick Crowe and Patrick Malone, for which see Rixon, 'Lonergan and Mysticism', 481, n 7. I shall refer to the 'Lapierre Retreat Notes' whenever appropriate.
25. 'Lapierre Retreat Notes', quoted in Rixon, 'Lonergan and Mysticism', 482. While Lonergan addressed his retreat to Jesuit students, we can see the same principle operating in any pattern of life. For a reflection on the single life, see Patricia A Sullivan, 'The Nonvowed Form of the Lay State In the Life of the Church', in *Theological Studies* 68 (2007): 320–47.
26. Rixon, 'Lonergan and Mysticism', 483.
27. Rixon, 'Lonergan and Mysticism', 483.
28. Rixon, 'Lonergan and Mysticism', 483.
29. 'Lapierre Retreat Notes', quoted in Rixon, 'Lonergan and Mysticism', 483.

with God requires sensitivity to 'the spontaneous movement of the soul towards God because of the workings of grace'.[30] This type of attentiveness is towards much more interior movements within the human soul than that of hearing a call to a new form of activity as in Balthasar's call-writ-large. I refer to these 'more interior movements' as the call-writ-small.

Lonergan considered that the *Spiritual Exercises* were 'a practical manual for cooperating with grace'.[31] This contrasted with the theology of the time. Such a theology offered merely 'metaphysical entities that could not be related "intelligibly and organically" to ordinary living'.[32] This approach was unhelpful and conceptualist.[33] Lonergan wanted theology to construct the 'conceptual network' needed to engage effectively with both Scripture and life.[34] He wanted theology to mediate between people in their particular circumstances and the religious values operative within those circumstances.[35] He wanted, thereby, to help people to cooperate with grace in the details of their daily living. Lonergan wanted, in other words, to help people attend to the call-writ-small.

Mysticism as a whole way of life

Lonergan came to see that attending to God's call meant attending to consciousness in the moment-by-moment details of daily life. He described such attentiveness as a 'mysticism' which was a 'whole way of life'.[36] Lonergan expressed the insight that mysticism could be lived as a 'whole way of life' in a letter he wrote in support of Harvey Egan's application for an associate professorship with tenure at Boston College.[37] In that letter, Lonergan reflects on the things he had learnt from Egan. Egan had sought,

30. Rixon, 'Lonergan and Mysticism', 484. Rixon here draws on archival material, specifically 'Folder 18'.
31. Lonergan cited in Rixon, 'Lonergan and Mysticism', 485; Archive, 'Folder 18'.
32. Rixon, 'Lonergan and Mysticism', 484–85. For further reflections on Lonergan's dissatisfaction with the prevailing theological world view which gave primacy to 'universal concepts', see Bernard JF Lonergan, 'Insight *Revisited*', in *A Second Collection*, edited by William FJ Ryan and Bernard J Tyrrell (Toronto: University of Toronto Press, 1974), 263.
33. Lonergan, 'Lonergan to O'Malley', 485.
34. For Lonergan's proposal of a 'conceptual network' which was later differentiated into general and special categories, see Rixon, 'Lonergan and Mysticism', 484.
35. Cf Bernard JF Lonergan, *Method in Theology* (Toronto: University of Toronto Press, 1971), xi.
36. Lonergan, 'Lonergan to O'Malley', 82.
37. See Lonergan, 'Lonergan to O'Malley', 77.

in his doctoral dissertation under Karl Rahner, to heighten awareness of the relevance of both mysticism and the tradition of the discernment of spirits within the Catholic world.[38] Following Rahner, Egan had identified the Ignatian concept of 'consolation-without-previous-cause' as crucial for discerning God's will in the details of daily living.[39] Before developing Lonergan's thinking, we need to clarify the notion of consolation-without-previous-cause in the *Spiritual Exercises* of St Ignatius of Loyola. Karl Rahner's reflections are most helpful for this purpose.

The 'consolation-without-previous-cause'

Ignatius tells us that we are able to know God's will through means other than rational reflection, drawing on reason and faith, or feelings and instincts.[40] While feelings and instincts are highly relevant for the call-writ-large, they will not serve the purpose for the call-writ-small, the dynamics of which we are now considering.

Other categories of human consciousness are needed for an adequate explanation. Elaborating on Ignatius' brief and somewhat dense presentation, Rahner proposed that knowing God's will is 'ultimately grounded in the simple presence to itself of the intrinsically intelligible subject'.[41] Rahner here highlights a significant dimension of human consciousness frequently overlooked in everyday functioning. It is the non-conceptual presence to self, which accompanies the intentionality of faith. For Rahner, the capacity to advert consciously to this dimension of interiority is essential for an 'everyday mysticism' alert to God's moment-by-moment calling.

Rahner seems to equate self-presence with the consolation-without-previous-cause. This is possible because the consolation-without-previous-cause penetrates to the core of the being and consequently

38. Egan's project was entitled 'An Anthropocentric-Christocentric Mystagogy: A Study of the Method and Basic Horizon of Thought and Experience in the *Spiritual Exercises* of Saint Ignatius of Loyola', for which see Lonergan, 'Lonergan to O'Malley', 81. For the subsequent publication of the dissertation, see Harvey D Egan, *The Spiritual Exercises and the Ignatian Mystical Horizon*, volume 5, *Series IV: Study Aids on Jesuit Topics* (St Louis, MI: The Institute of Jesuit Sources, 1976).
39. For Rahner's presentation of the importance of 'consolation-without-previous-cause' for discernment within the context of the Ignatian *Spiritual Exercises*, see Rahner, 'Logic', 84–170.
40. Rahner, 'Logic', 94 and 94, n 9.
41. Rahner, 'Logic', 94–95, n 9; emphasis mine.

presence to self cannot be separated from the experience given by God. Hence, Rahner can explain Ignatius' mode of discernment for the second 'time'. It is by repeated juxtaposition of the experience of the consolation-without-previous-cause with the object in question, and the ensuing harmony or disharmony, that we eventually discern which choice is in accord with God's will.[42] We move on now to Lonergan's insights into this Ignatian concept.

Examination of consciousness

Egan's development of Rahner's thought enabled Lonergan to understand the meaning of the words 'consolation without a previous cause'.[43] Lonergan tells us,

> I had been hearing those words since 1922 at the annual retreats made by Jesuits preparing for the priesthood . . . But now, after fifty-three years, I began for the first time to grasp what they meant. What had intervened was what Rahner describes as the anthropological turn, the turn from metaphysical objects to conscious subjects.[44]

Through Egan, Lonergan realised that the 'Ignatian *examen conscientiae*' meant not an 'examination of conscience but an examination of consciousness'.[45] With this insight, Lonergan came to appreciate that mysticism is 'not just a series of exceptional events. It is a whole way of life.'[46] Lonergan observed the same 'everyday mysticism'[47] was present in Paul's observation that 'all who are led by the Spirit of God are children of God' (Rom 8:14) and in Newman's 'Lead, Kindly Light, Lead Thou me on'.[48]

42. For the observation that the choice is determined by 'whether the will to the object of Election under scrutiny leaves intact that pure openness to God in the supernatural experience of transcendence', see Rahner, 'Logic', 158.
43. Lonergan, 'Lonergan to O'Malley', 81.
44. Lonergan, 'Lonergan to O'Malley', 81.
45. Lonergan, 'Lonergan to O'Malley', 81.
46. Lonergan, 'Lonergan to O'Malley', 82.
47. For this term, see McIntosh, *Mystical Theology*, 93.
48. Lonergan, 'Lonergan to O'Malley', 82. I consider that St John of the Cross referred to the same dynamic when he spoke of the light that burned in his heart and guided him to 'a place where no one appeared', for which see St John of the Cross, 'The Ascent of Mt Carmel', in *The Collected Works of St John of the Cross*, edited by Kieran Kavanagh and Otilio Rodriguez (Washington: ICS Publications, 1979), 69.

We noted above that Rahner referred to the dimension of consciousness pertinent to such everyday mysticism as a 'simple presence to itself of the intrinsically intelligible subject'.[49] The task now is to develop an appreciation of the meaning of Rahner's 'simple presence', and its implications for knowing God's will, by drawing on the work of Lonergan.

However, before presenting the categories that Lonergan offers us for understanding, I will reflect briefly on Balthasar's contrasting ambivalence to such analysis. Such a reflection helps us appreciate all the more the contribution that Lonergan has made to the analysis of our interiority.

Analysis of interiority and hearing the call of God

Hans Urs von Balthasar

While Hans Urs von Balthasar considers the call to be the 'very essence' of the Christian life,[50] he does not provide much help for people who want to grow in attentiveness to the call. On the one hand, Balthasar insists that 'psychological tests' cannot help to identify the dynamics constitutive of an obedient response to God's call. On the other hand, he stresses the importance of such psychological dynamics as self-surrender.[51]

Balthasar constantly conveys ambivalence when it comes to providing an explanatory account of the anthropological dimension of the divine-human exchange. We see this reflected also in his comments on the spirituality of his mystic and colleague, Adrienne von Speyr. Balthasar comments that Adrienne's '"mysticism" is one of pure maidenly service which any reflection upon self only diminishes'.[52] Hence, it is 'radically anti-psychological' insofar as 'psychological' is synonymous with 'egocentric isolation'.[53] In making such an observation, however, Balthasar does not adequately distinguish between egocentric, biased and inauthentic functioning and the authentic awareness of an interiority

49. Rahner, 'Logic', 94–95, n 9.
50. Balthasar, *State of Life*, 391.
51. For Balthasar's observations about the inadequacy of psychological tests for discerning a call, see Balthasar, *State of Life*, 396. For the point that the 'psychological realm is the concrete horizon of the human subject', see Mary Frohlich, *The Intersubjectivity of the Mystic: A Study of Teresa of Avila's* Interior Castle (Atlanta, Georgia: Scholars Press, 1993), 141.
52. Balthasar, *A First Glance*, 53.
53. Balthasar, *A First Glance*, 53.

engaged with God.[54] We must not dismiss attentiveness to the latter for fear of absorption in the former. Fine differentiations are required here, the lack of which can often mean overlooking important dimensions for 'living within God's engagement'; for living, in other words, alert to the movement of the Holy Spirit within our lives.[55]

Balthasar emphasises the dramatic consequences of the call-writ-large. He lacks, however, an adequate anthropological articulation of the call, the inadequacy of which leads him to overlook the dramatic implications of attending to the moment-by-moment call-writ-small. Balthasar's failure to engage in a formal analysis of the minutiae of human interiority limits his capacity to form Christians in attending to the call-writ-large.

This is a significant oversight, for authentic attentiveness to interiority, and the accompanying call-writ-small, is a reliable means of leading one to action in the here-and-now and ultimately to recognising the call-writ-large in the overall pattern of life. When we have been responsible stewards of our consciousness in small matters, then the Lord will give us responsibility for our consciousness in greater matters.[56] Such a consciousness will be attentive to the 'still, small voice'[57] of calling and will exercise responsible action accordingly. Only then will the 'state' of life and the 'role' one assumes be the fulfilling participation in Christ's life that Balthasar depicts for us. The realm wherein the call-writ-small is heard needs a formal articulation and appropriation if it is to contribute constructively to human living. Bernard Lonergan provides the categories for this articulation. So we return now to Lonergan's account of human consciousness and to the insights he can give us concerning what Rahner refers to as 'simple presence to itself'. I will introduce Lonergan's account with a consideration of the epistemological justification for the possibility of hearing God's call.

---

54. For the notion of the 'bias' that prevents authenticity, see *Collected Works of Bernard Lonergan*, volume 3, *Insight: A Study of Human Understanding*, edited by Frederick E Crowe and Robert M Doran (Toronto: University of Toronto Press, 1992), 191–207 (hereafter *CWL* 3 *Insight*).

55. Werner Löser points out that 'living within God's engagement' was the original German for the book subsequently translated as *Engagement with God*. Löser observes that choosing 'what God chooses leads intrinsically to a life within God's engagement', for which see Werner Löser, 'Hans Urs von Balthasar and Ignatius Loyola', in *The Way* 44, no 4 (October 2005): 119.

56. Cf Luke 16:10

57. Cf 1 Kings 19:11

Bernard Lonergan

Epistemological questions

How does one know one has received a call from God? What experiences do such people have? How can they be confident that their consequent decisions and actions are consonant with the call they purport to have received? It is insufficient simply to argue that scripture and the saints attest to such occurrences. Where can we find the empirical foundation for matter that purports to originate from a transcendent realm? Normally, empirical conclusions derive from measurement against a recognised standard.[58] What standard is there for determining the receipt of a 'call' from a realm transcendent to that of everyday consciousness?

Such a standard does exist. Bernard Lonergan has articulated this standard in the context of the presentation of his 'generalized empirical method' or transcendental method.[59]

We will not find the standard external to the subject who reports hearing God's call; we will, instead, find it within the subject's own consciousness.[60] The standard we seek will be that of the subject's appropriation of his or her own way of knowing. To refer to such 'knowledge of knowing' is to refer to a realm of interiority.[61] While there are other basic realms of meaning, such as the common-sense realm of everyday functioning, and the theoretical realm of scientific reflection, it is the realm of interiority that provides the measure against which we can assess functioning in the further realm of transcendence.[62] In the realm of transcendence, we move 'beyond the realms of common sense, theory, and interiority and into the realm in which God is known and loved'.[63] This realm 'can be understood

58. Frohlich, *The Intersubjectivity of the Mystic*, 21. I am indebted to Frohlich for the considerations in this and subsequent paragraphs.
59. For references to Lonergan's method variously referred to as transcendental or as generalised empirical method, see Lonergan, *Method*, 25; *CWL* 3 *Insight*, 72, 243.
60. For Frohlich's discussion of the corresponding issue of finding an objective status for mystical transformation, see Frohlich, *The Intersubjectivity of the Mystic*, 21–22.
61 Frohlich, *The Intersubjectivity of the Mystic*, 22.
62. For the presentation of the realms of common sense, theory and interiority as distinct realms of meaning, see Lonergan, *Method*, 81–83. For Lonergan's discussion of the realm of transcendence, see Lonergan, *Method*, 83–84, 265–66, 272; *CWL* 3 *Insight*, 634–730. While Lonergan differentiates only four *basic* realms of meaning, there are many other possible realms also, determined simply by the existence of a specific language, a 'distinct mode of apprehension', and a group speaking and apprehending accordingly, for which see Lonergan, *Method*, 272.
63. Lonergan, *Method*, 84.

either as the "ground" of all phenomena or as an "absolute whole" that sublates all phenomena'.[64] The immediate task, then, is to present Bernard Lonergan's generalised empirical method in order to identify the categories of interiority against which the experience of transcendence can be measured.

While originating in the realm of transcendence rather than from common sense, theory or interiority, the experience leading to a judgment that one has been called still resonates in human consciousness and must be processed through the usual channels of human consciousness. In other words, grace from 'above down' instigates the experience and, if we attend to the experience, we process it through a subsequent movement from 'below up'. Bernard Lonergan refers to the analysis of this movement as 'intentionality analysis'. I shall explain intentionality analysis within the context of a discussion of the different types of awareness which accompany the call-writ-large and the call-writ-small.

Different types of awareness accompany consciousness depending on whether that consciousness occurs at the empirical, intelligent, rational or responsible levels of consciousness.[65] Lonergan's major achievement was to identify the self-transcending dynamics of intentional consciousness constitutive of the 'successive stages in the unfolding of a single thrust, the eros of the human spirit'.[66] The 'basic fulfilment' of that thrust is being in love with God and once we are in love with God we are alert to the transcendent realm.[67]

To refer to the various forms of awareness accompanying the different levels of consciousness is to refer to 'general' categories that are transcultural and pertinent to the 'attending, inquiring, reflecting, deliberating subject'.[68] Once we refer to subjects in love with God, however, 'special' categories pertinent to the realm of transcendence are operative.[69] The experience foundational to understanding God's call can derive from numerous sources, all with meaning derived from the realm of transcendence. We turn now to the ways in which such experiences present themselves.

64. Frohlich, *The Intersubjectivity of the Mystic*, 115.
65. *CWL* 3 *Insight*, 322
66. Lonergan, *Method*, 13.
67. Lonergan, *Method*, 105.
68. Lonergan, *Method*, 285.
69. Lonergan, *Method*, 292.

Objectivity and the call-writ-large

The foundational experience for hearing the call-writ-large may be triggered by a conversation with a loved and respected person; it may be an ongoing desire or thought that constantly intrudes into awareness; it may be from a dream as it was in the case of Joseph's call to go to Egypt (Mt 1:20). The feelings aroused by this experience can be quite intense and they are typically adverted to readily. Most popular books encouraging sensitivity to the Holy Spirit refer to this type of inspiration.[70] In such instances, the 'object' eliciting one's attention is either without, in the case of circumstances, or within, in the case of thoughts and feelings. In this context, even one's sense of self is an interior 'object'[71] that derives, as Thomas Daly has pointed out, from making a judgment about our existence.[72] I refer to all these instances as examples of the call-writ-large.

An authentic response will derive from our basic orientation towards self-transcendence.[73] This orientation will elicit firstly, attentiveness to the experience, whether it is derived from an object within or without; secondly, intelligent understanding of that experience; thirdly, rational reflection on the understanding; and fourthly, responsible deliberation about possible courses of action in response to that reflection.[74] Each of these levels has its own 'self-taste', to follow Lonergan's allusion to Gerard Manley Hopkins.[75] Lonergan refers somewhat lyrically to the

> spontaneous vitality of our sensitivity, the shrewd intelligence of our inquiring, the detached rationality of our demand for evidence, the peace of a good conscience and the

---

70. See, for example, Ken Barker, *Becoming Fire: A Spiritual Journey of Faith* (Melbourne: Freedom, 2001), 150.
71. See Frohlich, *The Intersubjectivity of the Mystic*, 17. I am indebted to Mary Frohlich for many of the following reflections.
72. Thomas V Daly, 'Lonergan's "Epistemology" and "Theoretical Perspective"' (Personal Communication by email, 2007).
73. Bernard JF Lonergan, 'Second Lecture: Religious Knowledge', in *A Third Collection: Papers by Bernard JF Lonergan, SJ*, edited by Frederick E Crowe (New York: Paulist Press, 1985), 131.
74. For Lonergan's articulation of the dynamics of self-transcending intentionality, see, for example, Lonergan, *Method*; Bernard JF Lonergan, 'The Subject', in *A Second Collection: Papers by Bernard JF Lonergan, SJ*, edited by W Ryan and B Tyrrell (Toronto: University of Toronto Press, 1974); *CWL* 3 *Insight*; Lonergan, 'Religious Knowledge', 131–32.
75. Lonergan, 'Religious Knowledge', 132.

> disquiet released by memory of words wrongly said or deeds wrongly done.[76]

Training can give awareness of these different levels of consciousness. In all people there is, however, a 'unity' and 'harmony' to the experience of consciousness and the accompanying dynamic of self-transcendence before any such training occurs.[77] Lonergan explains that

> self-transcendence is so radically and so completely the inner dynamism of human reality that one cannot but be aware when one is moving towards it and, on the other hand, one cannot but feel constrained to conceal the fact when one is evading the abiding imperative of what it is to be human.[78]

Daly supports Lonergan's reflections here by his demonstration that 'morality is just as much a part of [one's] humanity as is . . . wonder or . . . inventiveness . . . or care about facts. And it can, and must, be integrated with these other powers'.[79] In other words, we *do* know when we are making good or bad decisions if we attend to the 'self-taste' when deciding. An authentic response to the exigence of self-transcendence will be the guarantor of objectivity for Lonergan explains, 'Objectivity is the fruit of authentic subjectivity' within the realm mediated by meaning.[80] The question to be addressed now is how to apply these principles to the call-writ-small.

76. Lonergan, 'Religious Knowledge', 132.
77. For the observation that the different kinds of awareness accompanying different acts 'cumulate into unities' see also Lonergan, *CWL* 3 *Insight*, 324–25.
78. Lonergan, 'Religious Knowledge', 133–34.
79. Thomas V Daly, 'Exercises in Responsibility: St Ignatius' Mediation of Morality', in *Australian Lonergan Workshop*, edited by Matthew C Ogilvie and William J Danaher (Sydney: Novum Organum Press, 2002), 13. This paper proposes that Ignatius, by urging retreatants to a constant reflectiveness about the decisions they make and how they carry out those decisions in the time of retreat, provides a series of exercises which raise the retreatant's consciousness about the interior processes involved in making responsible, conscience-based, decisions, akin to those Lonergan offers in relation to the act of understanding.
80. Lonergan, 'Religious Knowledge', 144. See also Lonergan, *Method*, 265. The realm mediated by meaning is differentiated from the realm of immediacy and of the 'already-out-there-now', for which see Lonergan, 'Religious Knowledge', 144.

Objectivity and the call-writ-small

Both types of call require attentiveness to experience. However, the experience foundational to the call-writ-large is an experience readily subject to the principles of intentionality analysis. It is an experience deriving from circumstances either within or without. This is not the case with the call-writ-small. In the call-writ-small, the experience involved in the process of intentionality analysis is what Rahner has referred to as the 'simple presence' to self.[81]

There are epistemological differences between Lonergan and Rahner. Rahner confuses self-presence with knowledge since for him self-presence is 'an area of unthematic knowing which is part of the condition of the possibility of knowing any categorical object' and hence is associated with knowledge.[82] Lonergan, on the other hand, has a more highly differentiated notion of self-presence or, in other words, of consciousness. For Lonergan, consciousness is the 'awareness immanent in cognitional acts' and must be distinguished from knowledge.[83] It 'constitutes and reveals the basic psychological unity of the subject-as-subject.'[84]

There are, then, epistemological differences between Rahner and Lonergan. Nevertheless, the experience relevant for our current enterprise is foundational for them both. Rahner's 'simple presence' or 'pure openness',[85] or what Lonergan refers to as 'self-presence'[86] or 'pure experience',[87] is the essence of the call-writ-small. Doran refers to this dimension as 'primordial immediacy'.[88] For Doran, Lonergan's method 'disengages' the 'basic structure of this primordial immediacy', enabling

81. Rahner, 'Logic', 94–95, n 9.
82. Raymond Moloney, 'The Mind of Christ in Transcendental Theology: Rahner, Lonergan and Crowe', in *The Heythrop Journal* 25 (1984): 289.
83. *CWL* 3 *Insight*, 320, 322.
84. Bernard JF Lonergan, 'Christ as Subject: A Reply', in *Collected Works of Bernard Lonergan*, volume 4, *Collection*, edited by Frederick E Crowe and Robert M Doran (Toronto: University of Toronto Press, 1988), 165; herafter *CWL* 4 *Collection*.
85. Rahner, 'Logic', 158.
86. Bernard JF Lonergan, *Collected Works of Bernard Lonergan*, volume 5, *Understanding and Being: The Halifax Lectures on* Insight, edited by Elizabeth A Morelli and Mark D Morelli (Toronto: University of Toronto Press, 1990), 15–17.
87. Bernard JF Lonergan, 'First Lecture: Religious Experience', in *A Third Collection*, 116. For the use of the term 'bare consciousness', see the work of James R Price, cited in Frohlich, *The Intersubjectivity of the Mystic*, 133, 147.
88. Robert M Doran, *Subject and Psyche: Ricoeur, Jung and the Search for Foundations* (Washington: University Press of America, 1979), 114.

a focus on the existential subject.[89] It is the 'self-taste' of the existential subject that must be aligned with the object for discernment. In other words, an experience which is usually the 'infrastructure' of knowledge becomes itself a significant part of the discernment process.[90]

In everyday functioning, the discernment of God's will in the moment requires four things. Firstly and essentially, it requires that we discover the 'self-taste' of the primordial or pure experience of ourselves before God. Secondly, we must be attentive to the experience triggered by the object presenting itself to us for discernment. Thirdly, we must juxtapose these two experiences with one another. Fourthly, we must be attentive to the experience that the juxtaposition elicits within us. In other words, we must learn to exercise a multivalent consciousness. While we do this in all sorts of ways every day, we do not always do it in a fully conscious way.

We need to develop a regular practice of contemplative prayer if we are to become familiar with the self-taste of our existential being before God. Only when we are familiar with this central reference point will we be able to make the ongoing discernments in the moment that constitute mysticism lived as a whole way of life. Lonergan referred to the development of such a capacity as 'openness'.[91] Lonergan's notion of 'mediation' and the accompanying notion of openness provide a bridge between the general categories of intentional consciousness and the special theological categories used to explain mystical experience.[92] So we turn now to a discussion of openness in the context of the mediation of Christ in prayer.

89. Doran, *Subject and Psyche*, 115.

90. Lonergan, 'Religious Experience', 116. For the observation that such experience is a 'preliminary unstructured sort of awareness', see *Collected Works of Bernard Lonergan*, volume 7, *The Ontological and the Psychological Constitution of Christ*, translated by Michael G Shields (Toronto: University of Toronto Press, 2002), 157 n 75.

91. See Bernard JF Lonergan, 'Openness and Religious Experience', in *CWL 4 Collection*, 185–87.

92. Frohlich, *The Intersubjectivity of the Mystic*, 26, 131, 135. See Bernard JF Lonergan, 'The Mediation of Christ in Prayer', in *Collected Works of Bernard Lonergan*, volume 6, *Philosophical and Theological Papers 1958–1964*, edited by Robert C Croken, Frederick E Crowe, and Robert M Doran (Toronto: University of Toronto Press, 1996), 160–82. For the application of Lonergan's notion of mediation to the study of mystical transformation, see Frohlich, *The Intersubjectivity of the Mystic*, 131–35.

Openness and contemplative prayer

Openness

I have referred to the necessity for openness to the transcendent dimension if we are to hear God's call. While we ourselves can work towards a natural level of openness, this is insufficient for engaging with the realm of transcendence, for grace is necessary here. Grace draws us with increasing consciousness into Christ, developing in us that which the Holy Spirit effected in Jesus Christ, namely a 'habitual and actual illumination of our understanding and of the orientation of our wills'.[93] How does this happen?

Rahner has spoken of the 'pure openness to God' that must be left intact if we are to discern that a particular object of choice is within God's will for us.[94] Lonergan refers to the way in which grace effects within us an openness to religious experience.[95] Foundationally, openness is the 'pure, detached, disinterested, unrestricted desire to know'.[96] It is the cause of wonder,[97] for its objective is being, *omnia,* which is both 'completely universal and completely concrete'.[98] While we are naturally capable of greater openness by enlarging our horizon, there is an 'ultimate enlargement' which is beyond our own resources and where God 'as unknown' is experienced as mystery.[99]

We require a receptive attitude to appropriate this new development. A number of thinkers address the issue of receptivity. Fred Crowe explains that such an attitude is 'basic both psychologically and ontologically'.[100] Balthasar argues that our ontological structure is designed to respond to

93. Lapierre Retreat notes cited in Rixon, 'Lonergan and Mysticism', 185.
94. Rahner, 'Logic', 158.
95. Bernard JF Lonergan, 'Openness and Religious Experience', 185–87.
96. Lonergan, 'Openness and Religious Experience', 186. See also *CWL* 3 *Insight*, passim.
97. Lonergan, 'Openness and Religious Experience', 186. For the importance of wonder in Balthasar see, for example, Balthasar, *TD* II, 286; Hans Urs von Balthasar, *Theo-Drama: Theological Dramatic Theory,* volume IV, *The Action* (San Francisco: Ignatius Press, 1994), 140.
98. *CWL* 3 *Insight*, 348; Lonergan, 'Openness and Religious Experience', 186. For Balthasar's observation that 'Jesus Christ is the *concrete* form within which the *universal* fullness of the love of God is . . . bound up' see Medard Kehl, 'Hans Urs von Balthasar: A Portrait', in *The Von Balthasar Reader*, edited by Medard Kehl and Werner Löser (Edinburgh: T&T Clark, 1982), 9.
99. Lonergan, *Method*, 107; 'Openness and Religious Experience', 186.
100. See Frederick E Crowe, 'Complacency and Concern in the Thought of St Thomas', in *Theological Studies* 20 (1959): 3.

God's initiative and hence gives primacy to receptivity.[101] Rahner clarifies Ignatius' teaching on the absence of the sense or knowledge of any object in the consolation-without-previous-cause by pointing out that this experience is actually 'utter receptivity to God'.[102] In such an experience, the whole person is drawn into God; the very ground of the person's being is drawn into God, 'into love, beyond any defined circumscribable object, into the infinity of God'.[103] The '*sine causa*' issues in the 'question of God and God alone'.[104] The absence of any object for sense or knowledge results in the fullness of the presence of God.

We need to develop the capacity for such receptivity and this will occur only through prayer. So we turn now to Lonergan's reflections on prayer.

Contemplative prayer

We are familiar with the transcendental precepts: Be attentive, be intelligent, be rational, be responsible and with a possible fifth precept for those whose lives are lived under the influence of grace: be in love.[105] Lonergan does, however, propose what we might consider to be a sixth precept. Citing 1 Thessalonians 5:17, he observes, 'The precept is: "Pray without ceasing"'.[106] This precept is particularly significant for our question of hearing God's call.

In his explanation of the various ways in which mediation occurs, Lonergan discusses the mediation of Christ in prayer.[107] In our immediacy to ourselves there are 'supernatural realities' infused by grace.[108] These realities can remain immediate, in which case we are part of the body of Christ 'but in a vegetative sort of way'.[109] Alternatively, we can make a

101. Hans Urs von Balthasar, *The Glory of the Lord: A Theological Aesthetics,* volume 1, *Seeing the Form* (Edinburgh: T&T Clark, 1982), 245–46.
102 Rahner, 'Logic', 135, 144, 149.
103. Rahner, 'Logic', 135.
104. Rahner, 'Logic', 135. Note that Anthony Kelly in his paper above refers to the receptivity that accompanies a phenomenological conversion. I suggest that a 'phenomenological conversion' is in fact the development of a differentiation of consciousness alert to receptivity before God.
105. Lonergan, *Method*, 20, 231, 105–7.
106. Lonergan, 'Mediation of Christ in Prayer', 180.
107. Lonergan, 'Mediation of Christ in Prayer', 176–82.
108. Lonergan, 'Mediation of Christ in Prayer', 178.
109. Lonergan, 'Mediation of Christ in Prayer', 179.

choice to live the life of grace consciously in such a way that we are readily 'distracted from worldliness' through our love for the Lord of our lives.[110]

It is prayer that effects that change, enabling the life of grace to transform us such that life in God becomes conscious, spontaneous and ultimately deliberate.[111] There is, however, a further development that occurs when we continue the work of becoming ourselves. This is the experience of letting ourselves be 'carried along'.[112] In our growing intimacy with God, we increasingly experience what Lonergan here refers to as a 'mutual self-mediation', for we find ourselves living more and more a life in relationship with Christ.[113] In that relationship, we grow in the capacity to be attentive to the consolation-without-previous-cause and move closer to living a mysticism as a 'whole way of life'.

Hans Urs von Balthasar's argument for a contemplative rather than discursive form of prayer to typify our prayer life supports Lonergan here.[114] Contemplative prayer is more receptive, more open to the movement from above. Discursive prayer, on the other hand, in its reflection on matters for understanding, tends to have the emphasis on a movement of consciousness from below. Both, of course, are necessary in our relationship with God. However, the receptivity that contemplative prayer encourages will enable the development of openness and awareness of the experience of the primordial immediacy of the subject-as-subject.[115] It will thereby enable attentiveness to the call-writ-small.

Conclusion

This paper has presented Hans Urs von Balthasar and Bernard Lonergan's approaches to hearing the call of God. For Balthasar, hearing the call determines one's role or mission in life and one's ultimate fulfilment. This is a 'call-writ-large'. For Lonergan, the call is 'writ-small' and is a matter of attending to movements of consciousness. In this instance, the person must learn, through contemplative prayer, to attend to the 'self-taste' of his or her pure experience before God. By so doing, such people are able to live

110. Lonergan, 'Mediation of Christ in Prayer', 179.
111. Lonergan, 'Mediation of Christ in Prayer', 179.
112. Lonergan, 'Mediation of Christ in Prayer', 180.
113. Lonergan, 'Mediation of Christ in Prayer', 180.
114. See Hans Urs von Balthasar, *Prayer*, translated by AV Littledale (New York: Paulist Press, 1967).
115. For the alternative terms of 'bare consciousness' developed by James R Price III, see Frohlich, *The Intersubjectivity of the Mystic*, 133–34.

their lives attentive to God in the details of daily life, a style of living that Lonergan characterised as 'mysticism' lived as 'a whole way of life'.

Chapter 8

Cosmology, Theology and the Universe: Lonergan's Insights

David Legg

The topic of this paper is the relationship between cosmology, theology and the universe, with a particular focus on the question: What is the universe? Starting from initial definitions of cosmology and theology and their common interest in the universe, I will examine why Kant (1724–1804) and Wittgenstein (1889–1951) separated cosmology from theology, before turning to Lonergan (1904–1984) and his understanding of the universe in *Insight*.[1]

The definition of cosmology I use can be found on NASA's website as 'the scientific study of the large scale properties of the Universe as a whole'.[2] Understandably the history of cosmology reflects the history of science and shows how theories of the universe originated, were refined, replaced and further developed. A well-known example of this ongoing development and replacement is the classical Greek geocentric theory, refined by Ptolemy, replaced by Copernicus's heliocentric theory, further developed by Galileo and Newton into the modern mechanistic view of the universe, and transformed into the contemporary expanding universe, along with competing multiverse[3] and plasma field theories.[4] It is important to note that though cosmologies change, the aim of cosmologists remains the same, that is, to give a comprehensive account of the universe as a

1. *Collected Works of Bernard Lonergan,* volume 3, *Insight: A Study of Human Understanding*, edited by Frederick E Crowe and Robert M Doran (Toronto: University of Toronto Press, 1992); hereafter *CWL* 3 *Insight.*
2. National Aeronautic and Space Administration, 'Universe 101: Big Bang Theory: Cosmology' at <http://map.gsfc.nasa.gov/m_uni.html>. Accessed 24 November 2008.
3. See, for example, Paul Davies, 'Multiverse Cosmological Models,' at <http://arxiv.org/ftp/astro-ph/papers/0403/0403047.pdf>. Accessed 24 November 2008.
4. See, for example, the website <http://www.plasmacosmology.net/>. Accessed 24 November 2008.

whole. And while most astronomers may not be motivated by such a grand ambition, some theoretical physicists are interested in the quasi-theological quest for a Grand Unified Theory of the Universe.[5]

The notion of theology that I refer to is natural theology that sits within the general field of religious inquiry, distinct from the special field of theological inquiry based on specific traditions of sacred scripture and doctrine. It is also distinct from the descriptive disciplines of World Religions that study the numerous expressions of beliefs, values and practices found in the religions of the world. Natural theology goes beyond description and historical account, beyond the sociology or psychology of religion, to understand and reflect critically on particular theologies, asking: how do they enhance or impede human development, and do they express an adequate understanding of the universe? It is this latter question that brings natural theology close to cosmology, for it asks why we ought to believe there is an ultimate ground of the existence and order of the universe.[6] And since it operates within the requirements of rational procedure, it criticises its own arguments and conclusions. However, this ideal is not always achieved and so there is a dialectical development in natural theology, similar to that found in cosmology.

There is a common link between cosmology and theology for both aim to give a comprehensive account of the universe as a whole. This common link can be found in the earliest recorded cultures; for example, in ancient Egypt people felt that their ancestors had gone up into the constellations in the sky and so 'the pyramids of Giza are laid out in the same formation as the three stars that make up Orion's belt. Orion is associated with Osiris and is the target for sending the righteous dead. The pyramids were aligned as launch pads.'[7] Another example is the opening sentence of the Book of Genesis, 'In the beginning God created the heavens and the earth'; here we see a theological claim linked to a cosmology of 'heaven and earth'. Later, in medieval Europe, Ptolemaic cosmology and Christian scripture were so closely entangled in Dante's imagination that he could produce his

5. See the definition of Grand Unified Theory at the following page of the York University (Toronto) website, 'An Introduction to Particle Physics' at <http://blueflag.phys.yorku.ca/yhep/gut.html>. Accessed 24 November 2008.
6. Joseph Magee, 'Thomistic Natural Theology', at <http://www.aquinasonline.com/Topics/nattheol.html>. Accessed 24 November 2008. For a range of online resources on Natural Theology, see 'Michael Sudduth's Natural Theology Website' at <http://www.homestead.com/naturaltheology/>. Accessed 24 November 2008.
7. Anon, 'Cosmology' at <http://4brightminds.info/cosmology.htm>. Accessed 24 November 2008.

grand unified vision of 'Cosmotheology'.[8] However, as we move beyond the feelings and imaginings of ancient and medieval people into modern times the shared concept of the universe, once common to cosmology and theology, was split apart with the development of modern science and philosophy. This separation was given one of its most influential justifications by Immanuel Kant.

Kant in his *Critique of Pure Reason*[9] argues that empirical science is conditioned by contingent human mental procedures and therefore cosmology as an empirical science could not be the basis for theological claims about a necessary unconditioned infinite Being, we call God. And if a cosmological argument were used to support a theological claim, it will fail in the same way the ontological argument fails, by misusing the concept of existence. Kant, it must be said, did not deny the reality of God, nor that rational argument can prepare us for faith in God, nor that moral aspirations postulate the need for God. What Kant denied was that we are able to deductively conclude on empirical or rational grounds, that a necessary unconditioned cause of the universe actually exists. As he said:

> I cannot even make the assumption—as practical interests of morality require—of God, Freedom, and Immortality, if I do not deprive speculative reason of its pretensions to transcendent insight. For to arrive at these, it must make use of principles which, in fact, extend only to the objects of possible experience, and which cannot be applied to objects beyond this sphere without converting them into appearances, and thus rendering the *practical extension* of pure reason impossible. I must, therefore, abolish *knowledge*, to make room for *faith*.[10]

What Kant meant by faith is exemplified in the conclusion to his *Critique of Practical Reason* where he famously said, 'Two things fill the mind with ever new and increasing admiration and awe, the more often and steadily

8. See Steven J Dick, 'Extraterrestial Life and Our Worldview at the Turn of the Millennium' (Dibner Library Lectures: Smithsonian Institution Libraries, May 2 2000), at <http://www.sil.si.edu/silpublications/dibner-library-lectures/extraterrestrial-life/ETcopy-KR.htm>. Accessed 24 November 2000.
9. Immanuel Kant, *Critique of Pure Reason (1781/1787),* translated by JMD Meiklejohn (London: Everyman, 1993); hereafter *CPR*.
10. *CPR*, B, xxx; emphasis original.

reflection is occupied with them: *the starry heaven above me and the moral law within me*'.[11] What Kant meant by knowledge is our immediate awareness of phenomena that are experientially identifiable, whether physical or mathematical. And about these experientially identifiable phenomena he said we have an 'unavoidable ignorance with regard to things in themselves'.[12] The reason he wanted to abolish all attempts to know what is beyond experience is because all such attempts convert what is real into appearances, making it impossible to know the real itself. That is why he insisted that a place must be made for faith and practical morality, for the practical extension of reason can legitimately aspire to ideals beyond human knowledge. It is worth recalling that Kant's early education[13] was within a strong pietistic Lutheran tradition that emphasised salvation by faith alone. Was his epistemology motivated by his theology? I leave that question to the historians, but what is known is that he rejected all attempts to prove the existence of God by using the ontological, cosmological or what he called physico-theological arguments.[14] However, what is noteworthy is that Kant was convinced that we are aware of more than what he called 'knowledge'.

Regarding the ontological argument, Kant argued that it failed as a proof for the existence of God because, 'the concept of an absolutely necessary being is a mere concept of reason, ie. a mere idea, the objective reality of which is far from being established by the mere fact that it is a need of reason'[15] and 'although an existence outside this sphere cannot be absolutely declared to be impossible, it is a hypothesis the truth of which we have no means of justifying'.[16] Kant compared the failure of the ontological argument to add to our knowledge, to a shopkeeper, who fails to add to his wealth by adding zeros to the end of his bank balance. Lonergan agreed with Kant because 'conception alone is an insufficient ground for judgment'.[17] However, the rejection of the ontological argument was not

11. Immanuel Kant, *Kritik der praktischen Vernunft (1788),* volume 5, *Akademieausgabe von Immanuel Kants Gesammelten Werken,* edited by Paul Natorp (Berlin: Berlin-Brandenburgische Akademie der Wissenschaften, 1900 Academy of Sciences, 1900), 161–62. English translation is by Paul Guyer in his book *Kant* (London: Routledge, 2006), 1; emphasis original.
12. *CPR*, B, xxx.
13. Paul Guyer, *Kant* (London and New York: Routledge, 2006), chapter 1.
14. *CPR*, A, 589/B, 617.
15. *CPR*, A, 591/B, 619.
16. *CPR*, A, 601/B, 629.
17. *CWL* 3 *Insight,* 695.

new; Aquinas (1225–1274) in the thirteenth century had argued that *for us humans* the existence of God is not self-evident, though it is self-evident for God, for even if we grant that a person understands the word 'God' to mean 'that than which nothing greater can be conceived' it does not follow that the same person understands that such a being actually exists, for one can think 'God' exists, but think of such existence in a manner that is still mental, not actual.[18] Aquinas furthermore held that the existence of what is well known to us is a necessary foundation for affirming the existence of God. And what is well known to us is *given* to us, as the universe is given to us, and no proof of its existence is needed. On this latter point, as we will see, Wittgenstein agreed with Aquinas that there are some things that need no proof of their existence, and he objected to Kant calling the existence of what is beyond experience a *hypothesis* that needs justifying.

Kant regarded the Cosmological and Physico-Theological arguments as the more natural way to argue for God's existence, for these arguments rely on the general contingency of the universe or the order found within it. And, since concepts alone are insufficient to prove the existence of anything, the correct procedure is to argue for the existence of God based on what we know about the universe. On this point he agreed with Aquinas, but surprisingly Kant went on to reject all cosmological arguments because we cannot experientially know how the principles of human knowledge apply to a necessarily existing infinite Being, since all experiential knowledge received by us is limited by our mental categories of space and time. Kant's rejection was a direct consequence of his perceptualist theory of knowledge that split the perceived appearance, from the thing in itself, and treated space and time as transcendental categories of mind that are not known experientially. As a consequence, Kant also rejected Newton's assumption that the universe is contained within objective space and time.

Having rejected the cosmological argument because human knowledge is limited to perceived knowledge, Kant seemed to have no trouble accepting the transcendental categories of space and time that are not known perceptually. This conflicting use of his criteria of knowledge is a major confusion in Kant's epistemology, and to the end of his life he struggled to gain acceptance of his version of transcendental idealism. Lonergan in *Insight*, aware of Kant's contributions and confusions, articulated a notion of objectivity[19] that did not fall into Kant's perceptualist position,

18. Thomas Aquinas, *Summa Theologiae*, I,q2,a1,re2.
19. *CWL* 3 *Insight*, Ch 13.

that identifies the real with what is 'already out there now'.[20] *Insight* points out that Kant's theory of knowledge is based on the 'ocular metaphor'[21] that equates knowing with looking, and thereby confused the conditions required for perception with the more complex conditions required for the conscious achievement called knowledge.

Lonergan in Chapter 5 of *Insight*, on Space and Time, left us a rich source of insights for thinking about the universe. After defining Space and Time as the ordered totality of concrete extensions and durations, he pointed out that only a fragment of all extensions and durations are actually experienced by human beings and therefore we can only experience a fragment of Space and Time. Yet, from a nucleus of experiences we can use frames of reference with different geometries of space and time to extend beyond our immediate experiences to an ordered universe of all space and time.[22] And as a creative process we can use this extrapolating technique to refer to any number of concrete, abstract, or imaginative universes. However, unless these different extrapolated universes, with their various conceptual logics are carefully distinguished, they become a source of endless ambiguity. Lonergan noted that this is what happened when Galileo and Newton divided qualities into *primary qualities* of extension and *secondary qualities* that were subjective, thereby confusing description with explanation. Lonergan correctly pointed out that all qualities are given by means of the senses and as such relate to the subject, but the difference is in how we use the data of the senses to describe or explain something.[23] To his credit Kant, who inherited the distinction between primary and secondary qualities, knew something was wrong with a Newtonian universe contained in so-called objective space and time, but not being able to give a correct account of space and time turned them into rigid mental categories. Unfortunately many of these confusions persist in the intellectual life of educators today and are passed on to generations of new students, especially when thinking about the universe. What *Insight* offers is not a simple rejection of Kant,[24] but a more elaborate set of techniques for clarifying the different levels of concepts we use, especially about the universe.

20. *CWL* 3 *Insight*, 276.
21. *CWL* 3 *Insight*, 344–45.
22. *CWL* 3 *Insight*, 184.
23. *CWL* 3 *Insight*, 107–9, 275–79.
24. *Collected Works of Bernard Lonergan*, volume 5, *Understanding and Being* (Toronto: University of Toronto Press, 1990), 389; hereafter *CWL* 5 *Understanding and Being*.

A similar position to Kant's, concerning our inability to argue from how the world is, to the reality of God, was held by Wittgenstein in his *Tractatus*,[25] where he argued, not from the limitation of knowledge, but from the limits of language. As he said, '*How* things are in the world is a matter of complete indifference for what is higher. God does not reveal himself *in* the world.'[26] For, he argued, '*the limits of my language* mean the limits of my world';[27] that is, 'the world is my world.'[28] It may seem as if Wittgenstein wanted to reduce cosmology to a personal *Weltanschauung*, however what he wanted to reduce was the aggrandizing of modern science, as he said, 'The whole modern conception of the world is founded on the illusion that the so-called laws of nature are the explanations of natural phenomena.'[29] Wittgenstein did not deny the reality of the universe, nor the reality of God, nor did he deny the value of faith and prayer; what he denied was our ability to explain the world and God within the limits of language. As he said, there is something mystical about how the world manifests itself, for 'There are, indeed, things that cannot be put into words. They make themselves manifest.'[30] 'It is not *how* things are in the world that is mystical, but *that* it exists.'[31]

Throughout his life Wittgenstein distinguished between what we can *say* and what *shows* itself,[32] and was adamant that we cannot say anything about the world as a whole. His position is well illustrated by his biographer Ray Monk[33] who recounts an occasion:

> Russell and Wittgenstein met in Holland and argued at great length, Russell was trying to persuade Wittgenstein that the sentence '*there are at least three things in the world*' was both 'meaningful and true'. Russell later recollected that during the discussion he took a sheet of white paper and made three blobs of ink on it, urging Wittgenstein to admit that, since there were three blobs, there must be at least three things

25. Ludwig Wittgenstein, *Tractatus Logico-Philosophicus*, translated by DF Pears & BF McGuinness (London: Routledge, 1961); hereafter *Tractatus*.
26. Wittgenstein, Tractatus, 6.432; emphasis original.
27. Wittgenstein, *Tractatus*, 5.6; emphasis original.
28. Wittgenstein, *Tractatus* ,5.641.
29. Wittgenstein, *Tractatus*, 6.371.
30. Wittgenstein, *Tractatus*, 6.522.
31. Wittgenstein, *Tractatus*, 6.44.
32. Anthony Kenny, *Wittgenstein* (London: Allen Lane Penguin Press, 1973), 218.
33. Ray Monk, *Ludwig Wittgenstein: The Duty of Genius* (London: Cape, 1990).

> in the world, *'but he refused resolutely . . . He would admit there were three things on the page, because that was a finite assertion, but he would not admit that anything at all could be said about the world as a whole.'* [34]

And yet Wittgenstein did not always remain silent about the world, since in the opening sentences of the *Tractatus* he said, 'The world is all that is the case. The world is the totality of facts, not of things.'[35] Was he distinguishing between 'the world' and 'the world as a whole'? Or is this a case where we should apply what he said at the end of the *Tractatus*, that anyone who understands what he is saying, 'must transcend these propositions, and then he will see the world aright'?[36] Granted there are different interpretations of Wittgenstein, it is clear that he sometimes blurred the *saying / showing* distinction to speak about what could not properly be said.

Now what can properly be said, is limited by the necessary conditions of meaning in a language. And these conditions of meaning must be shareable and publicly accessible, for without shareable criteria you could not understand what I am now saying, nor could I correctly remember the meaning of my own feelings and insights. Wittgenstein argued strongly against splitting meaning into inner and outer events, as the Private Language theory assumes, for we do not first have inner feelings and insights onto which we choose to stick outer words like labels. Rather we learn the meaning of words by using them in agreed public ways. For if there were no public semantic rules of usage, why should we use 'table' to refer to a table, and not to a light or a door? Now, these semantic limitations also apply to what we say about the world or universe; as he said, if words like 'world' have a use, it must be as humble a one as the words 'table', 'lamp', 'door'.[37] So the meaning of the 'universe' is learnt in the playground or not at all, for it is not learnt through an inner private mental affair. Lonergan too rejected the inner private mental view of meaning, though he expressed it differently, when he said, 'I do not believe that mental acts occur without a sustaining flow of expression. The expression may be

34. Ray Monk, *How to Read Wittgenstein* (London: Granta Publications, 2005), 39; emphasis original.
35. Wittgenstein, Tractatus, 1,1.1.
36. Wittgenstein, *Tractatus*, 6.54.
37. Ludwig Wittgenstein, *Philosophical Investigations*, translated by GEM Anscombe (Oxford: Blackwell, 1968), 97.

linguistic. It may be inadequate. It may not be presented to the attention of others. But it occurs. . . I have no doubt that the ordinary meaningfulness of ordinary language is essentially public and only derivatively private.'[38] If all this is correct, then our concept of the universe is a public affair we share with others, and if I want to say more about the universe than my language allows me to say, I must remain silent and let the universe show itself.

In his last writings *On Certainty* Wittgenstein spoke of the scientist's world as 'A world-picture and not a hypothesis, because it is the matter-of-course foundation for his research and as such goes unmentioned'.[39] Wittgenstein's point was that cosmologists take the universe for granted because in proposing hypotheses about the universe they implicitly acknowledge it exists. Lonergan also acknowledged that metaphysics, which is oriented toward everything, 'is implicit in everyone by the simple fact that he is a conscious subject that experiences, understands and judges'.[40] Kant too acknowledged the existence of the world-whole as an example of an *a priori* synthetic judgment.[41] About such judgments he said, 'this kind of knowledge must unquestionably be looked upon as *given*; in other words, metaphysics must be considered as really existing, if not as science, nevertheless as the natural disposition of the human mind (*metaphysica naturalis*)'.[42] So, Kant, Wittgenstein and Lonergan agreed that the existence of the universe is undeniable, it is the given foundation for science, and no proof of its existence is needed. Yet Kant and Wittgenstein denied that the existence of the universe could be used to prove that God exists. However, they accepted that we can be aware of the existence of God in the same way we are aware of the existence of the universe, with no proof needed. For they both acknowledged that we are aware of more than we can prove, about God and the universe, but exactly how we are aware of this more, they did not explain, except to hint at a natural disposition of the human mind, or at what manifests and shows itself. Lonergan's *Insight* makes central use of this 'awareness of more' to reconstruct a natural

38. Bernard Lonergan, *Method in Theology* (London: Darton Longman and Todd, 1972), 255.
39. Ludwig Wittgenstein, *On Certainty*, edited by GEM Anscombe and GH von Wright, translated by Denis Paul and GEM Anscombe (Oxford: Blackwell, 1974), 167.
40. *CWL 5 Understanding and Being*, 193.
41. See Guyer, *Kant*, 138–144, on 'The Metaphysics of the World'.
42. CPR, B 21; emphasis original.

theology, for it links the 'awareness of more' to Aristotle's[43] natural desire to know and the logic of unrestricted questioning.[44]

Lonergan acknowledged that we lived in different personal 'worlds' for 'Each one of us has his world: it is a solid structure; it is the result of our lives; it has a horizon. And this world is apt to define what I mean by the real.'[45] He also argued that since our consciousness operates at different levels of feeling, thinking and knowing, the universe is multi-dimensional. And so there are different cosmologies and theologies expressed in different stories and pictures, symbols and theories, or more often as a confused mix of these. However, there is a tension[46] in 'our world' felt by intelligent people whose ideal is to know what the universe really is, not just to live with a communal view of the world. He also agreed with Kant that the real universe is not an object floating around in space and time, for he knew the universe is more than a background grid, or vast Newtonian billiard table.

Lonergan also distinguished between *this universe* and *the universe of everything*. What he meant by *this universe* is what some contemporary cosmological arguments refer to when they claim, contrary to Kant and Wittgenstein, that there are features of the known universe that support the theologically relevant conclusion that *this universe* requires an intelligent ground. These arguments claim that the 'fine tuning' of the initial state of this universe, and its subsequent 'directionality', or as Lonergan put it, the 'upwardly but indeterminately directed dynamism of generalized emergent probability',[47] point to an order within this universe. In his discussions about probability and the intelligibility of this universe, Lonergan explained that 'you argue from the order of the universe not being accountable for by the universe; in other words, it's there as a fact, but if you have an intelligible order, the existence of that intelligible order is not accounted for without an intelligence. And so on. You are always arguing from some unaccounted for intelligibility of this universe.'[48]

43. Aristotle, Metaphysica, Book A in *Basic Works of Aristotle*, edited by Richard McKeon (New York: Random House, 1941), 980a.
44. David Legg, 'Questioning and Knowing: The Logic of Questioning in Bernard Lonergan's Theory of Knowing', PhD thesis, Department of Philosophy, University of Auckland, 2003.
45. *CWL* 5 *Understanding and Being*, 184.
46. *CWL* 5 *Understanding and Being*, 190.
47. *CWL* 3 *Insight*, 655–56.
48. *CWL* 5 *Understanding and Being*, 340.

Lonergan went on to argue that the lack of complete intelligibility in *this universe* does not imply a lack of complete intelligibility in the *universe of everything*, for if that were true then we would need to ask, is there another universe beyond the universe of everything that completes it, but that is impossible, because apart from everything there is simply nothing. Rather the lack of complete intelligibility in this universe is to be explained, not by assuming that everything is unintelligible, but by showing the limitations of classical and statistical, genetic and dialectical methods used in gaining knowledge. And to answer Kant's position, Lonergan in the early chapters of *Insight,* provided an exhaustive array of arguments to show why such methods are intrinsically unable to completely answer all our questions. And for anyone who has seriously studied both works, there is no doubt that *Insight* is a more adequate account of human knowledge than the *Critique of Pure Reason.*

Now it may surprise some to hear that Lonergan not only had several views of the universe, but his understanding of the *universe of everything* is of a unified concrete universe, which is unimaginable, and is not to be confused with the material universe. For Lonergan was a critical realist who rejected all fundamentally dualistic views of the universe and repeatedly said that apart from the real concrete universe there is simply nothing. The universe of everything is not an abstract idea but the most concrete reality; it is what is; it is being. As he said, 'Apart from being there is nothing. Again, being is completely concrete and completely universal. It is completely concrete: over and above the being of any thing, there is nothing more of that thing. It is completely universal; apart from the realm of being, there is simply nothing.'[49]. The view that there might be a radically other or transcendental universe outside the real concrete universe simply has no support in Lonergan's *Insight.* This is his position: if there were something apart from everything that is, then either that something is already encompassed within the universe of everything, or it is simply nothing. And that is the reason the universe of everything is a unity, for while we can identify different unities within everything, there is nothing outside the universe of everything that can divide it against itself.[50] Lonergan was a realist who drew a hard line between everything and nothing, which of course is not a line between two universes, between what is and what is not. Even a parallel universe, or a possible universe, is part of everything. And this, I think, is his deepest insight about the

49. *CWL* 3 *Insight*, 374–75.
50. *CWL* 3 *Insight*, 533–44.

universe and ourselves — that we stand in the universe open to everything and nothing, and because we are radically open to everything, we know that nothing can separate us from being encompassed by all that is. It is a position that is coherent with itself since ultimately there is nothing to contradict it.

Lonergan agreed with Kant that mere concepts are not the basis for knowing existence. And since the universe is not an abstract idea, we affirm the existence of the universe in the same way we affirm our own reality. As he said in his Halifax lectures on *Insight*, 'We have a sense of reality, and that sense of reality runs concomitantly with the being that we know in true judgments. When a judgment is true, normally the sense of reality is satisfied.'[51] Now each of us has a sense of reality that begins with objects and includes my own awareness of living in a real world. So too the stories of the Dreamtime, fuelled by an undifferentiated imagination, are about the real universe, not just about 'our world', for the Dreamtime openly wonders about the universe of everything. This open quality of wondering allows our sense of reality to be, not one-dimensional and fixed but multi-dimensional and dynamic; so too the universe we know and wonder about is multi-dimensional and dynamic. As we are open to everything, so is the universe, and as the universe encompasses everything, so do we, for there is nothing that separates us from the universe of everything.

While we know that the universe and ourselves exist, we also know that we do not completely know it or ourselves, and by knowing we are ignorant of many things we are aware there is more to know. So we speculate by inventing cosmologies and theologies expressed in pictures and theories, dance and dialectic, and when these pictures and theories lead to incoherent systems or dysfunctional consequences, our sense of reality is tested. Fortunately, we humans are not cognitively hard wired to think in species-specific ways, so we can re-set our cosmological and theological compasses and move out into wider and higher viewpoints.

This understanding of the universe of everything may seem overly optimistic today, for we hear about possible worlds and parallel universes, with multiverses having more dimensions than we can imagine, and plasma fields that challenge the dominant theory. I sometimes hear young people asking how do we know that there are not other universes with completely different types of reality in it, even anti-reality? Or, more despairingly I hear this question: is it not arrogant to think that the universe

51. *CWL* 5 *Understanding and Being*, 107.

exists with us in mind? And, from a new generation of students: Lonergan never saw the pictures we see today from the Hubble telescope, nor did he know of the latest results from NASA's satellite probes into microwave background radiation, so how can he tell us what the universe is?

Lonergan's answer to such questioning was to point to the difference between the heuristic and explanatory functions in knowing. The heuristic function is expressed in questioning, and although questioning techniques have developed over time, the unifying function of questioning remains the same. Take fire, for example. The earliest Greek physicists thought fire was an element. In the early seventeenth century fire was thought of as phlogiston, and after Lavoisier's work on combustion in 1783 chemists thought of fire as an oxidation process. But while they gave different explanations they all wanted to answer the same question: What is fire? What is its nature?[52] This questioning function Lonergan expressed metaphorically as the 'upper blade' in the 'scissors' of knowing, where the 'lower blade' is relevant data used to supply the answers.[53] Now Lonergan's notion of a *universe of everything* corresponds to the 'upper blade' that extrapolates to a horizon of answers that would satisfy all questions. The notion of *this universe* corresponds to the 'lower blade' of knowledge that we arrive at based on what is given and our ingenuity in gaining knowledge. Of course, *this universe* is in fact part of the *universe of everything.* It is that part of the runway we see disappearing over our horizon.

Finally, we ask, is the unrestricted desire to know sufficient ground for claiming that the *universe of everything* really exists, or is it just another bright idea? Well, by asking that question we show that the desire to know the universe of everything, is real. And since questioning expresses intelligence,[54] Lonergan used his intelligence to extrapolate from the openness of questioning to a view of the universe as the goal yet to be known when an unrestricted desire to know, correctly knows everything about everything.[55] This view of the universe is not knowledge, for we do not yet know what everything actually is, but it heuristically anticipates a *universe of everything.* And so, in answer to Kant and Wittgenstein, our concept of the universe need not be restricted to the concept of *this universe,* since the desire to know the *universe of everything* can be affirmed as a rational goal of a questioning intelligence. And while, like Socrates,

52. *CWL* 3 *Insight*, 759–61.
53. *CWL* 3 *Insight*, 337.
54. *CWL* 3 *Insight*, 372.
55. *CWL* 3 *Insight*, 372–74.

we acknowledge our deepest ignorance, we affirm the goal of wanting to know everything as it really is. Therefore, since an unrestricted desire to know is not the desire to know what I think, or imagine, is so, but to know what really is so, then I can affirm the reality of the universe of everything, as it really is to be known.

To imagine that the universe might be other than what we think it is; to doubt all answers that have been given; to know that we will never know enough to ask every question, does not in itself undermine the desire to know the *universe of everything* as it really is. And so, while Kant restricted our knowledge of the universe to his theory of 'perception', and Wittgenstein restricted what we could say about the world to the 'bubble' of language-games, Lonergan affirmed as real the yet-to-be-known universe of everything, since it is the intended object of the unrestricted desire to know, expressed in our questioning.

Chapter 9

Insight Within a New Global Culture

Philip McShane

This title expresses an ambitious project both of paper-writing and, if my projection is correct, of the historical process. How might I keep this chapter brief and accessible, yet not lose the unity of perspective I intend? Originally I wrote a first part, intending to add a second part, but Part II began to emerge as what I really wished to share. It is, however, altogether more dense and inaccessible, paradoxically much briefer than Part I. In that first Part I had already relegated to footnotes complexities that could not be developed, lurking in the text. Part II resembles, perhaps, a simple melody overwhelmed by footnote chords, cords, hearts of matter.[1]

Part I. Personal directions

By a new global culture I mean a culture that is established in the scientific mode invented by Lonergan in his creative leap of February 1965, when he conceived of a functional collaboration in the global search for progress.

1. A first footnote is necessary, hovering round the work *lurking* in the text above. It relates to a difficulty that occurs in axial cultures—a later topic. The difficulty is summarily described by Lonergan in his treatment of *haute vulgarization* (see *Collected Works of Bernard Lonergan*, volume 6, *Philosophical and Theological Papers 1958–1964,* edited by Robert C Croken, Frederick E Crowe, and Robert M Doran (Toronto: University of Toronto Press, 1996), 121, 155). But the difficulty haunts his entire life's work, and his *Collected Works*. I have made a stab at writing about it in 'Haute Vulgarization,' chapter 3 of *Lack in the Beingstalk: A Giants Causeway* (Cape Breton: Axial Publishing, 2007), and further in the first chapter of Part III of Pierrot Lambert and Philip McShane, *Bernard Lonergan: His Life and Leading Ideas*, forthcoming 2010 in English and French. I can make the completed drafts of my three chapters of Part III available on request, by e-mail. Below I also refer to writings on my website: the website is www.philipmcshane.ca; the books there are available free.

In Christian terms one might see him as bracketing Paul's hymn to charity of First Corinthians, chapter 13, with a sublation of the two bracketing chapters, 12 and 14, with a refinement of interpretation, a maturing of thinking: 'All do not interpret, do they?'(12: 30); and 'in your thinking be mature'(14: 20). But to that light-weight reading of a parallel in scripture there is to be added the deeper perspective of the effective unity of the mission of Jesus as it seeds the efficient unity of a human science. Lonergan argues: 'It is quite legitimate to seek in the efficient cause of the science, that is, in the scientist, the reason why a science forms a unified whole.'[2] And that efficiency places the global solution to Plato's ancient problem of the control of urban meaning in Lonergan's final identification of the human component of Cosmopolis.[3] Functional collaboration is to replace eventually the long muddled haphazard effort of thinking effectively forward in history.[4]

But what might I mean by *eventually*? It seems quite plausible to identify the third stage of meaning described by Lonergan in *Method in Theology* with the second time of the human subject that became a topic for him in the late 1950s.[5] The distinction between the first and second time of the temporal subject is quite simple yet profound. The first time is a time of spontaneous intelligence, intelligence used but not adverted to. The second time is the time of intelligence that is self-appreciative in a habitual manner, a quite different control of meaning. One can certainly think of that shift ontogenetically: the spontaneity of the young Aquinas or the young Lonergan, sharply intelligent but not seriously self-attentive. But the meaning to which I attend immediately is the phylogenetic meaning that leads one to a view of an Axial Period in human history that has its

2. *Collected Works of Bernard Lonergan,* volume 10, *Topics in Education,* edited by Robert M Doran and Frederick E Crowe (Toronto: University of Toronto Press, 1993), 160 (hereafter *CWL* 10 *Topics in Education*).
3. I discuss the manner in which the characteristics of Cosmopolis are realised in the strategy of functional specialisation in the second half of *Joistings 22* at <http://www.philipmcshane.ca/joistings.html>. Accessed 16 April 2010.
4. This haphazard strategy occurs in all disciplines. For an initial indication of the general problem see my *Method in Theology: Revisions and Implementations,* chapter 1 at <http://www.philipmcshane.ca/method.html>. Accessed 16 April 2010.
5. The first presentation of the topic occurs in *Quaestio XXI* of B Lonergan, *Divinarum Personarum Conceptio Analogica* (Rome: Gregorian University Press, 1957). It is repeated in the later version of the same work, *De Deo Trino II. Pars Systematica,* 1964, which is now available in English as *Collected Works of Lonergan,* volume 12, *The Triune God: Systematics,* translated by Michael G Shields, edited by Robert M Doran and H Daniel Monsour (Toronto: University of Toronto Press, 2007).

ontogenetic parallel.[6] This view solves a problem both in the thinking of Jaspers and in Lonergan's reflections on the second stage of meaning.

First, there was Jasper's problematic view. In his *Origins and Goals of History* he placed a basic axis of history in the period between 800 and 200 BCE when humans reached significant differentiation in Greece, Persia, Israel, India and China.[7] In the context of a later discussion of a contemporary culture, he raised the question of a second axial period.[8] Toynbee took issue with Jaspers in his last work, *Mankind and Mother Earth*:

> It would be misleading to set a chronological limit to the Axial Age that excluded the two mighty epigoni (i.e. Jesus and Muhammad) of Zarathustra and 'Deutero-Isaiah'. Thus the Axis Age expands from a period of about 120 years to one of about seventeen centuries running from *circa* 1060 B.C. down to A.D. 632, which is the date of the Prophet Muhammad's death.[9]

In the fourth volume of his work *Order and History*, entitled *The Ecumenic Age*, Eric Voegelin moves to a fuller view of the historical process which resembles broadly the one I propose here. A central feature of Voegelin's view is his emphasis on the 'In-Betweenness' of human existence, to which he gives the name *Metaxy*. There is an emergence of a tension of 'In-Betweenness' that Voegelin primarily associates with the noetic differentiation in the Greek tradition and the pneumatic differentiation in the Hebrew tradition. Clearly, Voegelin would consider this emergence into consciousness as axial in some temporal sense, so meshing his problem with ours, and it seems to me that a key pointer to the resolution of the debate regarding the meaning of axiality lies in his recurring questioning of the meaning of modernity. So, in noting the parallel falsifications of history in the Sumerian King List and in Hegel's *Philosophy of History*, Voegelin is led to query: 'And what is modern about modern mind, one may

6. One may think thus, ontogenetically and phylogenetically, of the claim of Lonergan in *Insight* regarding metaphysics as latent, problematic, explicit: see the index under *Metaphysics, Latent.*
7. Karl Jaspers, *The Origin and Goal of History* (London: Routledge & Kegan Paul, 1953), chapter 1.
8. Jaspers, *The Origin and Goal of History*, 97.
9. Arnold Toynbee, *Mankind and Mother Earth: A Narrative History of the World* (New York: Oxford University Press, 1976), 178.

ask, if Hegel, Comte, or Marx, in order to create an image of history that will support their ideological imperialism, still use the same techniques for distorting the reality of history as their Sumerian predecessors?'[10] In a later context he remarks:

> A 'modern age' in which the thinkers who ought to be philosophers prefer the role of imperial entrepreneurs will have to go through many convulsions before it has got rid of itself, together with the arrogance of its revolt, and found the way back to the dialogue of humanity with its humility.[11]

Voegelin asks, 'What is modern?' It is useful to advert to the meanings of the classical Latin word, *modo*, (merely, just, directly), and the derived medieval word, *modernitas*: present-dayness. Then—but I would note that the topic demands massive research of a functional kind—one, or rather mankind, can move to a dialogue with its humility and find ranges and varieties of fragmented consciousness as the character, or characters, of the long period of history between what Lonergan calls the first and second times of the temporal subject, making it possible to identify the first and third stages of meaning with these two and then to identify the Axial Period as the second stage of meaning, sublating Jaspers two axial periods.[12]

This is all too dense in its expression and its anticipation of later functional specialist cycling and re-cycling, but at least I can add the suggestion that the view can give a powerful heuristic grip on the tasks sketched on page 250 of *Method in Theology*. Part of that heuristic grasping will be the evolution of geohistorical estimative specifications of the Axial Period. But my first burst forward in the late seventies to this view, with its 5000 year span, from 2500 BCE to 2500 AD, gives us an initial image to ingest. Further, the second date serves to nudges us towards the issues raised in the final section of Chapter 7 of *Insight*: the date depends on

10. Eric Voegelin, *Order and History*, volume 4, *The Ecumenic Age* (Baton Rouge: Louisiana State University Press, 1974), 68; see also 7, 27–28, 173.
11. Voegelin, *The Ecumenic Age*, 192.
12. I would note that there is the apparently quite different problem of the nature of personal enlightenment. Note 6 gives the broader context. It is through self-attention in the personal problem of attaining enlightenment that one arrives at an initial basis for reflection on the historical problem. The issue of enlightenment in either case, however, is a complex topic that requires classifications of differentiations and cultures.

us, and on Lonergan's later functional identification of Cosmopolis as the instrument of humanity's dialogue with its humility.[13]

But it is also a dialogue of humanity with its greatness, its call to ontogenetic and phylogenetic growth in viewing its journey *sub specie aeternitatis.*[14] In an unpublished effort of 1965 to write a first chapter of *Method* Lonergan recalls Hegel:

> As the labour of introspection proceeds, one stumbles upon Hegel's insight that the full objectification of the human spirit is the history of the human race. It is in the sum of the products of common sense and common nonsense, of the sciences and the philosophies, of moralities and religions, of social orders and cultural achievements, that there is mediated, set before us the mirror in which we can behold, the originating principle of human aspiration and human attainment and failure.[15]

Further, in that same set of fragments he gives a clue to the maturing of the ongoing genesis of methods that occupied him later in identifying a third order of human consciousness:

> Second order intentionality has a second-order object that in a first order is not a datum of consciousness. Similarly, when as at present one introspects introspection, then there is a third-order consciousness and a third-order intentionality. There is a third-order consciousness, for consciously we

13. I associate the challenge of moving into functional specialised science as a participation in the satisfaction of Christ; see *Joistings 8*, 'Recycling Satisfaction' at <http://www.philipmcshane.ca/joistings.html>. Accessed 18 April 2010.
14. Recall the challenge of 'Finality, Love, Marriage': 'theologians, let alone parents, rarely think of the historical process' (*Collected Works of Bernard Lonergan*, volume 4, *Collection*, edited by Frederick E Crowe and Robert M Doran (Toronto: University of Toronto Press, 1988), 47 (hereafter *CWL* 4 *Collection*)). Recall notes 6 and 12 above. I would add that *sub specie aeternitatis* includes a perspective on a personal and phylogenetic genetic eschatology, a massive lacuna in present theology.
15. I quote from page 14 of a Lonergan archival file labelled A697. It contains a typescript numbered 8–23. Very plausibly it is a continuation of the sketch of a first chapter of *Method in Theology* that is contained in file V.7, the same file which contains the basic first scribbled version of functional specialisation. That file contains nine pages of typescript that is the beginning of a first chapter, and also a three-page scribbled outline of the entire chapter.

> advert to our adverting to our operations. There is a third-order intentionality whose third-order object was, in the second order, not an object but the datum of consciousness that is the introspection being introspected.[16]

Such a maturing of the Hegelian insight towards a luminous methodology obviously belongs to the second time of the temporal subject. Its naming no more carries us into that time than the slim identification of the need for self-knowledge fermenting in Confucius[17] or in Socrates, carries us into *Insight*. It is a distant hope, a hope wondrously expressed in the end of the book *Insight* that I would mesh into the statistics of its realisation: the complex of probabilities to be associated with the special auxiliary to humanity's question that is functional collaboration.[18] Hear Lonergan's reach in that final thirty-first place of chapter 20 of *Insight*: 'The antecedent willingness of hope has to advance from a generic reinforcement of the pure desire to an adapted and specialized auxiliary ever ready to offset every interference either with intellect's unrestricted finality or with its essential detachment and disinterestedness'.[19] It would be over eleven years later that the structure of that auxiliary would dawn on him, but it is wonderful to note that in that ten-page section of *Insight* he mentions *collaboration* twenty-nine times. Previously I have considered his solution of 1965 in relation to the demands of his suggestions about Cosmopolis, but it would be quite profitable—a task beyond this paper—to consider his suggestions here about collaboration in relation to that discovered functional auxiliary.

We should, however, pause further over his notion of a third order of consciousness in order to glimpse the character of the mature collaboration. That notion, to be slowly and empirically thematised, leads to a precision

16. I am quoting here from page 8 of the draft-chapter titled 'Method' referred to in the previous note.
17. 'When you meet persons of exceptional character / Think to stand shoulder to shoulder with them; / Meeting persons of little character, / look inward and examine yourself.' I quote from The Original Book IV (479 BC) of *The Analects*, translated by Jaime Barrera Parra in a paper read at the Loyola Marymount Fallon-Lonergan Conference, March 2007, 'Encountering Confucius's Ethics of Self Transcendence'.
18. One may start with the simple statistical shift that is related to cyclic recurrence: see *Collected Works of Bernard Lonergan*, volume 3, *Insight: A Study of Human Understanding*, edited by Frederick E Crowe and Robert M Doran (Toronto: University of Toronto Press, 1992), 145 (hereafter *CWL* 3 *Insight*).
19. *CWL* 3 *Insight*, 747.

regarding the meaning of methodology that both lifts it beyond Lonergan's later searchings[20] and at the same time roots back to his initial aspiration in tackling the adventure of writing *Insight*.[21] Second-order consciousness yields a luminous grip on a particular method. Third order consciousness grounds a luminous ordering of all methods. So, methodology's relation to methods is to resemble zoology's relation to the geohistory of animals.[22]

Furthermore, the distinction between nature and grace does not warrant a separation of methods or a fracturing of methodology. So we are back at Lonergan's bent in his tackling the writing of *Insight*. And we are back to the beginning of this present essay where I emphasised the Christian perspective on the search for method.

But what of the next fifty years, of Lonergan studies, of the global searchings that I wrote of in the summary anticipation of this paper? If this paper is to take its place in the pragmatics of effective method, then it had best add concrete appeal through proximate agenda.

Already in this fiftieth anniversary year I have mused over such an agenda at the West Coast Method Institute (Loyola Marymount University, LA, March 2007) and the summary expression given there of that agenda, placed as an addendum to this paper, would be a suitable start to my further reflections here.

Filling out that summary is no mean task, one I cannot undertake here. But the suggestion of minimal effort is the centrally important element. The global academic community is secretly gasping for the division of labour

20. See, for example, 'The Ongoing Genesis of Methods', in BJ Lonergan, *A Third Collection* (Paulist Press: Mahwah, NJ, 1985), 146–65.
21. A fuller reflection would add in consideration of the amazing achievement of *Insight* chapter 17 in defining the methodological strategy implicit in the universal viewpoint. That strategy is to be meshed with Lonergan's later strategy of reversing counterpositions in a manner that twists the dialectic component of the universal viewpoint into the ongoing sequence of genetic systematics that, meshed with the universal viewpoint, is to be the dominant perspective of the operation of functional specialisation: symbolically, UV + GS is to be the Standard Model operative in the cycle from Research to Communication and so on round. But that is a topic for a later work; see Lambert and McShane, *Bernard Lonergan*, Part 3, Chapter 3, 'Research, Interpretation, History, His Story', already mentioned in note 1 above. A further context is the two books mentioned in the Appendix here.
22. The fact that we are only on the fringe of this perspective should not excuse us from the effort to shift context into the explanatory mode hinted at in the previous note. See Appendix 3 of any of the three works mentioned in note 5 above, where Lonergan treats of the handicap of failing to reach an explanatory heuristic even in the early stages of a science.

described by Lonergan, and this is the place to start rather than with an invitation to tackle *Insight*, or at least supplementing that invitation with such a division.[23] The cycling of the full system will gradually—especially through the workings of *Method in Theology*, 250—move the challenge of *Insight* into the global culture, East, West and South.

This notion of gradualism leads me to two comments regarding what would appear to be over-hastiness. The first comment regards intellectual conversion, the second is on the work of Robert Doran.

Intellectual conversion is a massively complex human achievement ontogentically and phylogenetically. It is to be a dominant presence only in the community of culture, the creative community of functional specialisation, in the third stage of meaning. Certainly, it is a key challenge of *Insight* but, in my experience, it is beyond most of its present readers.[24] The fact of its difficulty is regularly noted by Lonergan so I leave you with his footnoted view.[25] The fact of its non-achievement by many experts in

23. The next note draws attention, both implicitly and explicitly—through the pointers from Mark Morelli—to the possibilities of both dialogue and dialectic with the Hegelian tradition.
24. The challenge is to get beyond a half-way house between sensism and idealisms that clings, perhaps with Kantian subtlety, to a naive realism on some level of sense or spirit, to reach beyond Hegel's inwardness to a more radical inwardness, a dark and extreme realism. On Hegel in this regard see Mark Morelli's very powerful and cogent paper in this volume, 'Lonergan's Debt to Hegel and the Appropriation of Critical Realism'. I would note that interviews of Lonergan by Professor JV Rice (1981), help to identify a more modest role for Kant in the drive of *Insight*. The driving element in *Insight* was an interest in methods, an eye on the distant future, an outreach for the thinking existential sufferer, but above all else a restructuring of thinking regarding the restructuring of all things in Christ. And among the elements of that drive there is to be found the truth of Ivo Coelho's claim: 'It could be said . . . that Lonergan's method is not only post-Aristotelian and post-Kantian, but also explicitly and consciously post-Hegelian' (Ivo Coehlo, *Hermeneutics and Method: The 'Universal Viewpoint' in Bernard Lonergan* (Toronto: University of Toronto Press, 2001), 194).
25. I need refer only to the single volume, *Collected Works of Bernard Lonergan,* volume 18, *Phenomenology and Logic, The Boston College Lectures on Mathematical Logic and Existentialism*, edited by Philip J McShane (Toronto: University of Toronto Press, 2001); (hereafter *CWL* 18 *Phenomenology and Logic*). See, for example, the index there, under *Augustine*. But the volume also draws attention to the possibility of axiomatic expression (121ff), and this possibility is to be exploited fully with regard to what Lonergan calls *The Position*. This is a largely uninvestigated region involving a sublation of the simple positional statement of *CWL* 3 *Insight*, 423, into an axiomatic form that involves axioms of intentionality, of the essay, *Prehumous 3*, 'Metagrams and Metaphysics' at <http://www.philipmcshane.ca/prehumous.html>. Accessed 10 May 2010.

Lonergan is beginning finally to be a topic,[26] and I had best leave it to ferment forward as such: I am already sufficiently unpopular! Again, the cycling of the full functional system is the hope of effective achievement.

Then there is the dedicated work of Robert Doran, worth singling out precisely because he stands out in his effort to see the task whole and to push forward in it, in relative solitude. In the conference at West Coast Method Institute, Loyola Marymount University, Los Angeles, 2007, and more elaborately at the Longeran Workshop, Boston College in June, 2007,[27] he presented his hopes of a move forward in systematic theology both through refinements of Lonergan's thematic of the absolutely supernatural and through the sublation of scripture scholarship such as that of NT Wright into a systematic context.[28]

I could not possibly do justice to the facets of his push forward here, nor to the refined disagreements that Bob and I have shared for more than two decades. To the note below I would only add the broad comment that such work as he is doing is desperately needed within a present pastoral effort to bring the subjectivity of a loving Three into the lives of the Christian community. But, as a move forwards towards the fresh systematics anticipated heuristically by Lonergan the effort is too hasty and too undifferentiated.[29] Doran fails; I have failed; we all have failed to

---

26. A key nudge here is the work of Richard Liddy, integrally presented in his book, *Startling Strangeness: Reading Lonergan's* Insight (Lanham, Maryland: University Press of America, 2006). Mark Morelli nudges further (see notes 23, 24, above) and there is the (Hegelian?) challenge (note 24, above) of the reach for a fuller logic.

27. His presentation there was simply titled 'Report on a Work in Progress'.

28. I note that Doran makes no mention, here or elsewhere, of the cleansing process involved in operations of the type suggested on page 250 of *Method in Theology* (London: Darton, Longman & Todd, 1971).

29. I would note that I find this true of other good work that is emerging at present. For instance, at that same Lonergan Workshop of 2007, Charles Hefling Jnr dealt magnificently with the topic 'Lonergan, Schleiermacher, and Christian Systematic Theology: Possibly Relevant Questions'. But he was compactly ranging over a half-dozen specialties: he would certainly admit this, but I would like that admission to emerge operatively, in community, as the central possibly relevant question. On Doran's work there are my extended reflections in *Method in Theology: Revisions and Implementations*, Part Three. See also my *Lonergan's Standard Model of Effective Global Inquiry*, chapters 9, 10 and 12 at <http://www.philipmcshane.ca/lonergansmodel.html>. Accessed 30 May 2010. Finally, *Joistings 18*, 'The Field and Unified Field Theories; God and I' and *Joistings 20*, 'Identifying Systematic Theology', focus on broader problems of identifying systematic theology, see <http://www.philipmcshane.ca/joistings.html>. Accessed 10 May 2010. A central key theological problem is his reading of Lonergan's hypothesis regarding graces' relations to the Eternal Processions as blossoming into 'a

meet the challenge of stumblingly attempting a climb to the differentiated thinking involved in working in any functional specialty. And have no doubts: the effort is to give rise eventually to precise and differentiated talk and writing, sentence by scientific sentence.[30]

An analogy with the difficulty of the cultural shift of economics helps here. The real crisis of transition in economics is not facing the complexities of a democratic economics that are latent in Lonergan's new political economy. The proximate operable—or should I say inoperable?—challenge is to get the distinction between two functions of money into the elementary searchings of economic realities, presently shabbily muddled. Similarly the proximate challenge in methodological thinking, in theology, philosophy, or any discipline, is not the facing of the complexities of a remote methodological horizon but the bringing into our present efforts an explicit talking and writing of the distinction between eight functions of talking and writing. We could make a start towards that by taking present written efforts, our own and others, and seeking pragmatic light of

---

new form of the psychological analogy'. I had best quote, in context, from his paper in what I hope is a helpful pointer towards reflection and discussion. 'I suggest that the hypothesis provides us with a new form of the psychological analogy for understanding the divine processions, an analogy within the order of graced experience itself. And I propose that systematic theology itself has evolved to the point where it can begin with a position that integrates the divine processions with the divine missions from the outset of the systematic enterprise' (Robert Doran, 'Envisioning a Systematic Theology'). There is a problem here regarding the meaning of 'from the outset,' a problem I dealt with in *Method in Theology: Revisions and Implementations*, by appealing to an analogy between the 4-hypothesis of Lonergan and the 4-hypothesis contained in Maxwell's 4 electrodynamic equations: from the outset, when fully understood, Maxwell's equations contain all the relations that are termed in investigable situations. So with the Eternal Processions' relations to the historical missions. Further, a full genetic systematics of systems would mesh fresh glimpses of the Relations into the entire structure, not as new but as missed, acknowledging the seeds of that freshness in earlier meanings of the tradition.

30. There is a further shift involved which is beyond the scope of this short article, the shift noted by Lonergan, *Method*, 88, note 34, towards linguistic feedback in subjectivity's destined reach for subject. This relates to the broad topic of a third definition of generalised empirical method, where the lonely subject is the centre of personal attention (see McShane, 'Research, Communications, Stages of Method', *Joistings* 21) and also to the topic of education crystallised in the slogan, 'When teaching children anything one is teaching children children'. (I note, in passing, a second reference to linguistic feedback in *Method*, page 92, omitted from the published texts—the omission is in italics: 'in the measure that linguistic *feed-back is achieved, that is in the measure that* explanations and statements provide the sensible presentations . . .')

how we ramble, prescientifically, sentence by sentence, from one function to another.

There are two broader starts worth mentioning. First, each of us may place ourselves, humbly and incompetently, in the discomfort of the challenge of *Method in Theology* page 250.[31] Surely that is a direction of what this self-appropriation business is all about: taking a luminous stand. Especially there is the issue that is most evidently raised in this paper: where do I stand with regard to functionally differentiated thinking and talking?[32]

Secondly, there is the need to push immediately and communally for luminosity with regard to key varieties of dialogue and dialectic. The oval circuit of functional dialogue, within the standard model even in its initial stages, does not turn to speak to other traditions. That speaking is one of the tasks of the eighth functional specialisation. But what, you might ask, is the nature of the dialogue of the specialty Dialectic? It is, or is to be, dialogue within and towards refinements of the 'cumulative and progressive results'[33] of the third stage of global meaning, results that are beyond present fantasy?

But what of our dialogue in this volume mediated by papers such as this? It falls within the tasks of the eighth functional specialty, a task that eventually may be seen as poorly done by me. I am drawing attention, in scattered or some might say scatty fashion, to Lonergan's answer to the challenge of rescuing *Insight*, both from its present shrinkage as a unified personal challenge and from its unavoidable incompleteness as a contemporary global methodology.[34]

31. I would note that the task of the page should now include Lonergan's achievement as expressed in *Method in Theology* 286ff, which is the result of his massive solitary dialectic effort.
32. I note that the list on page 287 of *Method* is incomplete: it is to include now a tenth challenge, (10), functional specialisation as the full methodological context of future culture.
33. *Method*, 4.
34. A fuller perspective on the present challenge—though earlier and so less sophisticated—is in my essay 'The Importance of Rescuing *Insight*', in *The Importance of Insight: Essays in Honour of Michael Vertin*, edited by John J Liptay and David S Liptay (Toronto: University of Toronto Press, 2007), 199–225. The issue of incompleteness is a fundamental theme throughout my study, *Lonergan's Standard Model of Effective Global Inquiry*. But I would draw attention, in conclusion, to that fundamental incompleteness to which Lonergan arrives at the end of chapter 19 of *Insight*, and return in that context to the Morelli essay mentioned above, notes 23 and 24. Morelli argues in his essay in his volume that if we are to achieve and inhabit the standpoint

Appendix to Part I: the paper's original outline.

The paper will place the book *Insight* within a culture of the third stage of meaning that I have attempted to sketch heuristically in the two books *Molecules, Minding, Meaning* (forthcoming University of Toronto Press) and its sequel *Lonergan's Standard Model of Effective Global Inquiry*. While the paper moves forward within these contexts it will sufficiently indicate their import to make intelligible the character of the relocation. So, it will take its start from the problem posed in 'Culture and Reversal', *Insight*, chapter 7, (that is, section 8.5) in Lonergan's reach for cosmopolis, and move through his later heuristic specification of cosmopolis (File V.7 of February 1965) to the new global cyclic system of culture that is implicit there. That cyclic system is to be redemptive of the cultural achievements of the previous two stages of meaning in a manner that sees history as better than it was (*Method in Theology*, 251). The cyclic dynamic is expected, under the laws of emergent probability, to be a slow labour of centuries. The paper will sketch, realistically but within the normativity of foundational fantasy, the core emergent foundational drive of the possible and concretely probable cyclic collaboration of the next fifty years. It will lift Robert Doran's work of these past decades into the context of a fuller system that will cycle current achievements of genetic systematics through a global community of culture. The cyclic aim, and the aim of the paper, is towards a pragmatics of ongoing effective gentle reversal of decline.

Part II: history's directions

I would, perhaps, better maintain an evident continuity with the first part if the title of this part were 'History's Directors'. There are the Three Directors of history collaborating exotically with the multitude of

---

of Critical Realism, not only must we reject incoherent realism, but we must enter into and go beyond Hegel's Absolute Idealism. Turn, now, in your imagination, to that old chestnut about the half-way house. The three way-stations obviously parallel the three that is matter, form, existence. But is their illumination not also related to the three stages of meaning? So Hegel brings into focus the question of form as a 'full objectification of the human spirit' (see the text at note 15 above). And is the third stage, swinging back to the Christian perspective, in some way related to hope and the luminous absence in history not only of the meaning of 'is' but of the First Person?

I recall, finally, a conversation I had with Lonergan one evening in July of 1971. 'When did you finally reach the meaning of "is"?' I asked. 'When I got that far in *Insight*', was Lonergan's reply. But how far was that?

humanity, each with a role in the dynamics of finitude, a vast and rich topic that we spin past in the conclusion.[35] But our interest here and now, is in some pragmatics of ourselves as directors.

I begin with an image which does not seem at all pragmatic, yet it seems to me to be massively so, and it is worth pondering more fully, indeed I would say habitually, if we are to reach that humility about which Voegelin wrote.[36] First, then, the strange but simple image.

I wrote above of the two times of the temporal subject, and with my focus on phylogeny rather than ontogeny, the obvious image is of linear time. I wish to complexify that image, but hold to the simplicity of a single line. We start with an image on the blackboard that is four meters long, each meter representing one thousand years, indeed the line representing the four thousand years from 1000 BCE to 3000 CE. Recall now the earlier discussion of the Axial Period and of the three stages of meaning.[37] Does the Axial Period span that four thousand years, something that jives with my suggested revision of the views of Jaspers, Toynbee, Voegelin? That is not what is important for our present effort, though it is not difficult to image various possibilities. What is important immediately is to go beyond the ends of the line.

The 'going beyond' is the catch, the tricky task, strangely related to the problem of general history, which is the real catch.[38] Certainly, drawing the line out further is not a difficult problem: the problem is in drawing the mind out in a massive slow interior growth. It is not a beginner's task or even, perhaps, a middle-aged achievement.[39] I liken the task to the task

35. After the conclusion I place the diagram that is central to the present text: the metagram called W3, taken from page 124 of Philip McShane, *A Brief History of Tongue: From Big Bang to Coloured Wholes* (Cape Breton: Axial Publishing, 1998).

36. See above, note 11. This is central to the intussusception into the Tower, or the Standard Model of collaboration, of the image that I deal with here. One reaches for a sense, a taste, of history that sublates Hegel's perspective (see the quotation from Lonergan at note 15 above) that casts a fresh light on these few millennia of Christianity. The time line also raises subtle questions about the longer cycle of decline, the unity of the universe, the place and character of the angels in Old Testament and present traditions (include here reverence for ancestors). These are topics quite beyond a short paper. Some further points are made relating to problems of eschatology in the concluding pages below.

37. See above, note 12.

38. *CWL* 10 *Topics in Education*, 236.

39. There is a deep cultural problem involved here: an axial period rejection of growth that normatively should echo the equation $d/dx\,(e^x) = e^x$. On this see *Lack in The Beingstalk*, 161–163; also *Eldorede 4*, 'Meaning-Growth'. Adult Growth in the Shakespeare of

that emerged peculiarly in chapter 19 of *Insight*: 'what, then, is being?' The question 'what is being?' emerged earlier, although in strange stages.[40] But my new question pivoting on the odd word, *then*, gives a new twist, indeed, I would claim, a new radical lift to the meaning of generalised empirical method.[41] But I will cut this identification of a new question short here and get on first with an apparently simple extension of the original image of a four-meter line.

I ask you to extend the four meters in your imagination. I wish you, in imaginative deed, to extend the line backwards 13.7 kilometres and forwards 2000 kilometres. The deed requires crutches, a human thing worth brooding over. I offer some immediately: take the four meters, in your imagination, and stand it on the ground beside you, like a pike or a spear. The backward extension goes, then, through the ground. How far? It comes out at the other side of the Earth and stands tall a further thousand kilometres. No great problem of measurement here: the Earth's diameter is about 12,700 kilometres. What of the forward extension, representing a piece of the future? Look up there into the blue, up the distance from Melbourne to Alice Springs in the centre of your Australia, or clasp some local distance that makes sense to you at home: a straight line joining the two ends of the coast of Peru, or two familiar cities' separation in Europe, Africa or Asia.

Where do my measurements come from? The backward measurement of 13,700 kilometres comes from the present estimate of the age of the universe: 13.7 billion years. A little mental effort brings one to the measurement 13,700,000 meters and so to 13,700,000,000 years. The

---

Pericles is magnificently presented by Patrick Kavanagh (see the lengthy quotation from a radio talk in *Lack in the Beingstalk*, 56–64). Adult growth in retirement is the central topic in McShane, 'The Importance of Rescuing *Insight*', 199–225.

40. The stages of Lonergan's dealing with the question of being seem to puzzle many, even people of serious authority. I dealt with the matter in 'The Contemporary Thomism of Bernard Lonergan', *Philosophical Studies* 11 (1961–62). The first stage involves a mere use of the word being; the real challenge occurs in an invitation to consent to the position on page 388 [413] of *CWL* 3 *Insight*. The challenge is that mentioned in notes 24 and 34 above. We return to it below, especially in notes 57–61and the text there.

41. I title the new lift GEM3, a shift from GEM2, which is defined in the first few lines of page 141 of *A Third Collection*, giving a view which requires a balanced attention to object and subject. GEM3 shifts to a mediation of the subject's self-appreciation. Further on this see *Joistings 21*, 'Research, Communications, States of Method', and the final chapter of *Bernard Lonergan: His Life and Leading Ideas*.

forward measurement is related to an estimate of the time left to Earth-life by sun's goings on.[42]

You stand there now, holding your spear, pointing forward. The issue I am raising is the issue of the holding, a heart-holding, sensed and tasted. A strange parallel may help. What is it to hold, be held by, the definition of a circle? You can rest naively in the view that it is given at the beginning of *Euclid*, even adding the self-attention of chapter 1 of *Insight*. But you may grow wiser, rise to the context[43] of the definition of a circle in a richer geometry, rise even further to hear the nudging image tell you of yourself and of God, so that indeed you have got the whole thing right in your intellectual paws,[44] in your curious bones, in your lonely nerves.[45]

So I bring you to the odd question that parallels that question of chapter 19 of *Insight*: 'What, then, is being?' The question is, 'What, then, is the empirical residue?'[46] Are we back at the ABC question of chapter 1 of *Insight*?[47] Rather we are forward to the question as you had not dreamt

42. There is, of course, the possibility of colonisation beyond the solar system. See, for example, Paul Davies' popular treatment of the topic, *The Last Three Minutes: Conjectures about the Ultimate Fate of the Universe* (New York: Phoenix, 2000), 139–46.
43. A key text to ponder here is: 'the concept emerges from understanding, not an isolated atom detached from all contexts, but precisely as part of a context, loaded with the relations that belong to it in virtue of a source which is equally the source of other concepts' (*Collected Works of Lonergan,* volume 2, *Verbum: Word and Idea in Aquinas,* edited by Frederick E Crowe and Robert M Doran (Toronto: University of Toronto Press, 1997), 238); hereafter *CWL* 2 *Verbum.*
44. *CWL* 18 *Phenomenology and Logic,* 357.
45. Our 'infinite craving' ('Finality, Love, Marriage', 49) is integral with the finality of the empirical residue. Its ongoing implementable discovery is a matter of the contemplation associated with the third form of generalised empirical method. This point raises a host of questions about completing Aquinas' work on 'natural resultance' (see *CWL* 2 *Verbum,* 147, note 236, but the entire text of Lonergan there is relevant). My concluding pages relate to this completion in the context of eschatology.
46. I only adverted to this twist in the meaning of *then* in September 2007, but it is an enlargement of a previous reflection on THEN, a lift of metaphysics beyond Ken and Zen; see Philip McShane, 'in Metaphysics THEN', *Cantower V* at <http://www.philipmcshane.ca/cantowers.html>. Accessed 30 May 2010.
47. McShane, *A Brief History of Tongue,* deals with the four presentations of this ABC exercise, including the verbatim version of the text from *Phenomenology and Logic,* in chapter 5. That chapter provides an existential reflection on the problem of *Insight*-in-hand raised in note 59 below, the problem of post-Hegelian style of living, thinking, talking. The four presentations of the ABC exercise are *CWL* 3 *Insight* 27 [51], 504 [527–528]; *CWL* 18 *Phenomenology and Logic,* 62; *Collected Works of Bernard Lonergan,* volume 5, *Understanding and Being,* edited by Elizabeth A Morelli and Mark

of it before, a question about the question, indeed (about)^3 the question.[48] The question? The quest? The 'subject as subject'?[49] Loneliness 'will be brought out into the open'.[50] But only if we recycle *Insight*, indeed in that recycling which is nature's and history's call, the surround of that page 250 just quoted.[51] We have, after all, had several generations of Lonergan studies to which the question, as thus posed, poised, is quite foreign: an evolutionary sport if it does occur, a random occurrence. 'If there are such random occurrences, then there is an instance of the merely empirical residue on the level of conjugate acts.'[52] It could 'occur systematically in virtue of the schemes, S_i', where the flexible circle of schemes are those that surround page 250 of *Method in Theology*. So, with luck—and it becomes alas a matter of luck—700 years later some Lonergan-like lady in the Orient may find Lonergan as Lonergan found Aquinas. This, surely, is no serious human control of emergent probability? What do you think? What is your stand?

There is, as my quotations about it in the previous paragraph hint, a richer and stranger view of the empirical residue in *Insight* than anyone has called attention to in fifty years.[53] It points to an embrace of the order of the universe in and with 'that order's dynamic joy and zeal'. It longs for a Tower identification of our 'Empirical Residence'[54] that would usher in the third stage of meaning, the second time of the temporal subject.

I had in mind to carry forward here towards an identification of functional specialisation and the regional culture of The Tower of Able

---

D Morelli (Toronto: University of Toronto Press, 1990), 57–58.

48. The peculiar terminology, (about)^3, was introduced in *Cantowers XXVIII –XXX* : it relates to the perspective on third-order consciousness that Lonergan reflected on in 1965 (see the quotation at note 16 above). A brief account is given in Philip McShane, *ChrISt in History*, chapter 2: 'The General Solution to Present Ineffective Fragmentation', section 2 at <http://www.philipmcshane.ca/christinhistory.html>. Accessed 30 May 2010.
49. *CWL* 18 *Phenomenology and Logic,* 226.
50. *Method,* 250.
51. I treat of history's call in chapter one of *Method in Theology: Revisions and Implementations.*
52. *CWL* 3 *Insight,* 464. I would note that the references in that section to the empirical residue need inclusion in the index.
53. The problem of energy's identification with the residue is another and more difficult matter. You may be consoled by the length of my own struggle there: a matter of forty years puttering. I treated the topic in the concluding section of *Cantower XXX*, 'The Conservation of Energy', and repeat that treatment in Chapter One, Part 3, of *Bernard Lonergan: His Life and Leading Ideas.*
54. The title and topic of *Cantower XXXII.*

as Lonergan's solution to 'the problem of history'. But it is a fresh topic, needing lengthy discussion. I have introduced it, all too briefly, elsewhere.[55] What is best is to conclude with that challenge of the next million years — why not start in this century? Placed in a more suggestive yet strangely precise context.

A first context, of course, is to be the positional context, transformed into a poisitional context[56] by a post-Hegelian existential collaboration[57] of Tower conversations that liberate Jack and Jill,[58] you and me, from the pressing and oppressive naïveté of lecture hall and handed book.[59] We live and move and have our being in the reality pointed to by the patterning of the given[60] given by the simple time-line. Does that time-line not merit the status of an added metagram?[61] But it is there already, raising deeper problems: for there is to be no last three minutes, nor mindless recyclings.[62] It is, or is to be, a heuristic but thoroughly mysterious[63] spear that pierces not the body of Jesus but the mind of Christ. That mind of Jesus, adequate

55. In the final chapter of *Bernard Lonergan: His Life and Leading Ideas.*
56. *Cantower IX*, 'Position, Poisition, Protopossession', is central to this discussion and problem.
57. I recall Morelli's challenge, mentioned in notes 24 and 34 above. See also his article, 'Obstacles to the Implementation of Lonergan's Solution to the Contemporary Crisis of Meaning', in *The Importance of Insight: Essays in Honor of Michael Vertin,* edited by John S Liptay and David S Liptay (Toronto: University of Toronto Press, 2007), 22–48, which relates to the issue of Protopossession referred to in the previous note.
58. Jack and Jill are characters in 'Cognitional Structure', *CWL* 4 *Collection*, 216, 219.
59. This, so to speak, places the problem literally and discomfortingly in your hand. Where is the book in your hand, and the print that surrounds, and is surrounded by, your curiosity? 'As the electron, so also the tree [and the book], in so far as it is considered a thing itself, [and nouns function that way] stands within a pattern of intelligible relations and offers no foothold for imagination' (*CWL* 3 *Insight*, 250 [275]).
60. *CWL* 3 *Insight*, 406–7.
61. I have made the case for metagrams regularly since the reflections on them in *Cantower XXXIII*, December 2004. The key appeal is to Lonergan's own appeal for adequate diagraming on page 80 of *De Constitutione Christi*, now available in English and Latin as *Collected Works of Bernard Lonergan*, volume 7, *The Ontological and the Psychological Constitution of Christ*, translated by Michael G Shields (Toronto: University of Toronto Press, 2002) 150, 151. A brief consideration of the need for such control is in my 'Obstacles to Metaphysical Control', in *Method: Journal of Lonergan Studies* 23 (2005): 187–95.
62. See, for example, *The Last Three Minutes*, the last two chapters.
63. The thorough mysteriousness is not, however, diffuse, in a fully explanatory context. See thesis 5 of Lonergan's Doctrinal Work, *De Deo Trino I*, on the Trinity. Add the context of the first section of *Insight* Chapter 17.

in its pilgrim content for the befriending of you and me,[64] is the central meaning of that graced dynamic content,[65] but the dynamic must grip, be gripped and clasped,[66] by the glorious everlasting incompleteness[67] of that Jesus-minding, to which we are called, cosmic-cauled.[68] The Eschaton is a state of Infinite Surprise[69] in which all[70] instances[71] of the empirical residue are wafted into a Trinitarian spiral.[72]

64. Relevant here are Lonergan's theses in *The Incarnate Word* on the knowledge and care of the pilgrim Jesus. The incompleteness of Jesus' comprehension of the divine essence is a general theorem of Aquinas regarding human minding's relation to the divine essence. He did not exploit this perspective in treating of eschatology. See also note 45 above.
65. The centrality of the secondary esse, creation's glorious participation in the Divine Speaker's Relating, is the focus of Philip McShane, 'Grace: The Final Frontier', chapter 7: *The Redress of Poise*, 107–120 at <www.philipmcshane.ca/redress.pdf>. Accessed 30 May 2010.
66. I recall here my reach for contemporary names for the triplicity of the divine mystery in *Joistings 23*, 'Teaching, Preaching and Cherishing the Triune God': *Speak, Spoke, Clasp*.
67. We need to think here of theorems of incompleteness both in the zone of the empirical residue and in the reach of finite mind for the complexly-infinite divine essence. *Lonergan's Standard Model of Effective Global Inquiry* has incompleteness as a key topic.
68. 'Skin within are molecules of cos mi c all, cauled, calling' (McShane, *Lack in the Beingstalk*, 66). To this add the context of note 40 above. The meaning and significance of *anastomosis* is raised also in on page 183, note 73.
69. The phrase 'Infinite Surprise' concludes 'Being and Loneliness', the Epilogue to Philip McShane, *Wealth of Self and Wealth of Nations: Axis of the Great Ascent*, at <http://www.philipmcshane.ca/books.html>. Accessed 30 May 2010. However, the meaning is altogether more complex now. One moves in that direction by following up analogies with the various infinities associated with the empirical residue.
70. 'All' raises Origen's question of inclusivity freshly, and grace's effectiveness in an open eschatology.
71. This is a large and complex question, ranging, in Thomas' early efforts, from growing toe-nails on resurrected bodies to sexual activities. But the deeper issue is the possibility of a type of Eucharistic supernaturality in which acts of lower beings are gloriously lifted beyond substantiality and sustained, in the infinite surprise, through Divine Incarnational causality.
72. The context is Lonergan's Systematics of the Trinity, especially the discussions of circumincession and its finite imitations.

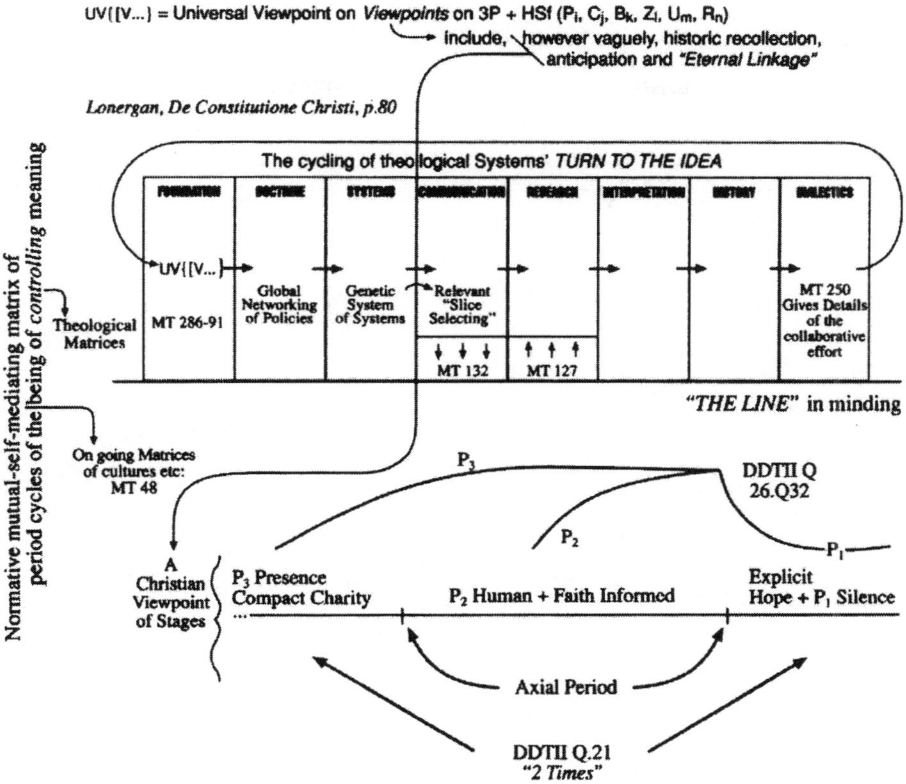

MT = B. Lonergan, *Method in Theology* 1972
DDTII = B. Lonergan, *De Deo Trino II* 1964

3P = The TryPty Divinity of Understanding,

Creator { P1 = Speaker = Attractor
P2 = Spokener = Informer
P3 = Listener = Gift

W3

ADDENDUM

Placing and replacing *Insight* after fifty years: a case of three interlocked primers

Possible and probably mutual self-mediations of present global culture and Lonergan's three priming communities grounded in [1] *Method in Theology* (1972); [2] *Insight* (1957); [3] *Circulation Analysis* (1944). Strategic minimalisms.

[1] Lonergan as foster-father to history's mothering of functional collaboration (*Method, Minding, Meaning*, University of Texas Press, 2008, chapters 1, 6): Plato's Athenian reach, Thomas' *Quaestio Prima* of the *Summa Theologica* and the issue of the efficient beauty of metaphysics (Lonergan Archives, batch 5 section 7; *Topics in Education*, 160, line 16, and *Lonergan's Standard Model of Effective Global Inquiry)*. Minimalist beginnings in apparently isolated disciplines: Physics as lead instrument of orchestra, and a fruitful digression on functional research. [See McShane, 'The Elevating of Insight: Space-Time as Paradigm Problem', in *Method Journal*, 19 (2001)]. Educational psychology as zone of vulnerability in [2]; economics' vulnerable zones for [3].

[2] A minimalist effective strategy for *Insight* (See *A Second Collection*, 222 top, and *Method in Theology*, last sentence of note on page 336). A focus on school texts, grades 11 and 12, and first year university texts. Functional researchers interlocking efforts (2011; 2111, as reflected on in *Lonergan's Standard Model*): see 'Stray Points' below, especially (3) re ethos.

[3] The narrower strategy of interlocking texts on economics for Grade 12. See 'Grade Twelve Economics: A Common Quest Manifesto' (Prehumous 1 on Website). The minimalism here of two circuits of analysis and of present descriptive weakness of texts and policies (*For a New Political Economic*, chapter 1, and *The Systematics of the Trinity*, end section, on explanatory heuristics needed in beginnings of science). Details in Prehumous 1.

Some Stray Points:

(1) The need for an elementary metagramic control of metaphysics (see 'Metaphysical Control of Meaning', *Method: Journal of Lonergan Studies* 23, 2005 and Appendix A of *Method, Molecules and Meaning* [to appear on the website as Prehumous 2: <http://www.philipmcshane.ca/prehumous.html>]. Parallel with chemistry).

(2) The cyclic horizon shifting as ongoing genesis, total ('conceptualization . . . as system . . . context' (*Verbum*, 238)), as well as complexly and

geographically genetic (Doran's pointers of *What is Systematic Theology?* within the larger functional, global and foundationless cycle-system).

(3) The practical genesis of the mutual self-mediative communities:

Detailed efforts are to emerge eg my own re Australia, Korea, etc, as compactly expressed in the thirteen *Eldorede.* It seems to me that the problem here is one of *ethos* and group-commitment eg to Lonergan's dedication to bring forth a democratic and enlightened political economy. We need pragmatic outreach to those in our circle of teaching friends, teenagers, etc etc, in the mood of an 'aesthetic apprehension of the group's origin and story . . . operative . . . especially in a crisis' (*Topics in Education*, 230).

(4) The long axial road to the mature second-stage meaning of Conversion to Word, the Divine Explanation (an embracing': see (*Insight*, 417 [442], 514 [537], 699 [721-2]; W3 and W5).

Chapter 10

Lonergan's Economic Theory: A Template which Challenges Current Social and Economic Research

Sean McNelis

Introduction

Lonergan's heuristic anticipates the understood as a complex ecology of schemes of recurrence. Such a heuristic also underpins his understanding of society as a complex ecology of technological, economic, political and cultural schemes of recurrence.

Lonergan's economics provides a template, an example of how we can shift from a common sense understanding of our society to a theoretical understanding. To understand our society is to understand both the systematic elements of these schemes of recurrence (through classical method) and the non-systematic elements of these schemes of recurrence (through statistical method), their complex inter-relationships and their development. Implementation of social and economic policy through which progress will be realised requires an integration of the ethic operative in various schemes of recurrence.

A common sense understanding of economics does not distinguish between technological, economic, political and cultural schemes of recurrence. Rather, it deals with these schemes in an undifferentiated way. Lonergan, on the other hand, in his 'pure' analysis of the exchange economy, distinguishes between economic and political schemes of recurrence and in so doing discovers the ethic immanent in economics.

I work in the field of housing studies. As a housing researcher, I am particularly interested in solving problems, many of which appear intractable. This is often attributed to the parameters for problem-solving set by those in power or by the powerlessness of those affected. But there is, I believe, a further issue: the problem is often not properly understood. Herein lies my interest in Lonergan's writings: understanding an issue properly as the basis for implementing sound changes in policy and practices.

Let me begin by posing a problem—one which I will come back to later in this paper.

In Australia most people live in a household which owns or is in the process of purchasing its own house. No doubt you have seen the headlines about current problems in housing affordability due to high house prices and increasing interest rates. But we also have a small but very important social housing sector—public housing and community housing.[1]

There is and always has been since public housing first began in the late 1930s a problem with public housing rents. The current problem—a problem which has recurred many times in the past seven decades—is that public housing providers are no longer financially viable (primarily because they have increasingly targeted households on lower incomes). So the pressure is on once again to establish a new method of determining rents, one which will increase rental revenue for public housing providers. One possible consequence of this strategy is that rents will be increased for those who are already in poverty. So what do we do? Can we implement a new method of determining rents which will achieve both increased rental revenue for public housing providers (and ensure their financial viability) and, at the same time, ensure that rents are affordable?

The usual mode of social research aims to find some way through this issue that will provide financial viability for public housing providers and housing affordability for public tenants. The aim of the research is often about trying to find a way in which to make trade-offs acceptable, about finding a way in which the interests of both parties can be achieved or in which the interests of one party can be achieved without upsetting the other party too much. The primary context here is political. But if we are to work out a longer-term solution to problems such as this, then we need to get beyond this context to an understanding of what is happening and

1. The term social housing is used for forms of rental housing which are financed, owned and managed in ways that ensure this housing meets social objectives and social obligations. In Australia, public housing which is owned and managed by a state government is the predominant form of social housing. Other forms, such as community housing and local government housing, are growing. In many overseas countries, 'council' housing or housing owned and managed by not-for-profit organisations are the predominant forms of social housing. See Sean McNelis, *Social Housing: a Future Direction for Housing* (Melbourne, Victorian Council of Social Service 1992).

address the root of the problem. And the root of the problem is not simply one of self-interest or greed; and the solution, a call for restraint and care for the disadvantaged and abused in our society.

So, you will note an oddity about this paper. Most, if not all, the papers in this collection have discussed some aspect of Lonergan's work in the context of philosophy and theology. The interest behind this paper is in reaching an understanding of social and economic problems and in implementing new practices which address these problems. This title of this paper points to Lonergan's economics. I am certainly no economist but do have a passable understanding of how social housing works in Australia. I suspect that the importance of Lonergan's very limited economic writings lies not simply in his economic theory but in the example he has provided as to what needs to be done in the social sciences more broadly.

First, I will outline briefly Lonergan's notion of a scheme of recurrence.

Second, I will note some important aspects of Lonergan's economics which are relevant to social and economic research.

Third, by using the problem of financial viability for public housing as summarily outlined above, I will illustrate Lonergan's heuristic in the social sciences.

Finally, I will make some concluding comments drawing out the challenges posed by Lonergan's heuristic to current social and economic research.

Lonergan's heuristic—a scheme of recurrence

Insight is a discovery, 'an "internal" psychological event in which something *new* becomes psychologically present.'[2] Lonergan's book *Insight* is a study of the different types of insight or understanding. In its classical form, an 'insight grasps a relation or set of relations' between elements; this is a grasp of what is essential and excludes what is incidental.[3] In its statistical form, insight grasps that this relationship will only occur under certain conditions, that the relationship between these conditions and the

2. Kenneth R Melchin, *History, Ethics, and Emergent Probability: Ethics, Society, and History in the Work of Bernard Lonergan*, second edition (Ottawa: Lonergan Web Site, 1999), 63.
3. Melchin, *History, Ethics, and Emergent Probability*, 63. Also see *Collected Works of Bernard Lonergan,* volume 3, *Insight: A Study of Human Understanding*, edited by Frederick E Crowe and Robert M Doran (Toronto: University of Toronto Press, 1992), 36, 57–70; hereafter *CWL* 3 *Insight.*

set of relations is random, not systematic, and that there is a probability of these conditions occurring.[4]

Lonergan then goes on to develop the notion of a scheme of recurrence, 'a series of events that occur in a specific pattern or order' where this pattern or order coils around in a circle and recurs over and over again.[5] In this series of events, the occurrence of one event fulfils the conditions for the occurrence of the next event, with the last in the series fulfilling the conditions for the occurrence of the first. It is from the integration of classic insight that grasps this recurring scheme, and statistical insight that grasps how often the conditions are actually present for the scheme to function, that Lonergan develops the notion of emergent probability.[6]

> Emergent probability would understand world processes in terms of conditioned series of schemes of recurrence that emerge, continue functioning and disappear in accordance with successive schedules of probability. And it is the acts of intelligence which grasp the absence of system in the coincidental manifold of laws operative in the environment, on the one hand, and the operation of system linking the events of the scheme and explaining its recurrence, on the other hand, which distinguish the explanatory structure of this account.[7]

But there is one particular aspect of the notion of a scheme of recurrence that I wish to point to. It is not just a matter of one scheme of recurrence, but rather sets of schemes of recurrence that are structured in a particular way. I point to two examples of this in *Insight*.

Insight is concerned with elaborating the scheme of recurrence that constitutes knowing and doing. This scheme is constituted by a series of sub-schemes: the sub-scheme of experience, the sub-scheme of understanding, the sub-scheme of judgment and the sub-scheme of making decisions. (In turn, each of these sub-schemes is itself constituted by a further series of schemes of recurrence.) Each of these sub-schemes contributes something to the process of knowing and doing and, in so doing, those activities which constitute knowing and doing are distinguished

4. Melchin, *History, Ethics and Emergent Probability*, 64ff. See also *CWL* 3 *Insight*, 76–81.
5. Melchin, *History, Ethics and Emergent Probability*, 105. See also *CWL* 3 *Insight*, 141–43.
6. *CWL* 3 *Insight*, 144–48.
7. Melchin, *History, Ethics and Emergent Probability*, 108; emphasis mine.

from those activities which do not, which are coincidental to the process and which inhibit or undermine that process. The success of the higher scheme of knowing and doing depends upon the successful achievement of each of the sub-schemes. These sub-schemes of experience, understanding, judgment and decision-making are structured in such a way that the sub-schemes of understanding sublate those of experience, those of judgment sublate those of understanding and those of decision-making sublate those of judgment. In using that word 'sublate', I am noting two things. First, the schemes that are sublated continue to have their own intelligibility or autonomy, and this sublation does not destroy this intelligibility and autonomy. Second, the higher scheme integrates these lower autonomous schemes and goes beyond them.[8]

A second example is the way in which Lonergan uses the scheme of recurrence to distinguish the different levels of science: physics, chemistry, biology and psychology:[9]

> If the non-systematic exists on the level of physics, then on that level there are coincidental manifolds that can be systematised by a higher chemical level without violating any physical law. If the non-systematic exists on the level of chemistry, then on that level there are coincidental manifolds that can be systematised by a higher biological level without violating any chemical law . . .[10]

Again the relationship between the different schemes is one of sublation. At each level, a range of schemes and sub-schemes operates and the higher schemes sublate the lower. Each science has its own autonomy, its own schemes, its own purpose. The higher science systematises what is non-systematic on the prior level. Different sciences seek to understand different types of schemes of recurrence. And particular types of such schemes operate within an entity. Thus, as illustrated in Figure 1, they provide a structured heuristic for understanding human living. A human being is

8. *CWL* 3 *Insight,* 291–92; Bernard JF Lonergan, 'Cognitional Structure', in *Collected Works of Bernard Lonergan,* volume 4, *Collection,* edited by Frederick E Crowe and Robert M Doran (Toronto: University of Toronto Press, 1988), 205–21; Lonergan, *Method,* 316.
9. *CWL* 3 *Insight,* 229–30, 280–83.
10. *CWL* 3 *Insight,* 229–30.

constituted by a series of schemes of recurrence at different levels: physical, chemical, biological, psychological, intellectual and being-in-love.[11]

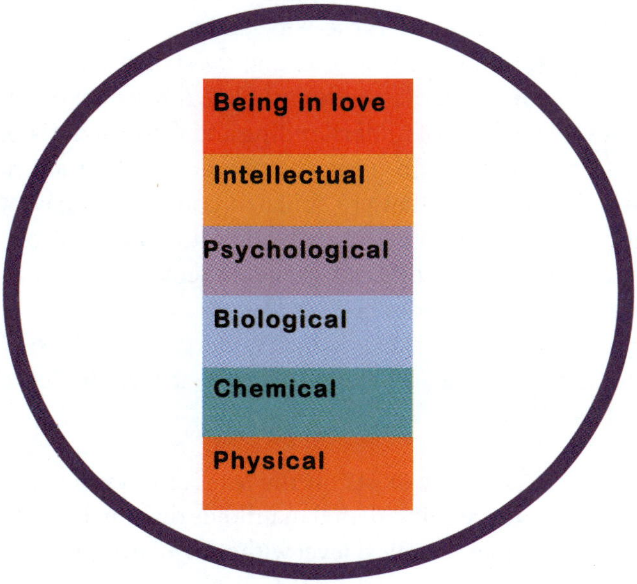

Figure 1: A structured heuristic for understanding human living

Schemes of recurrence not only distinguish different levels of science but also operate within human activities:

> Human actions are recurrent; their recurrence is regular; and the regularity is the functioning of a scheme, of a patterned set of relations that yields conclusions of the type: If an X occurs, then an X will recur . . . Clearly, schemes of recurrence exist and function. No less clearly, their functioning is not inevitable.[12]

But how are we to understand these human schemes of recurrence? Among the manifold of human activities, some, if not most, human actions are recurrent and regular. Now we could group these activities according to some characteristic of the person undertaking them—workers

11. *CWL* 3 *Insight*, 291–92, 494–504.
12. *CWL* 3 *Insight*, 235.

or businessmen, employed or unemployed, consumers or producers, happy, sad, angry, psychotic. Alternatively, we could group them according to the function of different types of activities. We can then proceed to look for patterns within these groups of activities, patterns that link groups of activities together, patterns that are recurring, patterns and processes that link with other patterns and processes. Some groups of activities operate in series. Some groups of activities control or produce other activities. In this way, we co-operate with one another so that one set of activities by one person or group relate to and add to the activities of another set.[13]

So rather than focusing on the participants and their particular characteristics,[14] Lonergan's heuristic focuses on their activities and the function of these activities. To understand a human scheme of recurrence is to grasp the functional relationship between a whole series of activities or processes. In grasping this relationship we are grasping the function of each type of activity or process within the whole scheme. The scheme is constituted by many linked activities or processes, but what unifies the scheme is its meaning or its internal purpose. The scheme, then, consists of two elements: a series of activities or processes; and a particular purpose which is commensurate with the scheme or, in other words, this purpose is internal to the processes and unifies it.[15] Individual schemes are interlinked with other schemes.

Now, *Insight* illustrates this notion of a scheme of recurrence with many examples from mathematics and physics, Lonergan's understated sublation of Hobbes, Marx and Freud in those deceptively simple but unavoidably short chapters 6 and 7. It seems to me, however, that Lonergan's economics presents us with one of the prime illustrations of these notions

13. Melchin, *History, Ethics and Emergent Probability*, 203.
14. In the common sense world, this is very important if we are to respond immediately to events and situations. In the social sciences, this common sense view emerges in analyses where the individual (as subject) is juxtaposed against the community (as object). See for example Andrew Sayer, *Method in Social Science: A Realist Approach*, second edition (London: Routledge, 1992). Gibson Winter, *Elements for a Social Ethic: Scientific and Ethical Perspectives on Social Process* (New York: Macmillan, 1966), provides an alternative view in his analysis of three different approaches (behaviourist, functionalist and voluntarist) to the human sciences in the USA in the 1950s. He shows how these approaches highlight different types of schemes of recurrence within human activities. Winter's analysis seeks to integrate these different approaches by showing how these schemes operate at different levels, with the higher schemes sublating the lower schemes.
15. Kenneth R Melchin, *Living with Other People: An Introduction to Christian Ethics Based on Bernard Lonergan* (Ottawa: Novalis, 1998), 53ff.

within the context of a human empirical science. Without some sense of the notion of a scheme of recurrence, it is very difficult to read Lonergan's economics.

Lonergan's economics

So what was Lonergan up to in his economics? Here is not the place to go into the complexities of Lonergan's economics and his achievement in this area.[16] Lonergan's economics is the end result of a long process of dialectical analysis, an integration of past achievements into something radically new. We can only understand and appreciate Lonergan's achievement if we understand what of this past is being integrated and how it is being integrated. It is this that he is at pains to point out in the very first chapter of *For a New Political Economy (*henceforth *FNPE);* he says:

> The problem, I think, is clear. We cannot rely on the old political economy: it was democratic but has been found wrong. We cannot rely on the new economics: it is accurate but it can solve real problems only by eliminating democracy. What is needed is a new political economy that is free from the mistakes of the old, a democratic economics that can issue practical imperatives to plain men.[17]

And later he adds, 'It is, I believe, a scientific generalisation of the old political economy and of modern economics that will yield the new political economy which we need.[18]

The following indicates five unique aspects of Lonergan's economics.

16. Frederick G Lawrence, 'Editor's Introduction', in *Collected Works of Bernard Lonergan,* volume 15, *Macroeconomic Dynamics: An Essay in Circulation Analysis,* edited by Frederick G Lawrence, Patrick H Byrne, and Charles Hefling (Toronto: Toronto University Press, 1999), xxv–lxxii (hereafter, *CWL* 15 *Macroeconomic Dynamics*). See also Philip McShane, *Pastkeynes Pastmodern Economics: A Fresh Pragmatism* (Halifax, Nova Scotia: Axial Press, 2002).
17. Bernard JF Lonergan, *Collected Works of Bernard Lonergan,* volume 21, *For a New Political Economy,* edited by Philip McShane (Toronto: University of Toronto Press, 1998). 5 (hereafter, *CWL* 21 *New Political Economy*).
18. *CWL* 21 *New Political Economy,* 7.

(1) Distinguishing technology, economics and politics

A first difference between current economic theory and Lonergan's theory is that Lonergan distinguishes between technology, economics and politics according to their particular purpose.[19] Indeed technology, economics and politics form an ordered hierarchy:

> . . . technology, which is the society's concrete possibility for transforming the potentialities of nature into the standard of living, is subordinate to economy, which is the process for producing and distributing the best possible standard of living; and economy is subordinated to a political order embodying a democratic, free-enterprise economy.[20]

By distinguishing between economics and politics, Lonergan in his economic analysis initially uncouples economic processes from politics and the exercise of power. So just as biology has its own autonomy as a science, so too does economics. Technology is concerned with our control over nature; economics is concerned with the transformation of natural materials into a standard of living; politics is concerned with the ways in which we collectively reach agreement about who is to do what to achieve what. In this way, Lonergan separates out an analysis of structures of technology, economics and politics and their respective schemes of recurrence and then deals with their inter-relationships.

A common sense understanding of economics does not distinguish between technological, economic, political and cultural schemes of recurrence. Rather, it deals with these schemes in an undifferentiated way. Subsequently, today we find that economics dominates politics, to the detriment of both.

(2) Economic processes not human motivations

A second difference from traditional economics is that Lonergan uncouples economic processes from human psychology, or in other words, from human motivations such as self-interest, perceived by current economics as the basic driving force of our economies. As he writes in FNPE:

---

19. *CWL* 3 *Insight*, 232–39. See also Lawrence, 'Editor's Introduction,' xxxi–xxxii.
20. Lawrence, 'Editor's Introduction,' xxxi.

> Our inquiry differs radically from traditional economics, in which the ultimate premises are not production and exchange but rather exchange and self-interest, or later, exchange and a vaguely defined psychological situation. Our aim is to prescind from human psychology that, in the first place, we may define the objective situation with which man has to deal, and, in the second place, define the psychological attitude that has to be adopted if man is to deal successfully with economic problems. Thus something of a Copernican revolution is attempted: instead of taking man as he is or as he may be thought to be and from that deducting what economic phenomena are going to be, we take the exchange process in its greatest generality and attempt to deduce the human adaptations necessary for survival.[21]

So Lonergan distinguishes between the activities that constitute an economy and the motivations whereby persons and organisations participate in that economy. In relation to the economy, the motivations such as self-interest provide the conditions that determine whether particular economic processes will actually operate. They are the random events which are to be understood through statistical method rather than classical method. For example, the motivations of investors tell us nothing about how the private rental market works, but they do tell us under what circumstances investors will actually participate in the processes that constitute the private rental market; or again, the many and varied motivations of public transport users are not relevant to understanding how the public transport system works, but they are important to that system actually working.[22]

---

21. *CWL* 21 *New Political Economy*, 42–43.
22. Note that the economic scheme is distinguished from other schemes, including those which constitute the motivations of investors, consumers, businesses and government. It seems to me that this confusion between the systematic (the scheme of recurrence) and the coincidental or random (such as motivations in relation to the economic scheme of recurrence) is a basic confusion within current social and economic research. Renowned British sociologist, Anthony Giddens, attempts to address this ongoing problem with social sciences in his theory of structuration which distinguishes between structure and agency. For example, see A Giddens, *Central Problems in Social Theory: Action, Structure and Contradiction in Social Analysis* (London: Macmillan, 1979).

(3) Economics as functional relations

A third difference, one to which we have already alluded, is that Lonergan's economics focuses on groups of activities and their functional relationships within an economy.

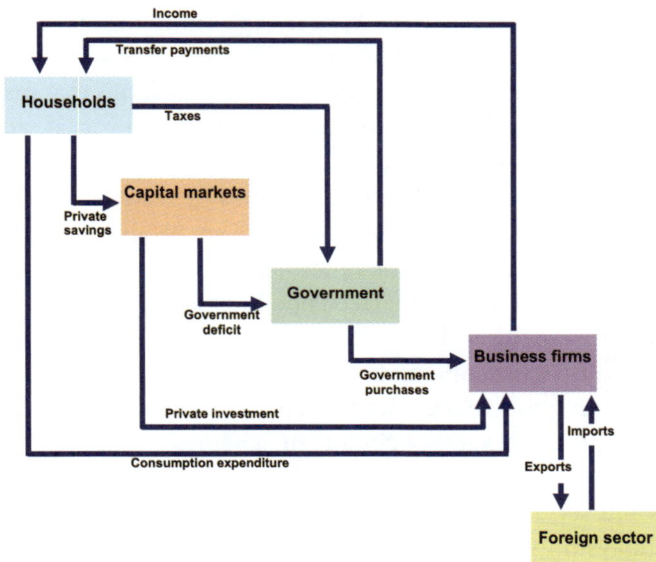

Figure 2: Financial flows between entities (standard economics)

In contrast, as illustrated in Figure 2, current macroeconomic theory focuses on activities as they emanate from entities such as households, firms and government and the flow of funds between these entities. It seeks explanations as to why these entities operate in the way they do.

Lonergan, however, focuses on the function of particular activities rather than the entities that undertake these activities. It is this clear focus on functional relationships that differentiates Lonergan's economics analysis from others. It is disconcerting because it moves away from those institutions we deal with on a day-to-day basis; it shifts the focus away from government, from firms and from households. And, after all, if we are concerned with the business of the world, we spend most of our lives trying to manage/deal with people, corporations, governments and other institutions which are 'whole bodies' over against us—and sometimes with us.

Lonergan begins his economic analysis by focusing on the process of production—not the prices of goods and services. He distinguishes between two circuits of production, each with a different function within the economy. The basic circuit produces goods and services which enter into our standard of living, for example, food, shelter, clothing, cars and bikes, and amusements such as TV, radio and computers.[23] A second circuit, the surplus circuit, produces goods and services which support or indeed accelerate the basic circuit, for example, machines that make shoes and shirts, computers which control the production process, and trucks which deliver machines.

Each of these circuits consists of schemes of recurrence: on the one hand, the processes whereby shoes and shirts are produced and enter into our standard of living and on the other hand, the processes whereby machines are built, maintained, replaced and upgraded.

Once he distinguishes these two circuits of production, Lonergan then goes on to examine the concomitant financial flows as illustrated in Figure 2. Corresponding to the schemes which produce goods and services are the flows of money, monetary circuits or schemes. So in the basic circuit there is a flow of funds from the basic demand function as expenditure on goods and services, and the flow of funds from the basic supply function as outlays on wages and profits (WP), as well as on the acquisition, maintenance and replacement of machinery and equipment (MR). In the surplus circuit there is a similar flow of funds from the surplus demand function as expenditure on the acquisition, maintenance and replacement of machinery and equipment (MR), the flow of funds from the surplus supply function as outlays on wages and profits (WP), as well as on the goods and services required to produce machinery and equipment.

The two circuits of production are connected in two ways (or crossovers): some outlays of the basic supply function are for the acquisition of new machinery and for its maintenance and replacement from the surplus circuit; some outlays of the surplus supply function are for wages and profits which add to the basic demand function in the basic circuit.

In addition to the two circuits of production, Lonergan postulates a large and complex function—the distributive function—through which second-hand goods such as land and shares are traded, loans are raised and income is redistributed via governments. In this view, goods and ser-

23. An important point to note here is that not all goods and services of a particular type have a function in relation to our standard of living. Some will be used within the second circuit of production to produce equipment and machinery.

vices have a function in relation to the standard of living (the basic circuit of production) or in relation to the processes which accelerate the production of these goods and services (the surplus circuit of production). It is this distinction in function which transforms Lonergan's economics from a static view of economics (which characterises current economic theories) to a dynamic view. By functionally separating out those processes which accelerate the production of goods and services and their transformation over time, Lonergan's dynamic analysis explains how economies evolve and develop over time.

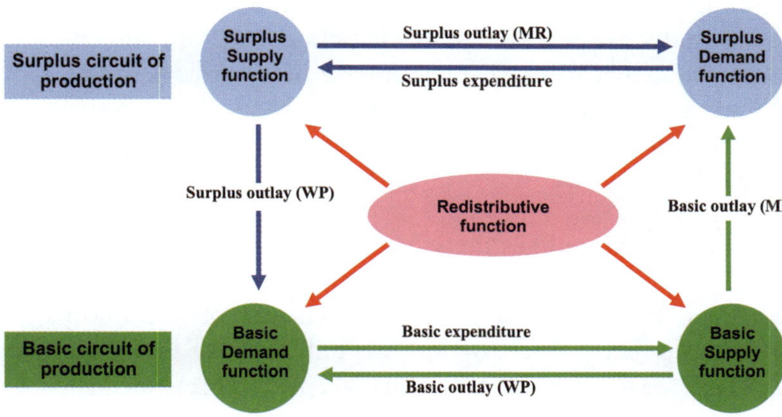

Figure 3: Financial flows by function

Moreover, this functional analysis allows Lonergan to go on and propose different economic phases and to explain some contemporary economic problems such as cyclical recessions and depressions. But what I want to note in this simplistic presentation of Lonergan's starting point in macroeconomics is the way in which different schemes of recurrence are distinguished: two different schemes of production, basic and surplus which are related to one another through some basic outlays on the one hand and some surplus outlays on the other; two corresponding schemes of financial flows; a range of schemes within the redistributive function which are related to the two different schemes of production, in specific ways.

(4) Normativity of schemes of recurrence

Not only does Lonergan uncouple economic processes from human psychology and from politics, but a fourth difference is the way in which he discerns an ethic within these economic processes. For instance, in his introduction to *Macroeconomic Dynamics: An Essay in Circulation Analysis*, he notes:

> Our title regards not only macroeconomics but also the dialectic of history. By dialectic I understand a process that is at once concrete, dynamic and contradictory. The concrete and dynamic component is supplied by human individuals . . . This dialectic connects immediately with the macroeconomic analysis. There, there are discernible criteria immanent in the productive process. But the dialectic arises from the contradiction that arises when the criteria are adverted to or not, understood or not, affirmed or denied, observed responsibly or disregarded, by a community of love or a community of egoists.[24]

In *Insight* Lonergan outlines the schemes of recurrence concerned with knowing and doing—the schemes of experience, the schemes of understanding, the schemes of judgment, the schemes of decision-making. Knowing is a scheme of recurrence. It is only through this scheme that we can know something (insofar as this scheme has been adequately understood and articulated). The scheme is not only recurrent but it is also normative. The purpose of the scheme is to know.

In *Method*, these schemes of knowing and doing become the foundation for the schemes of functional specialisation. At the outset Lonergan defines method as 'a *normative* pattern of recurrent and related operations yielding cumulative and progressive results.'[25] The purpose of the schemes of functional specialisation is the yielding of cumulative and progressive results. It is only through the schemes of functional specialisation as outlined in *Method* that this purpose will be achieved (insofar as *Method* is an adequate understanding and articulation of these schemes).

Similarly, the schemes of recurrence that are economic processes have a purpose. If we want to produce something, then this production consists of a number of schemes of recurrence. Each scheme has an ethic, an internal purpose. Unless each scheme of recurrence occurs, then this internal purpose will not be achieved. If we want the economy to work through its

24. *CWL 15 Macroeconomic Dynamics*, 4–5; emphasis mine.
25. Lonergan, *Method*, 4; emphasis mine.

various phases and continually add to our standard of living, then immanent within that is an ethic.

Not only is there an ethic of production of goods and services, an ethic of circulation of money (of maintaining a balance between the crossovers between the two circuits of production), an ethic of economic transformation (of the transition between phases in the economy), there is also an ethic or purpose to the economy as whole. What, then, is the ethic or purpose of an economy as a whole? Surprisingly, Lonergan proposes that the purpose is 'leisure'.[26] An economy consists not simply of the processes of production whereby goods and services enter into our standard of living. The transformation of these processes and the economy make these processes of production more efficient, so that we have more leisure—not as we might understand leisure today—but leisure as personal, social and cultural development. Contrary to what many economists would have us believe, the purpose of business is not to make profits, though that may be the motivation of investors and businesses, rather it is to produce goods and services that enter into our standard of living. The purpose of the economy as a whole is not to make profits. Rather, it is leisure. It is for this purpose that that various schemes of recurrence are constituted as the economy.

(5) Democracy not central planning

If you remember an earlier quote, Lonergan pointed to one of the basic dilemmas in economic policy, indeed in any policy:

> The problem, I think, is clear. We cannot rely on the old political economy: it was democratic but has been found wrong. We cannot rely on the new economics: it is accurate but it can solve real problems only by eliminating democracy. What is needed is a new political economy that is free from the mistakes of the old, a democratic economics that can issue practical imperatives to plain men.[27]

Most policy that stems from social and economic research is directed at our governments. They should do this or that. A fifth difference in Lonergan's economics is its foundation in liberty and democracy. Many dif-

26. *CWL* 21 *New Political Economy*, 20ff.
27. *CWL* 21 *New Political Economy*, 5.

ferent participants—consumers, businesses and government—operate in the economy. Each undertakes activities that play a particular role in the economy. The responsibility for what happens lies not simply with government but with a whole range of players.

Lonergan does not propose an unregulated economy, rather an economy which is regulated by all participants. His analysis of economic activities points to the role of the many participants in making an economy work. The task we face in making our economies serve their purpose, leisure, and higher political, cultural and religious goals is 'so vast that only the creative imagination of all individuals in all democracies will be able to construct at once the full conception and the full realisation of the new order.'[28]

An illustration: social housing rental systems

But what does all this mean to social and economic research? It seems to me that it is only in the struggle to implement Lonergan's heuristic that we can begin to understand and gradually develop an understanding of what it is all about.

The challenge of *Insight* is a challenge to implementation.[29]

So, let us go back to the problem I presented in the introduction: the problem of establishing a new way of determining rents which will not only ensure the financial viability of public housing providers but also rents which are affordable to public housing tenants. My search to understand this problem illustrates my attempt to implement Lonergan's heuristic of the scheme of recurrence. Among the multitude of problems that the world faces, this may seem a simple issue but, bearing in mind the wisdom of Descartes on page one of *Insight*, I hope it will serve to illustrate some of the different aspects of Lonergan's heuristic.

In doing this, I am confronted with a difficulty—I am presenting the results of some research and at the same time trying to convey something about the approach, the heuristic that underpins this research. So the following presents some complex material which is difficult even for those who are familiar with social housing finance. Hopefully, however, it will serve to indicate the general pointers to Lonergan's heuristic and the challenge it poses for current social and economic research.[30]

---

28. *CWL* 21 *New Political Economy*, 37.
29. *CWL* 3 *Insight*, 416, 581–82.
30. For a fuller outline of this complex material, see S McNelis and T Burke, *Rental Systems*

Rental systems in social housing: an introduction

The problem briefly outlined above can be tackled in various ways. We could examine the inherent conflict over rents between tenants and social housing providers, or what rents are charged and how they correlate with particular characteristics of tenants such as income and household type, or the discourses around rent, how rent emerged as an issue and its genealogy, or the role of government in setting rents. The particular issue I am going to explore is how rents are determined. This exploration is not limited to the experience of public housing providers in Australia, but also draws upon the experience of other forms of social housing in Australia as well as that of various forms of social housing overseas, particularly in New Zealand, the United Kingdom, Sweden, the Netherlands, the United States and Canada.

As a starting point we can describe rent as the payment made by a tenant to a landlord. We can understand it in the context of the relationship between a landlord and a tenant. Social housing providers can determine this rent in many different ways. Each way results in a different rent and thus has a different impact on the tenant. Some will result in a rent which is unaffordable, some will not. Some ways will influence the decisions a tenant makes about whether to stay in public housing or go elsewhere, whether to stay in the current dwelling or seek another dwelling in another place. On the other hand, from the perspective of the social housing provider, some ways will result in surpluses, others in financial ruin.

The determination of rent involves sets of routines or processes which regularly occur, are serially related and dependent upon one another.[31] These are regularly recurring schemes whereby particular things happen. They are co-operative schemes whereby one set of activities relate to and add to the activities of another set.[32]

---

in Australia and Overseas: Positioning Paper (Melbourne: Australian Housing and Urban Research Institute, 2004), available at <http://www.ahuri.edu.au/publications/download/50226_pp>. Accessed 25 June 2010 and, in particular, S McNelis, *Rental Systems in Australia and Overseas: Final Report* (Melbourne: Australian Housing and Urban Research Institute, 2006), available at <http://www.ahuri.edu.au/publications/download/50226_fr>. Accessed 25 June 2010.

31. See McNelis and Burke, *Rental Systems.*

32. Melchin, *History, Ethics and Emergent Probability*. Also Kenneth R Melchin, 'Exploring the Idea of Private Property: A Small Step Along the Road from Common Sense to Theory,' *Journal of Macrodynamic Analysis* 3 (2003): 287–301, available at <http://www.mun.ca/jmda/vol3/melchin.pdf>. Accessed 25 June 2010.

What rental system should we adopt in social housing? Will this system achieve affordability for the tenant? Will it achieve financial viability for the social housing provider?

Whatever way is adopted, the purpose of a rental system and the processes that constitute this system is to determine a rent. These processes with their unifying purpose constitute a rental system as a scheme of recurrence. The unresolved question is: which rental system, among the available or possible systems, should be adopted? This question shifts us to a new context.

Rent and ongoing costs

A starting point for this new context is the relationship between the rent revenue of social housing and the ongoing costs of social housing. In this new context, rent has to be determined in such a way that aggregate rent is sufficient to cover ongoing costs. As illustrated in Figure 4, the purpose of rent, as distinct from the purpose of a rental system, is to meet the ongoing costs of social housing. The purpose of rent sublates the purpose of a rental system: the rental system will determine rents in such a way that social housing providers can meet the ongoing costs of social housing.

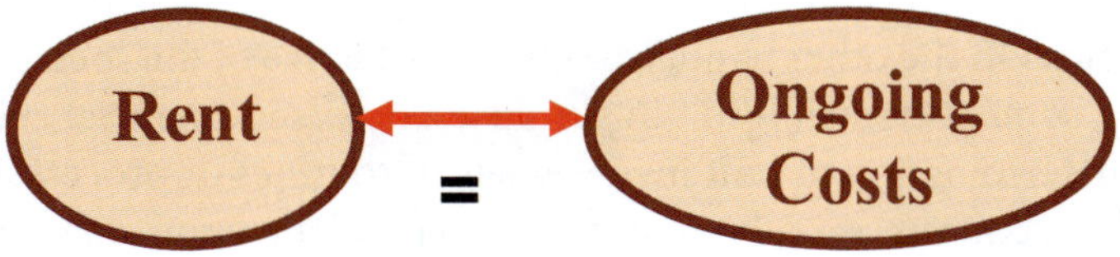

Figure 4: Rent and ongoing costs

Again, there are a series of unresolved questions: what are the ongoing costs which aggregate rents must meet? On what basis can rents be determined? This question shifts us to the broader context of the social housing finance system.

Rent within the social housing finance system

What we have proposed here is a functional relationship between the way in which rents are determined, aggregate rent and ongoing costs. The normative aspect of this relationship is that rents are determined in such a way that aggregate rent will meet the ongoing costs of providing social housing.

Just as 'insight' is placed in the larger context of knowing by relating it to experience and judgment, we can place this relationship between rent and ongoing costs in a larger context, the context of a social housing finance system. What function does a rental system play within a social housing finance system? We can seek to answer this question by relating rent to income and rent to the specific ongoing costs of social housing, as illustrated in Figure 5.

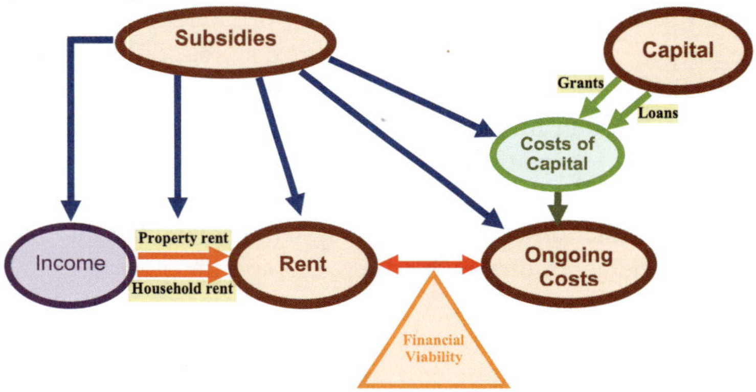

Figure 5: Social housing finance scheme

So, firstly, we can note the two different bases on which rent can be determined: by reference to the property or by reference to the household occupying the property. Whether one or the other operates depends upon the income arrangements and whether income is specifically supplemented for housing purposes. The way in which rent is determined will depend upon the income arrangements.

Secondly, we can note that the scheme of recurrence that determines rents intersects with the schemes of recurrence within ongoing costs. There are different types of costs with different schemes of recurrence: annual insurance payments, quarterly rates payments, irregular ad hoc repairs, regularly recurring payments for internal and external painting, for replacement of heaters and hot water services etc, the employment of staff to manage tenancies and to manage dwellings.

Most of these ongoing costs are pretty standard and regular. But one, the cost of capital, can vary significantly depending upon the capital arrangements used to acquire social housing. So capital sourced from (interest-free) grants will have a different impact on the rental system than capital raised through loans.

But there is a further element. Subsidies can be delivered in a variety of forms, and thus function differently within the overall social housing financial system. Subsidies can be general in nature, and tenants can determine the goods and services on which they are expended. They can be provided specifically to tenants for housing purposes only. They can be provided to social housing providers directly in lieu of or partly in lieu of rents paid by tenants, as assistance in meeting their ongoing costs, or specifically as assistance in meeting the costs of capital.

The purpose of the social housing finance system (and the recurrent processes that constitute it) is to maintain the financial viability of social housing. Without financial viability, social housing will be unable to continue. All the elements of the social housing finance system must be arranged in such a way that they achieve this purpose. So while different countries and different social housing systems have different combinations of these elements, they each achieve this specific purpose of financial viability.

While the purpose of a rental system is to determine rent in such a way that it meets the ongoing costs of social housing, it operates within the larger context of a social housing finance system. The role of a rental system and how rents are determined vary according to this context and its purpose of financial viability.

Rent within social housing

We have been talking of the role of a rental system within the context of a social housing finance system. But there is an even larger context within which new questions emerge about rental systems. The finance scheme is but one among a number of schemes that constitute social housing. Each of these schemes has its specific purpose.

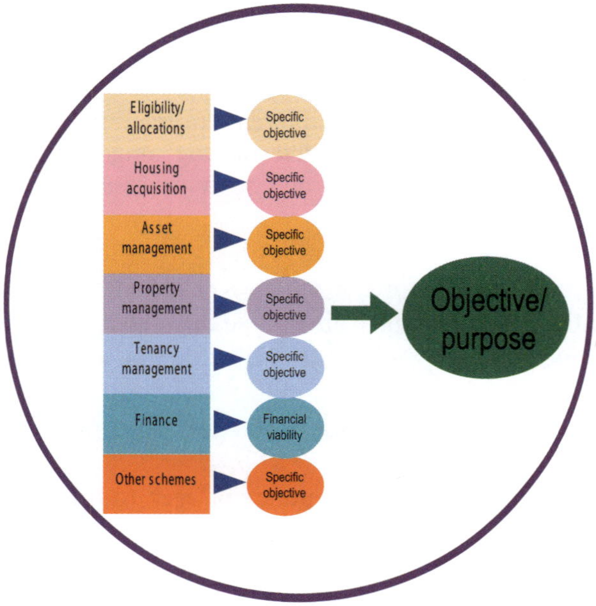

Figure 6: Schemes within social housing

As illustrated in Figure 6, among the possible schemes that constitute social housing we can distinguish:

- An *eligibility/allocations scheme* which relates specific characteristics of applicants with the processes for determining who is eligible for social housing, the processes for determining their priority and the processes by which dwellings are chosen by or allocated to applicants;
- A *housing acquisition scheme* which relates a standard of housing with the processes for raising of capital funds, the processes for determining these standards and the processes by which land and dwellings are acquired;
- An *asset management scheme* which relates a standard of housing with the processes for maintaining that standard, the processes for bringing dwellings up to that standard and the processes for deciding whether and when to upgrade, demolish or sell dwellings;
- A *property management scheme* which relates an ongoing standard of maintenance and repair of properties with the processes whereby they are maintained;

- A *tenancy management scheme* which relates management of tenancies with processes whereby tenants and staff can interact and whereby tenants' rights are ensured;
- A *finance scheme* which relates different transactions – capital and operating—with processes for determining ongoing costs, with processes for determining rents and with processes for allocating subsidies.

And no doubt there are other major schemes of recurrence, each constituted by particular processes which are unified through a specific purpose.

This new context raises questions as to the function of a rental system in relation to each of these schemes and to social housing as a whole. A central preceding question here concerns the overall purpose or objective of social housing.

When we develop social housing policy or seek to implement some social housing strategy, we presume some view of what social housing is about and what we are trying to achieve through it; we presume that social housing has some particular objective. If we ask a range of participants in social housing, 'What is the objective of social housing?', we receive a multitude of answers: some competing and contradictory, some which complement one another. These objectives emerge out of the immediate and practical interest of each of the stakeholders.

The common sense approach would list these objectives, distinguish between the various stakeholders, work out what is common to each stakeholder and then work out how the different objectives can be traded off.[33] In the common sense approach, what happens to social housing will depend upon the prevailing politics among the stakeholders.

But when we are speaking of the objective of social housing in a theoretical context, we are seeking an objective or purpose which constitutes the recurring schemes as a unity.

These schemes are applicable, in some way, to any type of housing, including private rental and owner-occupied housing. The question about the objective of social housing is one which is seeking to identify the dis-

33. G Bramley, *Public Sector Housing Rents and Subsidies: Alternative Approaches and Their Applications to Selected Localities*, Working Paper No 92 (Bristol: School for Advanced Urban Studies, University of Bristol, 1991); J Yates, 'Strategic Directions for Reforms of Public Housing Rent Policy: A Response to the Industry Commission's Report on Public Housing' (unpublished mimeo, c1994); S McNelis, *Social Housing: A Future Direction for Housing, Social Housing Project*, Paper No. 1 (Melbourne: Victorian Council of Social Service, 1992).

tinguishing characteristic of social housing, one which unifies these various schemes—bringing them together. Such an objective is not the objective or purpose of one of the sub-schemes, nor will it supersede or destroy these schemes and their particular purpose or objective; indeed, social housing depends upon their proper functioning if it is to achieve its objective. Such an objective will make sense of the schemes within social housing but will also make sense of social housing as one of the various ways in which our society ensures that families and individuals are housed.

In this larger social housing context, the way in which rent is determined is sublated by this objective. A rental system will not only determine a rent, not only determine a rent in such a way that aggregate rent will cover the ongoing costs of providing social housing, not only determine a rent in such a way as to maintain the financial viability of social housing, but it will also contribute to the achievement of the overall objective of social housing. It is here that the question about housing affordability emerges.[34]

What is important to note about this analysis is the transformation of the original problem in a new context. Previously, the issue for social housing providers is whether to trade off housing affordability for financial viability, that is, introduce a new rental system which would increase rental revenue but would, marginally for some, more for others, make social housing unaffordable. What emerges from this analysis where schemes of recurrence are built one upon another as the context expands is that there can be no trade-off between housing affordability and financial viability. Financial viability relates to the purpose of one particular scheme of recurrence within social housing—the social housing finance system. The achievement of financial viability is the specific objective of this scheme, and the achievement of this specific objective, as with the achievement of specific objectives in other schemes, is a precondition for the achievement of the overall objective of social housing. In short, if social housing is not financially viable, it just goes out of business. Housing affordability,

34. How housing affordability is related to the overall objective of social housing is a complex question. Currently most housing activists and academics regard affordability as the core objective of social housing. My view, however, is that the overall objective of social housing is 'to ensure that households have access to housing which is adequate and appropriate as a key component of an equitable standard of living'. Housing affordability is an indicator as to whether this objective is being achieved. See McNelis and Burke, *Rental Systems,* 64–71, for a discussion of this issue.

however, relates to the overall objective of social housing. If social housing does not achieve this objective, then it is no longer social housing.

Rental system and other internal and external schemes

A rental system not only operates within the context of the overall objective of social housing, it also operates within the context of a range of other internal schemes (as illustrated in Figure 7). Both the social housing financial system and these other internal schemes operate in the larger context of schemes external to social housing. These form a complex ecology of the schemes that operate both within and outside social housing. What is the relationship between the rental system and these internal and external schemes?

Figure indicates the specific points at which different aspects of the social housing finance system connect with other schemes and thus impact on how rents are determined within social housing.

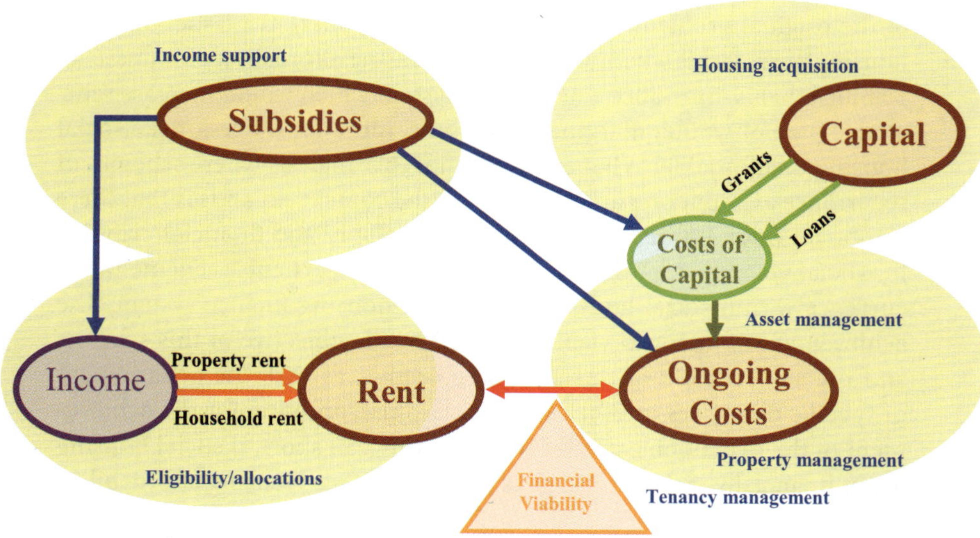

Figure 7: Finance and its relationship with internal and external schemes

So, through income, the rental system is related to the eligibility/allocations schemes.

Through ongoing costs, the rental system is related to tenancy management schemes, property management schemes and asset management schemes.

Through capital, the rental system is related to housing acquisition schemes.

Through subsidies, the rental system is related to income support schemes.

In turn, each of these internal schemes operates within the broader context of schemes external to social housing. For example, social housing providers purchase and construct dwellings within a broader housing market; they raise capital funds from financial institutions; they employ people etc.

Rather than a general reference to factors impacting on rents, this analysis pinpoints connections and the subsequent task of understanding the relationships.

We can go on … towards a theology of rental systems

The foregoing has sought to illustrate Lonergan's heuristic within social science through the development of a theory of social housing rental systems. In doing so, it has focused on the functional relationships between activities rather than the relationship between participants (tenants and social housing providers). The theory shifts from a concern about the random motivations and perspectives of participants to a concern to understand the role and the function of groups of activities in relation to one another. The theory has distinguished different levels of analysis rather than conflating them (a distinction akin to Lonergan's distinction between technology, economics and politics). It has highlighted the normativity immanent in the schemes of recurrence as well as the role of many different players. In doing this, it has outlined a series of contexts within which rental systems can be understood: within ongoing costs; within a social housing finance system; within social housing and within the production of housing. This series of contexts forms a structured complex ecology of schemes of recurrence. It is structured because the schemes of recurrence at the lower level are sublated by those at the higher. Yet, the success of these higher schemes depends upon the achievement of the lower schemes. The normativity of a rental system is also structured as different aspects of this normativity are operative at each level. It is a complex ecology of schemes as elements of one scheme interlock with other schemes.

This type of analysis of schemes with their constituent sub-schemes demands a very specific and detailed analysis of what is happening. It is simply not enough to note *that* different factors affect the elements of an analysis. What is demanded is an understanding of the specific relationship between the elements, *how* different factors affect an element and through what mechanism.

But we could go on and speculate about our understanding of social housing rental systems within even broader contexts: within the economics of housing, the politics of rental systems, the culture of rental systems . . . even towards a theology of rental systems. We can ask about their significance within God's plan, within the Kingdom of God. In this way we can build up our understanding of rental systems and their specific purpose at different levels as illustrated in Figure 8.

Understanding within each of these levels depends upon and is conditioned by an understanding of the lower level, an understanding of the schemes of recurrence as they link together into a complex structured ecology. Further, policy can emerge at any level insofar as it does incorporate a higher level. Any formulation of policy and its implementation in new practices will integrate or sublate the lower levels in the service of something new, the emergence of new possibilities.

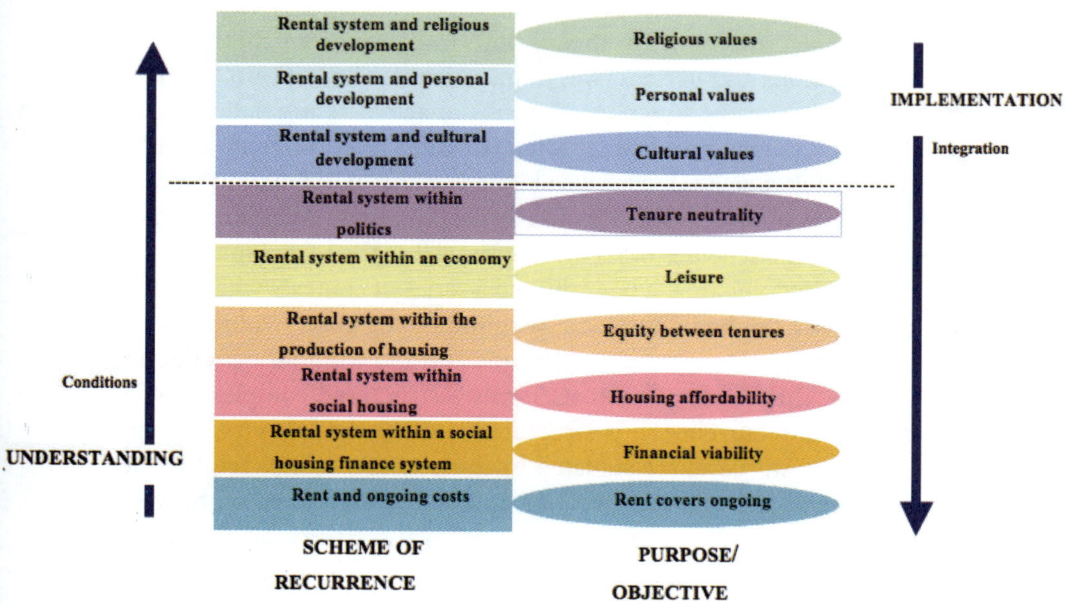

Figure 8: We can go on ... towards a theology of rental systems?

Social research and Lonergan's collaborative division of labour

As I noted above, Lonergan's economic theory emerged as he sought to integrate two traditions of economics: the old political economy and the new economics. He envisaged this new political economy as 'the movement from a less to a more general level of thought' like the movement from Ptolemaic astronomy through Copernicus, Kepler, Galileo, Kepler and Newton to Einstein. Since writing FNPE, Lonergan's understanding of the scientific process underwent a major transformation and bore fruit in his collaborative division of labour, functional specialisation. This scheme of recurrence functionally relates the process from data to results.

It is within this much larger scheme of recurrence that social and economic research operate.[35] The following briefly illustrates this scheme with reference to my illustration about rental systems. It is within this larger scheme of recurrence that we can move progressively and cumulatively to a better understanding of social housing rental systems and the implementation of better social housing rental systems.

Research

In my illustration I have been proposing an interpretation of rental systems. I have been proposing an hypothesis based upon a range of materials which described a variety of social housing rental systems in Australia, New Zealand, the United Kingdom, Canada, the United States, Sweden and the Netherlands.

This hypothesis provides a basis for further research on social housing rental systems, one which would reach for and discover activities which confirm, complement or bring into question this understanding or theory of a social housing rental system. It would extend beyond the countries just mentioned—it would extend to social housing globally.

35. Lonergan, *Method.* See also Chapter 3 of Philip McShane, *Pastkeynes Pastmodern Economics: A Fresh Pragmatism* (Halifax: Axial Press, 2002), and Philip McShane, *The Origins and Goals of Functional Specialization* (Montreal: Lonergan Centre for Ethical Reflection, Concordia University, 2004), available at <http://lonergan.concordia.ca/reprints/mcshane/McShane_Functional_Specialization_2004.pdf>. Accessed 25 June 2010.

Interpretation

This new research would ground new understandings of rental systems, alternate or more comprehensive hypotheses which account for any new data or integrate the proposed theory of rental systems into a higher viewpoint.

History: development of social housing rental systems

The scheme with its specific objective and constituted by sub-schemes with their specific objectives gives us a clue to the puzzle of the development of a scheme such as the social housing rental system. The rental system of 1950s public housing is not the same as it is today. Both the sub-schemes that constitute the rental system and the context within which it operates have changed. (We could ask to what extent this has been a development or a decline, but let me not get into that complex question here.) The distinction between the two aspects of social housing rental systems—the scheme of recurrence and its purpose or objective—provides a basis for understanding the changing nature of social housing while at the same time affirming that what was known as a social housing rental system in the 1950s continues to be known as a social housing rental system today. What drives this development is both the specific objective of the rental system and the objectives of those schemes which form the context within which the rental system operates. These objectives operate as values—something valuable to be achieved—that drive change in the schemes so that they better achieve what is intended by the value.

Dialectics: evaluation

The specific objective of a scheme and its role in contributing to the objectives of higher schemes provide a basis for an evaluation of the scheme. This evaluation does not bring in criteria from the outside such as the criteria of the participants. Rather, the specific objective of each scheme and its role in the achievement of the objectives of higher schemes are normative and provide the criteria by which to evaluate the scheme.

Dialectics also evaluates the different theories of social housing rental systems insofar as they imply differing views as to the purpose and value of social housing. In this way, the heuristic that underpins my understanding of rental systems—at least as it has been operative in developing this theory of rental systems— is subject to evaluation.

Such an evaluation invites a shift to more adequate heuristic, a more adequate viewpoint.

Foundations

Such a viewpoint is foundational and operative within housing researchers, and an evaluation of differing viewpoints invites a transformation of researchers/policy makers and their world-view. It is from this transformed viewpoint that housing researchers/policy makers can go on to implement new practices, whether this is the practice of undertaking further research on social housing rental systems or implementing new social housing rental system practices.

Policy

On these new foundations, housing researchers/policy makers can envision the development of a new social housing rental system. The detailed analysis of the schemes of recurrence that constitute a social housing rental system opens up a broad range of possible new directions for further development. The scheme and its constituent sub-schemes have a normative or policy element. Here, the term 'policy' is being used in a technical sense—policy as it relates to abstract theory. It is not policy in the more commonly accepted meaning of the term—as the stance of government or an organization. This type of policy emerges from executive reflection (as outlined below).

Strategic planning

The analysis of social housing rental systems is very limited. For instance, it has prescinded from the politics of social housing rental systems, from discourses about rent, from the relationship of rent to other internal and external schemes within social housing, from the organisational context.

While policy as it relates to an abstract theory provides guidance in relation to development or direction of particular schemes or sub-schemes, changes cannot be implemented without integration with other schemes and sub-schemes. Any new rental system has to be compatible with and integrated with possible changes in other constituent schemes and sub-schemes.

Executive reflection

Finally, the implementation of these future housing directions and strategies has to occur within particular institutions, organizations and the roles people play within them. The implementation of new practices demands change in what individuals do and how these new activities relate to those of others.

Concluding remarks

Lonergan's heuristic anticipates the understood as a complex but structured ecology of schemes of recurrence. As structured, the understood is constituted by multi-layered schemes of recurrence whereby the scheme is constituted by a range of sub-schemes, each of which has a particular internal purpose, with each of these sub-schemes constituted by further sub-schemes with a particular purpose. The higher schemes integrate the lower schemes yet depend upon the proper operation of these lower schemes if they are to achieve their particular purpose.

Lonergan's economic theory is a prime example of this heuristic recurrence within social sciences. It illustrates some unique aspects of this heuristic: the ordered hierarchy of technology, economics and politics; the distinction between the patterns of an economy and the coincidental motivations of participants; the functional relations between series of groups of activities; the normativity immanent within the productive process; and the democratic focus of his analysis.

By trying to understand social phenomena in this way we are shifting from a common sense understanding of our society to a theoretical understanding where this structured complex ecology of schemes is concerned with understanding things as they are related to one another.

Lonergan's heuristic as illustrated firstly through his economic writings and secondly through his collaborative division of labour presents a challenge for current social and economic research.

Chapter 11

Finality, *Insight*, and Method: My Stand on Lonergan's Contribution to Philosophy and Theology[1]

Tom Halloran

For some the title of my paper brings to mind 'Finality, Love, Marriage', the title of one of Lonergan's earlier contributions to theological praxis.[2] More than the title, I want to recall—re-read—that article insofar as the opening sentences intimate the functional specialty, Dialectic.[3] The first part of my paper is an exercise in functional interpretation bringing to light Lonergan's stand and stance in 1943.

I will endeavour to follow an analogous[4] procedure in part two, presenting my stand on Lonergan's contribution to philosophy and

1. This paper differs from the initial abstract, the initial writing, and the actual delivery. It benefits from the context of the Conference of which it was a small part. I take the liberty of referring then to some of the other presenters whose papers are included in this publication.
2. Bernard Lonergan, 'Finality, Love, Marriage', in *Collected Works of Bernard Lonergan*, volume 4, *Collection*, edited by Frederick E Crowe and Robert M Doran (Toronto: University of Toronto Press, 1988), 17–52 (hereafter *CWL* 4 *Collection*). Next July marks the fortieth anniversary of *Humanae Vitae*—will there be celebrations of that event? Would 'things' be different today, indeed, would *Humane Vitae* have been different if this 1943 contribution and the invitation to collaboration had elicited a collaborative response?
3. See Bernard Lonergan, *Method in Theology* (London: Darton, Longman & Todd, 1971), 249–50 (hereafter *Method*). Other helpful references to what Lonergan means by dialectic can be found at Chapter 17 in *Collected Works of Bernard Lonergan*, volume 3, *Insight: A Study of Human Understanding*, edited by Frederick E Crowe and Robert M Doran (Toronto: University of Toronto Press, 1992); (hereafter *CWL* 3 *Insight*), and at Chapter 14 in *Collected Works of Bernard Lonergan*, volume 18, *Phenomenology and Logic: The Boston College Lectures on Mathematical Logic and Existentialism*, edited by Philip J McShane (Toronto: University of Toronto Press, 2001); (hereafter *CWL* 18 *Phenomenology and Logic*).
4. It is an 'analogy of proportion'.

theology—the 'theme' for this present volume.[5] I argue that Lonergan's contribution to philosophy and theology is contextualised by a differentiated, historical and systematic understanding of these two fields.[6]

Finally, I propose that the most adequate celebration of Lonergan's contribution would be to accept the challenge of functional specialisation. This would be adequate for two reasons: it respects Father Lonergan's incarnate desire for good 'non-disciples';[7] it evokes the 'infinite craving' of every human heart and invokes a division of labour that integrates freedom and grace.[8] Absolute finality refers all things to God, the (vertical) finality of functional specialisation intends concrete solidarity in history which Christians conceive as restoring all things in Christ.

Finality, Love, Marriage: a 'functional interpretation'

I have read 'Finality, Love, Marriage' many times over many years. In the 70s, I found it 'pastorally' helpful in the negotiating the confusion and crisis brought about by *Humanae Vitae*. My proximate context then focused on the 'preliminary speculative outline' which is, in fact, the concern of the article.

---

5. It is somewhat ironic that the 'actual' publication day for *Insight* was 1 April, 1958. In 1997—the fortieth anniversary—I bought a pristine copy of *Insight* for a dollar when the Marist brothers sold their library at a secondary school fete. So, quite 'politely' we re-call neither the publication nor the success of the book but the contribution of the author and remember his call for collaboration—a re-membering of the mystical body of Christ.
6. The field of philosophy is proportionate being; the field of theology is transcendent being. Though these fields imply differentiated conjugate forms, generalised empirical method embraces both: 'it is quite legitimate to seek in the efficient cause of the science, that is, in the scientist, the reason why a science forms a unified whole. It is at that point that the significance of group theory comes into view'. *Collected Works of Bernard Lonergan,* volume 10, *Topics in Education*, edited by Robert M. Doran and Frederick E Crowe (Toronto: University of Toronto Press, 1993), 160. For further reference to the significance of group theory see 'Time and Meaning' in *Collected Works of Bernard Lonergan,* volume 6, *Philosophical and Theological Papers 1958–1964,* edited by Robert C Croken, Frederick E Crowe, and Robert M Doran (Toronto: University of Toronto Press, 1996), 94–121 (hereafter *CWL 6 Philosophical and Theological Papers*).
7. Lonergan did not intend to found a school of 'Lonerganians'; and he would not rejoice at such founding. See his remarks about 'schools' in *CWL* 18 *Phenomenology and Logic*, 281. I recall Lonergan's *parting words* at the first Lonergan Workshop at Boston College in 1974: 'Be good non-disciples'.
8. On the several ways in which our 'infinite craving' can be recovered and restored see of Lonergan, 'Finality, Love, Marriage', 49.

Now, however, I attempt a 'functional interpretation' of the first two sentences which communicate Lonergan's *stance* in 'Finality, Love, Marriage'. As illustrating 'functional interpretation', I am 'interpreting' the so-called 'early Lonergan' in the light of my understanding of the so-called 'later Lonergan'.[9] So, interpretation is done by the 'current Halloran'. This interpretation seeks to find 'evidence' of the six 'operations' which are thematic on pages 249 and 250 of *Method in Theology* and in that context 'structure' the functional specialty Dialectic, *qua* functional.[10] The operations are named: Assembly, Completion, Comparison, Reduction, Classification, and Selection.[11]

Notwithstanding the correctness of my understanding of 'functional interpretation', it is standard scientific procedure to look for evidence of the *thématique* in the *vécu*,[12] to look for evidence that supports the theory.[13] I am interpreting 'Lonergan at work', seeking evidence of the six operations which some twenty years later he makes thematic. This is not an unreasonable procedure, as both *Insight* and *Method in Theology* are the product of one man and a reflexion on *his own* 'practice' over the preceding decades—and those texts 'invite' me and you to do the same with regard to our own practice.[14]

9. The 'later Crowe'—gentleman scholar, incarnate serious student—remarks in a footnote (somewhere in the *Collected Works*) that perhaps the Crowe of 1974 was not 'entirely correct' in referring to Lonergan's 'new' notion of value in *Method*. A functional interpretation of Lonergan's writings hands on its findings to the functional historian of Lonergan's intellectual biography.
10. Dialectic *qua* functional as distinct but not separate from dialectic *qua* existentially spontaneous or even psychologically differentiated.
11. 'The structure of dialectic has two levels. On the upper level are the operators. On a lower level are assembled the materials to be operated on . . . Before being operated on, the materials have to be *assembled, completed, compared, reduced, classified, selected*' (*Method*, 249; emphasis mine).
12. The distinction between *vécu* and *thématique*, between one's living and loving and one's thinking about that living and loving—and indeed one's thinking about that thinking of one's thinking, living and loving—occurs regularly in the Lonergan *corpus*, but see especially 'The Mediation of Christ in Prayer' in *CWL* 6 *Philosophical and Theological Papers*, 160–82.
13. Lonergan attributes the relevance of Piaget's detailed data on child development to the fact that Piaget had a theory. See 'Time and Meaning' in *CWL* 6 *Philosophical and Theological Papers*, 109; references to the importance of Piaget's theory for understanding the data are multiple.
14. This is an issue which is years beyond the context of this paper. The relationship between 'interpretation' as normally understood and practiced and 'functional interpretation' is complex. For example, Lonergan's achievement in the Verbum articles can be conceived of as 'interpretation'; it can also be construed as 'functional

The text for my[15] 'exercise' in 'functional interpretation' is the first two sentences:

> In the recent fermentation of Catholic thought on the meaning and ends of marriage, the basic component of novelty would seem to be a development in biological science. Quite other factors, no doubt, account for the intense and widespread interest aroused; but the ground of the intellectual problem must be placed, I think, in a new scientific insight.[16]

What is *assembled* is the 'recent fermentation of Catholic thought on the meaning and ends of marriage'.[17] So Lonergan attends to what has been 'fermenting', bubbling up. The assembly of materials is not restricted to contemporary (1943) 'controversies' or 'disputed questions' but gives broader historical scope to the meaning of 'recent'.[18] Performatively—as becomes clear in the main part of the article—the term 'Catholic thought' refers to the *field* of the supernatural.[19]

Adding 'evaluative interpretation and evaluative history',[20] *completion* brings or *anticipates bringing* the fermentation process to the 'brew' for some 'tasting'. Completion adds evaluation insofar as it 'picks out the one hundred and one good things' and their opposites; it can be contrafactual insofar as it remembers things better than what they were.[21] In this context, completion refers concretely to Leo XIII's "*vetera novis augere*

research'; Dialectic as conceived in Chapter 10 of *Method* transposes Hermeneutics as conceived in Chapter 17 of *Insight*.

15. But also your own exercise.
16. *CWL* 4 *Collection*, 17.
17. The proximate context is that of Doctors Dom and Ford; the more remote context is Catholic thought.
18. I take 'recent' to be co-extensive with Lonergan's 'psychological present' in 1943 as expressed in 'the cosmic breadth of a simultaneous context of nature, history, and grace' and detailed in the editorial notes of this article.
19. Although 'written' many years later, in Chapter 10 of *Collected Works of Bernard Lonergan*, volume 10, *Topics in Education*, Lonergan is quite clear in saying that 'the supernatural' as understood by Catholics, specifies the *field* of theology.
20. *Method*, 250.
21. *Method*, 250. In treating of evaluative interpretation and evaluative history, Lonergan alludes to history in the style of Burckhardt rather than Ranke and devotes two chapters in *Method* to the functional specialty, History. To 'get' the allusion one must 'get at' both of these styles; I have found it helpful to allude to personal history and the place of forgiveness in an ongoing withdrawal from inauthenticity. In this latter context 'forgiving the past' does not mean 'forgetting' but 'remembering differently'.

et perficere"—insofar as that maxim provides a holistic view, a pragmatic grasp[22] of the universal viewpoint.[23]

As is the case with completion, so *comparison* as operative here is similarly less differentiated, more compact. As, I claim, *Aeterni Patris* provided the pragmatic context for 'completion' in 1943, so one goes on to 'compare' the 'positive and doctrinal'—'more important to us as Catholics' with the 'analytic and explanatory'—more 'relevant to the solution of problems'.[24] The interplay between completion and comparison as operative in Dialectic as a 'functional specialty' remains a complex issue.

Reduction 'finds the same affinity and the same opposition manifested in a number of different manners; from the many manifestations it moves to the underlying root'.[25] The underlying 'root'—here 'the basic component of novelty'—is 'a development in biological science'. This is the critical issue, and appropriating the development is the root of the difficulty but also the key to meeting the 'intellectual' problem head-on. The key feature of the 'reduction' is the recognition and grasp of the 'development'.

Classification:[26] 'Quite other factors, no doubt, account for the intense and widespread interest aroused; but the ground of the intellectual problem must be placed, I think, in a new scientific insight'. So the various aspects of the 'fermentation' are classified with respect to their affinity with the 'root', the development. Further classification seeks to discern whether that relationship to the 'root' has its origin in a dialectically opposed horizon or has other grounds.

'*Selection*, finally, picks out the affinities and oppositions grounded in dialectically opposed horizons and dismisses other affinities and

---

22. As evidence, Lonergan says: 'one can agree with Fr. Ford in desiring the assimilation of new insights into the traditional theoretical framework' ('Finality, Love, Marriage', 18).
23. Lonergan's notion of *complete* is heuristic and, for that reason, ongoing. Lonergan's notion of complete is far from being simple. See, in this regard, Philip McShane, 'Lonergan's Meaning of Complete in the Fifth Canon of Scientific Method', in *Journal of Macrodynamic Analysis* 4 (2004): 53-81 available at <www.mun.ca/jmda>. Accessed 1 June 2010.
24. Lonergan, 'Finality, Love, Marriage', 18. Lonergan's notion of *comparison* operates proximately within the remote context of the constitutive meaning of *complete* which intends a universal viewpoint. The contemporary practice of 'comparison'—comparing X and Y on A—falls far short of what, I believe, Lonergan is intending as a cog in the wheel of dialectic.
25. *Method*, 250.
26. 'Classification determines which of these sources of affinity or opposition results from dialectically opposed horizons and which have other grounds' (*Method*, 250).

oppositions.'[27] Lonergan's 'I think' indicates that he is satisfied that the dialectic function has objectified the field and his horizon so that he can go on, go forward, take a stance with regard to the future, by providing a 'preliminary speculative outline [which] aims at no more than a brusque occupation of *strategic theoretical* points on finality, on love, and on marriage'.[28] These opening sentences indicate that Lonergan is anything but *voraussetzunglos*.

The strategic points are the first stage in 'a large and long task'[29] oriented to 'inserting the *vertical tendency* of love from sex to divine charity into the *horizontal process* of fecundity to offspring; and such insertion has to be made on the background of the *general field* of human process'.[30] 'But as theologians, let alone parents, rarely think of the historical process, it must be noted that we speak not of a *finis operantis* but of a *finis operis* and we do so in its most general terms.'[31]

The fact that such thinking on the part of theologians is rare is a statistical fact. That it happens at all is marvellous for 'no one will find a motive in the historical process as such. What moves men and women is some concrete aspect of history'.[32] And, I would add, that such concrete aspects of history emerge in the context of a 'crisis' in the routines of persons or communities.[33]

I do not wish to dwell on the crisis which Lonergan's invitation to collaborate may have avoided. My sole concern here was to conduct an exercise in 'functional interpretation' of two sentences with which Lonergan prefaces his outline but which indicate his stand and his stance. The aim was to find evidence of the six operations which constitute the structure of the functional specialty Dialectic. While evidence here of completion and comparison is circumstantial, it seems reasonable to affirm that these two sentences exemplify what Lonergan means by 'functional dialectic'.

---

27. *Method*, 250.
28. *CWL* 4 *Collection*, 18; emphasis mine.
29. Lonergan, 'Finality, Love, Marriage', 18. Recall *CWL* 3 *Insight*, the Epilogue.
30. Lonergan, 'Finality, Love, Marriage', 18–19; emphasis mine.
31. Lonergan, 'Finality, Love, Marriage', 47. See Morelli's essay in this volume for the relationship of Hegel's absolute idealism and historical process.
32. Lonergan, 'Finality, Love, Marriage', 47.
33. With every 'crisis' spontaneously we ask: How did we get into this mess? Where did things start to go wrong? What was the original sin? The answers to those questions and the evidence that supports the answers provide a context for the solution.

My stand on Lonergan's contribution to philosophy and theology

Similars are understood similarly. I express my stand in a similar 'format' to what I have 'functionally interpreted' as Lonergan's stand in 'Finality, Love, Marriage'.

In the *recent fermentation* of *catholic praxis* on the *meaning and redemption of history*, the basic component of novelty would seem to be a *development in methodical collaboration.* Quite other factors, no doubt, account for the intense and widespread interest aroused in so-called Lonergan studies, but the ground of *the existential problem* must be placed, I think, in *one's judgement of value*[34] with respect to functional specialisation.

Some significant *differences* between Lonergan's stand in 1943 and mine in 2007 need to be indicated to support the analogous nature of the similarity.

'Recent fermentation' is objectively indeterminate; subjectively it is my and your psychological present. So, for example, one might 'start' with Vatican II as the locus of 'recent fermentation'[35] or with the Reformation, or with modern science as does Butterfield (and Lonergan). Proximate *and remote* contexts orientate one's reading. Indeed the reference to 'catholic praxis' and the 'meaning and redemption of history' may indicate a plethora of seemingly recent concerns but praxis, the meaning of history, and the redemption of history have been present in the catholic fermentation since the 'fullness of time'.[36]

'Development in methodical collaboration' is the basic component of novelty. The moving viewpoint of *Insight* invites the reader to develop—in accord with a spontaneous but historically conditioned[37] *critical* exigence—self-appropriation, self-mediation. The attempt to come to grips with the development of theory and the consequent fact that there are two realms of meaning—two fields—two radically opposed worlds gives rise to the

34. Perhaps better expressed as 'one's consent to the value of functional specialisation'.
35. Recall Vatican II and the *assembly* which '*completed*' an evaluative interpretation and evaluative history of the historical movements (biblical, liturgical, patristic). Was there a component of novelty in the deliberations of the Council? Was this and were indeed prior councils operating in the functional specialty of dialectic? How does the notion of dialectic apply to conciliar deliberations down the ages?
36. Galatians 4:4–6.
37. The critical exigence emerges in the historical context of an apparent conflict between common sense and theory to take a stand with regard to objectivity and reality. The complete 'stand' emerges in Chapter 17 of *Insight* and faces forward in Chapters 18, 19, 20 calling for an implementation of that stand in the Epilogue.

epistemological context of critical philosophy—a *spontaneous* critical exigence.[38]

In accord with this spontaneous critical exigence one moves into a world of interiority in which the *capacities*[39] of human subjectivity are identified, heightened, lightened, and appropriated; one takes possession of oneself as rationally self-conscious, as autonomous, as responsible for oneself. Although the appropriation is a personal achievement, it is historically conditioned by the achievement of those who have gone before in accord with the reach of spontaneous human capacities. In mounting to the level of one's times, one has to move beyond the milk wood of *haute vulgarisation*[40] to a genuine appreciation of the world of theory.

Every instance of cooperation and collaboration involves evoking spontaneous intersubjectivity to achieve a practical outcome as part of an aggregate and recurrent good of order. In every instance, corresponding to a specific goal there is a commonly understood and accepted set of procedures for collaborating. Methodic collaboration invokes the normativity of human interiority as the procedure for achieving *a* cosmopolis[41] which would reverse the longer cycle of decline. Thus while

38. I refer the reader to the contributions of Mark Morelli and Elizabeth Murray in this volume. In their respective approaches, they enlarge the scope of the spontaneous critical exigence to move beyond a solution to the problems of idealist Kantian epistemology and address the issues of Hegel's absolute idealism (Morelli) and the appropriation of rational self-consciousness (Murray). Chapter 18 of *Insight* identifies the possibility of Ethics with the self-appropriation of what Lonergan terms there rational self-consciousness and later terms the existential moment when one decides for oneself what to make of oneself. It remains that freedom is exercised in the company of others; *Insight* 'brackets' interpersonal relations and so prescinds from the effective exercise of liberty.

39. See *Method,* 48. Although beyond the scope of this paper to present a persuasive argument, I would contend that it is the hierarchy of capacities which determines the scale of preference associated with terminal value, not, as some would suggest, a hierarchy of needs.

40. 'Haute vulgarisation' acknowledges 'both theory and common sense but the acknowledgement of theory is a devalued acknowledgment [because there is] no personal experience of the intellectual pattern of living, of living the way a theorist lives' ('Time and Meaning' in *CWL* 6 *Philosophical and Theological Papers*, 121). In the same volume see 'Exegesis and Dogma' at 155.

41. Many readers of *Insight* have experienced and expressed difficulty in working through the first five chapters. Strategies that would ignore this preliminary work to 'fast track' a summary introduction to Lonergan's meaning do so at the expense of an appreciation of theory! Few, however, have failed to *resonate* with the two chapters on Common Sense and, in particular, Lonergan's depiction of the *malaise* to which *a* cosmopolis is the heuristic generic solution.

the achievement in accord with a spontaneous critical exigence opens a third stage of meaning, to go through that opening is to exercise a methodic exigence 'return' to exteriority, to the realms of both common sense and theory. *Method in Theology* pivots[42] on authentic self-mediation as foundation as 'background'[43] to provide a doctrine to direct *mutual* self-mediation—one consequence of which is to disavow common sense of its mythic omnicompetence but draw out the proper orientation of common sense to mystery.

'The existential problem' is the gap between one's subjective horizon and the objective field. The 'existential problem' can be 'bracketed' in the natural sciences[44] but it cannot be avoided in the human sciences among which are philosophy and theology.

'One's judgment of value with respect to functional specialisation' is the final item of difference. Why a judgement *of value* with respect to functional specialisation? It is possible to find evidence of the nominal specialties in the current products but it is not functional;[45] there is evidence of collaboration but it is not methodical.[46] Is there enough evidence to make a judgement of fact about functional specialisation? A judgement of value takes the facts into account—about what is the case—as well as the fact of one's freedom to 'leap' forward towards 'what could be the case'. A judgement of value implies 'risk'.[47]

In the Epilogue of *Insight*, Lonergan 'looks forward':

> If I have written as a humanist, as one dominated by the desire not only to understand but also, through understanding understanding, to reach a grasp of the main lines of all there is to be understood, still the very shape of things as they are has

42. Or 'twists' to cut, scissors-like. The upper blade is interiority, the lower blade is the complex of exteriority (theory *and* practice).
43. The five background chapters of *Method* pivot on Chapter 18 of *Insight*; *Method* begins with the Structure of the Human Good.
44. And *perhaps* in the first three functional specialties. Does it emerge in Communications? Or is it 'sublated downwards'?
45. 'Interpretation' is often 'functional research'.
46. Methodical collaboration specifies the audience as the 'next' group of functional specialists in the ongoing eight.
47. A judgement of value refers all things to an absolute finality which is unconditional in its worth-while-ness—implying an optimism about the passionateness of being, an eschatology, which would orient a theology of hope; a judgement of value takes the risk that a yet-to-be-realised state of affairs is worth-MY-while in accord with the statistics of the Law of the Cross.

> compelled me to end with a question at once too basic and too detailed to admit a brief answer. The self-appropriation of one's own intellectual and rational self-consciousness begins as cognitional theory, expands into a metaphysics and an ethics, mounts to a conception and an affirmation of God, only to be confronted with a problem of evil that demands the transformation of self-reliant intelligence into an *intellectus quaerens fidem*. Only at the term of that search for faith, for the new and higher collaboration of minds that has God as its author and its guide, could the desired summary and completion be undertaken; and then, I believe, it would prove to be, not some brief appendage to the present work, but the inception of a far larger one.[48]

Metaphysics *implements* the integral heuristic structure of proportionate being. Chapter 18 of *Insight* asks whether Ethics can be conceived in the same way. The *remote* possibility of ethics is grounded in the ontological structure of the good which parallels the method of metaphysics and in the fact of essential freedom, autonomy; the *proximate* possibility is conditioned by effective freedom. Chapter 18 'rounds off' by returning to the questions that emerged in the chapters on common sense, now raised again in the context of the possibility of effective freedom.

In Chapters 19 and 20 further questions evoke a remote context—the remote possibility of *a* cosmopolis[49]—which is transcendent,[50] absolutely supernatural.

Method in Theology continues 'the inception of the far larger collaboration' by placing the (vertical) finality of *fides quaerens intellectum* into the (horizontal) finality of *intellectus quaerens fidem.*[51] Chapter 18 of *Insight* raises the possibility of ethics in the context of the integral heuristic structure of proportionate being as made thematic in metaphysics;

48. *CWL* 3 *Insight*, 753–54.
49. The indefinite article indicates that Cosmopolis is a genus. For example, is Augustine's City of God a species?
50. See however Chapter 17 and the discussion of mystery and myth for the cosmic evidence of the remote transcendent context as the fact of further questions.
51. The terminology is obverse, the meaning is via a 'strange twist' (think of the Moebius strip) which is dimensionally obverse. *Insight* moves in accord with the critical exigence which emerges in relation to two types of knowing; *Method* pivots, twists, on interiority as background to pursue foreground methodical exigence which would unite theory and common sense in praxis.

Chapter 2 of *Method in Theology* returns to a discussion of the human good and its structure as the first element in the Background and provides the context for the 'retrieval' of insight as multi-dimensional, multi-functional meaning in Chapter 3.

But back to the beginning: 'theology mediates between a cultural matrix and the significance and role of a religion in that matrix'.[52] Does *religion* intend the same terminal value as *a* cosmopolis? If so, as mediating between the significance of religion and a given cultural matrix, the role of theology is heuristically practical—a cosmopolis. For Christians, on the one hand theology is *fides quaerens intellectum* and on the other it is 'restoring all things in Christ'—not the myth[53] of 'one hand clapping'!

Celebrating Lonergan's contribution: our stance?

I am convinced that functional specialisation is Lonergan's greatest contribution[54] to philosophy and theology—considered as a complex field. I find little evidence that serious appreciation of that contribution has yet been acknowledged. The most adequate celebration of Lonergan's contribution would be the implementation of functional specialisation.

'We' must gather again in another fifty or perhaps a hundred years.[55]

The 'we' that gathers *then* will be like the 'we' that is gathered *now* insofar as all stand on the 'us' of history, the mystical body of Christ. But whether the 'we' *then* will be better off depends on whether or not 'we' *now* opt for the better way, the more excellent finality, of functional specialisation. The remote audience for theology is the 'next' millennium; the proximate audience for the functional specialist theologian is the 'next' functional specialty—irrespective of time.

---

52. *Method*, xi.
53. Myth is removed permanently by correct understanding; mystery displaces—cumulatively and cyclically—limited understandings. See Vatican I *Dei Filius*—DS 3016.
54. Like the 1943 article on which I commented in part one, there are other contributions, other leads, that can be gleaned from Lonergan's writings and self-attentive reflection on what he is *about* in those expressions.
55. Fifty years is a very optimistic view. The prevailing wisdom among management gurus is that the 'week' not the 'day' is the smallest unit of effective 'to-do' sheets. Even with the division of labour which functional specialisation facilitates, one has to think in terms of 'generations' with regard to cultural change. In the meantime—mean times—we pray to the Father of Jesus for the coming kingdom as well as our daily bread.

Then, having made a 'preferential option for functional specialisation' *now*, we will gather not as 'Lonerganians' but as 'functional specialists'—good non-disciples of Father Lonergan—to celebrate a cultural change in which 'a preferential option for the poor *in spirit*' is more evident . . . mediating a restoration of all things in Christ.

Index